Social Innovation and Sustainable Consumption

T0270827

This book showcases strategic policies *for* and processes *of* societal transformation, which are required to address the challenge of sustainability. Based on the latest thinking at the interface of social innovation, sustainable consumption and the transformation of society, the book provides:

- in-depth discussions at the nexus of sustainable consumption, social innovation and social transformation, highlighting their significance to sustainability-related policy and practice;
- detailed case studies of social innovation in energy, food, housing and policy which illustrate emerging practice and promising policy, business and civil society interventions; and
- critical reflections and commentaries on the contribution of social innovation to societal transformation.

Bringing together aspiring scholars and leading thinkers on this topic, this book leads to compelling new insights for an international audience into the potential of social innovation for sustainable consumption and the transformation of society. It will be of great interest to students and scholars of sustainable consumption, sustainable development, (social) innovation studies and environmental sociology.

Julia Backhaus is a doctoral researcher at the International Centre for Integrated Assessment and Sustainable Development (ICIS) at Maastricht University, the Netherlands.

Audley Genus is professor of innovation and technology management at Kingston University, UK.

Sylvia Lorek holds a Ph.D. in consumer economics and is trained to work on the interlinkages of the individual micro-economic and the societal macro-economic perspective in which the scientific and societal discourses about sustainable consumption take place.

Edina Vadovics is research director of GreenDependent Institute and president of GreenDependent Association in Hungary.

Julia M. Wittmayer works as senior researcher at DRIFT, the Dutch Research Institute for Transitions at the Erasmus University Rotterdam, the Netherlands.

Routledge–SCORAI Studies in Sustainable Consumption

Comprising edited collections, co-authored volumes and single author monographs, *Routledge–SCORAI Studies in Sustainable Consumption* aim to advance conceptual and empirical contributions to this new and important field of study. In particular, this series will explore key issues such as the emergence of new modes of household provisioning, the evolution toward post-consumerist systems of social organisation, novel approaches to consumption governance and innovative business models for sustainable lifestyles.

The Sustainable Consumption Research and Action Initiative (SCORAI) is an international knowledge network of approximately 1,000 scholars and policy practitioners working at the interface of material consumption, human well-being and technological and cultural change. For more information about SCORAI and its activities please visit www.scorai.org.

Series editors:

Maurie J. Cohen, Professor of Sustainability Studies and Director of the Program in Science, Technology, and Society in the Department of Humanities at the New Jersey Institute of Technology, USA.

Halina Szejnwald Brown, Professor of Environmental Science and Policy at Clark University and a Fellow at the Tellus Institute, USA.

Philip J. Vergragt, Professor Emeritus of Technology Assessment at Delft University, the Netherlands, and currently a Fellow at the Tellus Institute and a Research Fellow at Clark University, USA.

Titles in this series include:

Responsible Citizens and Sustainable Consumer Behaviour
New Interpretative Frameworks
Pietro Lanzini

Social Innovation and Sustainable Consumption
Research and Action for Societal Transformation
Edited by Julia Backhaus, Audley Genus, Sylvia Lorek, Edina Vadovics and Julia M. Wittmayer

Social Innovation and Sustainable Consumption

Research and Action for Societal Transformation

Edited by Julia Backhaus, Audley Genus, Sylvia Lorek, Edina Vadovics and Julia M. Wittmayer

LONDON AND NEW YORK

from Routledge

First published 2018 by Routledge

2 Park Square, Milton Park, Abingdon, Oxfordshire OX14 4RN
52 Vanderbilt Avenue, New York, NY 10017

Routledge is an imprint of the Taylor & Francis Group, an informa business

First issued in paperback 2019

British Library Cataloguing in Publication Data
A catalogue record for this book is available from the British Library

Library of Congress Cataloging in Publication Data
A catalog record for this book has been requested

ISBN: 978-1-138-70694-1 (hbk)
ISBN: 978-0-367-34015-5 (pbk)

Typeset in Goudy
by Wearset Ltd, Boldon, Tyne and Wear

Contents

Contributors

Flor Avelino has a background in political science and works as a transition researcher and lecturer at DRIFT, Erasmus University Rotterdam. Her research focuses on the role of power and empowerment in sustainability transitions. As scientific coordinator of the Transformative Social Innovation Theory (TRANSIT) research project, she currently investigates how grassroots initiatives and trans-local social innovation networks challenge existing institutions. As the academic director of the Transition Academy, Flor strives to co-create new learning environments to challenge people to think and act for radical change.

Julia Backhaus is a doctoral researcher at the International Centre for Integrated Assessment and Sustainable Development (ICIS) at Maastricht University, exploring theories of change and the role of assumptions in change processes towards more just and sustainable societies. Much of her work draws on her involvement in European research projects on resource efficiency (POLFREE), transformative social innovation (TRANSIT) and sustainable energy use (ENERGISE). Next to her research, Julia teaches at bachelor and master level and regularly supervises undergraduate and graduate research projects. In addition, she is a member of the steering committee of the European branch of the Sustainable Consumption Research and Action Initiative (SCORAI). Julia holds an interdisciplinary B.Sc. (cum laude) and an M.Phil. in science and technology studies, both from Maastricht University.

Bálint Balázs is senior research fellow and managing director of the Environmental Social Science Research Group and lecturer of environmental sociology at the Department of Environmental Economics, Institute for Nature Conservation and Landscape Management, St. István University, Gödöllő, Hungary. He has international research experience in the field of sustainable and local food systems, transition to sustainability and policy analysis, as well as public engagement, science-policy dialogues, cooperative research and participatory action research. He is a member of the International Network for Community Supported Agriculture Research Group.

Marcelline Bonneau is a facilitator of societal transition processes. While seeking to make the bridge between theory and practice, she is working both on research and analysis and on experimentation projects. She is well-versed in the co-creation of new (urban) governance principles. As such, she was co-coordinating the work on social innovation in cities for the European programme of cities, URBACT, and is co-leading the expertise of the URBACT network on the temporary use of vacant spaces, REFILL. Through an Innoviris Co-Create grant within the VILCO project, she is also researching ways to improve the cooperation of public authorities and citizens' initiatives to improve the resilience of local dynamics in favour of the environment. Marcelline holds a master's degree in management of the environment from IGEAT/ULB (Brussels, Belgium) and a master's degree in European public policy from UCL (London, UK).

Adina Dumitru is a postdoctoral researcher at the University of A Coruña, Spain, and an assistant professor of social psychology at the West University of Timisoara, Romania. Her current research focuses on the psychological determinants of pro-environmental behaviour and sustainable lifestyle choices, the relationship between nature-based solutions, pro-environmental behaviour and wellbeing and the psychological dimensions of social innovation, empowerment and social cohesion. She is the scientific coordinator of the GLAMURS FP7 project, which focuses on sustainable lifestyles and a green economy in Europe. She is also a lead researcher in the TRANSIT FP7 project, focusing on the psychological dimensions of agency, empowerment and social learning in social innovation. She is also working on developing a reference framework for the evaluation of nature-based solutions in cities. She was a junior Fulbright Scholar and received her master's degree in political science (with a track in political psychology) from Washington State University.

Audley Genus is professor of innovation and technology management at Kingston University. He researches sustainability-related innovation, community entrepreneurship and technology policy. Audley is the editor of *Sustainable Consumption: Design, Innovation and Practice*, published by Springer, three single-authored books and numerous peer-reviewed articles in leading journals. He is currently working with SCORAI Europe colleagues and others on a €3.2 million pan-European project (known as ENERGISE), which has a focus on sustainable consumption and innovations in energy use practices, and is funded by the European Commission's Horizon 2020 initiative. Audley is a member of the editorial board of Technology Analysis and Strategic Management, the steering committee of the Sustainable Consumption Research and Action Initiative (SCORAI Europe) and a member of the European Association for the Study of Science and Technology, the British Academy of Management, the Sustainable Development Research Network and the Sustainability Transitions Research Network.

Emese Gulyás has a degree in economic sciences and sociology, and a Ph.D. in sociology from the Corvinus University of Budapest. She is one of the founders and still a board member of the Association of Conscious Consumers (ACC) in Hungary. The ACC is a significant civil society organisation for sustainable consumption in Hungary. Since its foundation in 2001, it has been running various activities to achieve a more sustainable society. Emese is active in research activities and in international cooperation for sustainability and social fairness. She is has been doing qualitative and quantitative research on several aspects of sustainability in order to provide input for the organisational strategy of the ACC. She also took part in designing and realising innovative organisational activities that aimed to progress sustainable consumption in Hungary. Recently her activities moved from large-scale communication projects towards fostering and facilitating actual behaviour change programs on the household and on the community level.

Alex Haxeltine is a senior research fellow in the 3S group at the University of East Anglia. His main research interests concern the deep psychological, social and cultural changes that may be associated with sustainability transformations in the coming years. Over the last ten years he has led research on sustainability and societal transitions in several key European research projects. In the EC-funded (FP7) Transformative Social Innovation Theory (TRANSIT) research project he is leading a work-package charged with developing a new empirically grounded theory of transformative social innovation.

François Jégou graduated in 1989 from the national design high school, ENSCI Paris. François is the founder and head of Strategic Design Scenarios. He has twenty years of experience in strategic design, participative scenario building and new product-services system definition. He is professor of strategic design at La Cambre, Brussels and design manager of the Lab of Usage and Innovative Practices at the Cité du Design in Saint-Etienne, France. He is lead expert of the UBACT REFILL network and was co-coordinator of the work on social innovation in cities for the European programme of cities, URBACT. He was also lead expert of URBACT Sustainable Food in Urban Communities network and founding member of the DESIS Design for Social Innovation and Sustainability network.

Michael Jonas is a senior researcher at the Institute for Advanced Studies (IHS), Vienna. Following a praxeological perspective, he is currently researching social inequality, injustice and unsustainability in world society as well as searching for answers as to how these might be changed. He seeks to combine a wide range of approaches from various disciplines, including sociology, philosophy, economic sciences, political sciences and geography. In June 2013, he completed his post-doctoral lecturing qualification (habilitation) at the Europe University Viadrina Frankfurt/Oder.

René Kemp is professor of innovation and sustainable development in Maastricht. He is interested in the link between micro-change and macro-change. He is well known for his work on strategic niche management, socio-technical regime shifts and transition management. René has a background in (environmental) economics and innovation studies and is a self-taught expert on the sociology of knowledge, public policy and political economy. As a multidisciplinary researcher, he has published in innovation journals, ecological economics journals, policy journals, transport and energy journals and sustainable development journals. He is advisory editor of *Research Policy*, editor of *Sustainability Science* and editor of *Environmental Innovation and Societal Transitions*. He currently works on transformative social innovation and urban labs.

Iris Kunze has a Ph.D. in geography and sociology. She is a senior researcher at the Center for Global Change and Sustainability at the University of Natural Resources and Life Sciences (BOKU), Vienna. Iris is currently researching transformative social innovations within the EU-FP7 project TRANSIT, community-based climate mitigation practices for the Austrian project COSIMA and transition for leadership in a practitioner project. After completing her doctoral studies on sustainable ways of living at the University of Münster, she coordinated the doctoral school of sustainable development while researching on concepts of human–nature relationship at BOKU until 2014. Her expertise and research activities relate to sustainable ways of living, empirical research on social movements, intentional communities and ecovillages, as well as transition studies, social ecology and governance.

Michaela Leitner has been a researcher and project manager at the Austrian Institute for Sustainable Development in Vienna since 2010. She obtained her master's degree in sociology in 2008 at the University of Vienna, where she specialised in urban and housing research. She coordinated and carried out research projects dealing with sustainability (e.g. regarding housing, (energy) consumption, lifestyles and climate change), participation processes in housing (e.g. co-housing) and social innovation. In her research, she applies quantitative and qualitative socio-scientific methods and the theory of social practices. She is interested in innovative practice-oriented social research to better understand and promote social, ecological and economic sustainability by collaborating with actors from various societal areas. Currently she is on an educational leave attending interdisciplinary distance studies of environmental sciences (infernum) at the FernUniversität, Hagen, and the Fraunhofer Institute for Environmental, Safety and Energy Technology, UMSICHT.

Harro van Lente is full professor of science and technology studies and head of department at Maastricht University, Faculty of Arts and Social Sciences. He graduated in physics and philosophy and holds a Ph.D. in the sociology of technical change (University of Twente, 1993). He has published widely on technology dynamics, innovation policy, technology assessment and the politics of knowledge production. He is one of the founding fathers of the sociology of expectations, which studies how representations of the future shape current developments. He is programme director of technology assessment of NanoNextNL, the leading Dutch research consortium in nanotechnology, and secretary of the European Association for the Studies of Science and Technology (EASST). In 2013, he was a guest professor at the Center for Nanotechnology and Society at UCSB, Santa Barbara, California.

Beate Littig is head of the Department of Socio-Ecological Transformation Research at the Institute for Advanced Studies in Vienna. Her research agenda since 2009 has focused on practice studies and sustainability. She studied sociology (history, philosophy and psychology) at the Universities of Göttingen, Hamburg and Berlin. In 1995, she finished her Ph.D. at the Fern-Universität, Hagen. Since February 1996, she was a senior researcher in the Department of Sociology at the Institute for Advanced Studies in Vienna. In 2001, she finished the habilitation procedure at the University of Vienna and became lecturer of sociology at the University of Vienna. From 2005 until 2009, she was vice-president of the Austrian Sociology Association (ÖGS). Beate coordinated many national and international research projects mainly in the areas of environmental sociology, gender studies and participatory technology assessment. She teaches at Austrian universities as well as in international summer schools and workshops.

Noel Longhurst is an economic geographer by training whose research focuses on the intersections between technological change, economic inclusion and sustainability. Empirically, his recent research has focused on fuel poverty, energy transitions, alternative currencies and the Transition Network environmental movement. His Ph.D. research was an ethnographic study of how a countercultural 'alternative milieu' developed in the vicinity of the town of Totnes in the UK, and the extent to which the existence of this milieu supports the emergence of grassroots economic experiments and/or enhances their longevity.

Sylvia Lorek holds a Ph.D. in consumer economics and is trained to work on the interlinkages of the individual micro-economic and the societal macro-economic perspective in which the scientific and societal discourses about sustainable consumption take place. As head of SERI Germany e.V., she is working on studies and as consultant for national and international organisations. She has a lecturer position at the University of Applied Science in Münster and held classes at the University of Helsinki, the Baltic University Program (BUP) and the Asia-Europe Foundation University. Sylvia is an organising member of SCORAI Europe, the Global Research Forum on Sustainable Consumption and Production (GRF-SCP), and the Society for the European Roundtable on Sustainable Consumption and Production (ERSCP).

Keighley McFarland has spent several years involved in the research and prac-tice of transformations in the food system. She has worked at the Ecologic Institute in Berlin since 2012, researching topics in biodiversity policy, food systems, and sustainability transformations. In 2014 and 2015, she completed a research internship at the Dutch Research Institute for Transitions (DRIFT), where she investigated food-system transitions and socially innov-ative alternative food networks. She received her M.Sc. in integrated natural resource management from Humboldt University of Berlin in 2015, follow-ing a B.A. in political economy and German at the University of California, Berkeley. Alongside her professional and academic work, she is an active member of Slow Food Youth Germany, a non-profit organisation engaging with young people for a good, clean and fair food system.

Simon Milton is one of the founding members of GreenDependent Association in Hungary. He has participated as a researcher in international projects on the topics of natural resource management and evaluation, corporate sustain-ability and CSR, and sustainable communities and initiatives, and has authored or co-authored a number of publications on these topics. As an assistant professor at the Corvinus University of Budapest, his primary interest was CSR and business ethics.

Satoru Mizuguchi holds a bachelor's degree in law from Tokyo's Waseda Uni-versity (1981) and works as journalist and communication consultant. Since 2015, he has been a co-editor and co-author of the series Theory and Prac-tice of Urban Sustainability Transitions published by Springer and chairman of the Japanese Forum of Environmental Journalists (founded in 1991). As a media consultant, he has undertaken outreach activities for the fourth and fifth assessment reports of the IPCC (working for Japan's Ministry of Environment), and for the Kyoto Protocol (working for UNEP).

Tim O'Riordan is emeritus professor of environmental sciences at the Univer-sity of East Anglia. He received an OBE in 2010, is a deputy lieutenant of the County of Norfolk, served as sheriff of Norwich (2009–10), and is a fellow of the British Academy. He holds an M.A. in geography from the Uni-versity of Edinburgh, an M.Sc. in water resources engineering from Cornell University, and a Ph.D. in geography from the University of Cambridge. Tim is actively involved in research addressing the themes associated with better governance for sustainability. He is also active in the evolution of sustain-ability science partnerships. His direct work relates to designing future coast-lines in East Anglia in England and in Portugal, so that they are ready for sea-level rises and the creation of sound economies and societies for a sus-tainable future.

Iain Soutar is a research fellow within the Energy Policy Group at the Univer-sity of Exeter. His research focuses on the interplay between innovation pro-cesses and inertia within the context of energy system transformation. Specifically, he is interested in how processes of social and technological innovation are influenced by a range of actors, including 'niche' agents, incumbents and wider society and the conditions and implications of transformational change in the energy system. Iain's Ph.D. examined the value of community energy and a 'citizen-oriented' energy system in terms of both facilitating local energy system change and more broadly in helping to overcome system inertia.

Edina Vadovics is research director of GreenDependent Institute and president of GreenDependent Association in Hungary, both with the mission to promote and research sustainable lifestyles, focusing on facilitating dialogue between research and practice. Edina manages GreenDependent's work in international research projects and campaigns. While her research focuses on sustainable communities and lifestyles, she is also involved in action projects. Previously, she worked in corporate sustainability management and taught related courses at various universities. She also worked as an external expert to the European Environment Agency and UNEP and contributed to some of their key publications. She is member of the advisory board of the Transformative Social Innovation Theory (TRANSIT) research project, and an expert in the URBACT capitalisation project on social innovation in cities. Edina is a member of the SCORAI Europe steering committee, and has contributed to several SCORAI workshops and co-organised SCORAI special sessions at conferences.

Philip J. Vergragt is an associate fellow at the Tellus Institute, a research professor at Marsh Institute, Clark University, and a professor emeritus of technology assessment at Delft University of Technology, the Netherlands. He has co-authored more than ninety scientific publications and four books. His research focuses on sustainable technological and social innovations in transportation, energy and housing; grassroots innovations; socio-technical transitions; sustainable consumption and production; and technology assessment of emerging technologies. In the last ten years, he has co-founded the North American (and European) Sustainable Consumption Research and Action Initiative (SCORAI), the North American Roundtable on Sustainable Production and Consumption (NARSPAC), and the Global Research Forum on Sustainable Production and Consumption (GRF-SPaC). Philip obtained his Ph.D. in chemistry from the University of Leiden in 1976.

Julia M. Wittmayer works as senior researcher at DRIFT, the Dutch Research Institute for Transitions at the Erasmus University Rotterdam, the Netherlands. She holds an M.Sc. in social and cultural anthropology (cum laude) and her research focuses on social innovation and social sustainability in urban areas and on a local scale. Her research interest is in roles, social relations and interactions of actors involved in transition (management) processes and initiatives, with a specific interest for the role of research and transdisciplinary engagements. She also lectures at DRIFT's Transition Academy, leading the theme 'Transformative Research'.

Acknowledgements

Most of the chapters of this book were originally presented at a workshop which took place at the Impact Hub in Vienna, in November 2015.[1] The focus of the workshop was to improve our understanding of the interaction of social innovation, transformation of society and sustainable – or lower – consumption, and to identify strategies to influence this nexus whilst addressing fundamental societal challenges. The editors wish to thank members and funders of a cross-national research project and a global research and practitioner network, representatives of which jointly organised and led the workshop, and the preparation of the book.

Our thanks therefore go to the partners and funder (the EU Commission) of the TRANSIT project, which is dedicated to increasing our understanding of the processes through which social innovation may lead to transformative change (referred to as transformative social innovation).[2] Second our thanks go to members of the SCORAI,[3] which is an ever-growing global network of close to a thousand researchers and practitioners committed, since its inception in 2008, to a better analysis of consumer society and its challenges and diagnosis of ways in which more sustainable societies and economies may be realised in practice. The editorial team of this book included members of the TRANSIT research and advisory team and members of the steering committee of SCORAI's European network, SCORAI Europe.[4] We thank members of SCORAI and partners of TRANSIT for their intellectual and practical support. Our gratitude also goes to the staff of the Impact Hub in Vienna who hosted us so well at the workshop.

The editorial team[5] would like to thank the following: all of the contributing authors, for their efforts and patience during the rounds of revision necessary to convert workshop papers into final book chapters; the series editors of the Routledge–SCORAI Studies in Sustainable Consumption, Halina Szejnwald Brown, Maurie Cohen and Philip Vergragt; the anonymous reviewers of the proposal for the book; and the workshop participants who contributed to our lively discussions in Vienna. All of the aforementioned encouraged and helped us to reflect on the purpose of the book, as well as its content and organisation. Finally, we wish to acknowledge the support of the commissioning and production teams at Routledge, including Annabelle Harris and Margaret Farrelly.

JB, AG, SL, EV, JMW
Maastricht, London, Overath, Budapest, Rotterdam
June 2017

Notes

1 Further information about the Vienna workshop may be found at http://scorai.org/vienna-2015.
2 The editorial work on this book by Julia M. Wittmayer has been carried out as part of the TRANSIT project funded by the European Union's Seventh Framework Programme (FP7) under grant agreement 613169. The views expressed in this article are the sole responsibility of the authors and do not necessarily reflect the views of the European Union.
3 More details on the global SCORAI network can be found at http://scorai.org.
4 Further information about the SCORAI Europe community can be found at http://scorai.org/europe.
5 The editors share equal responsibility for the preparation of this volume: names are listed alphabetically on the front cover to reflect this sharing of effort.

1 Introduction

The nexus of social innovation, sustainable consumption and societal transformation

Julia Backhaus, Audley Genus and Julia M. Wittmayer[1]

1 Background

Globalised consumption and production patterns contribute to environmental change and damage, most noticeably in the form of anthropogenic climate change, resource depletion and the pollution of water and air. In addition to environmental degradation, societies worldwide are facing deep challenges including political unrest, instability or even crises, a widening gap in income and security between wealthier and poorer population segments and the erosion of social cohesion in the face of mass migration. It has been argued (Lundvall forthcoming) that these are not isolated phenomena but consequences of a global, capitalist system which emphasises the pursuit of economic growth based on market competition as measured by indicators such as GDP. Despite global, national and local efforts to protect the environment and citizens from the hazardous effects of an – in terms of spread and volume – ever-expanding global market for capital, services and goods, 'bad news' appears to outweigh 'good news', whereas a relatively small number of people make enormous financial gains. In a number of countries, the political establishment struggles between hardening frontlines dividing those who support national(istic) approaches and those who promote international cooperation to face the crises and challenges of the twenty-first century.

Until recently, there seemed to be a global consensus on the necessity to undertake concerted action on climate change, as stipulated for example in the Paris Agreement that was signed at COP21 in 2015. With the impending withdrawal of the United Kingdom from the European Union ('Brexit') and the 2016 presidential election in the USA, the global political context has since become less predictable. US policies under President Trump have changed and are expected to change further, with climate change 'denial' a pervasive element of relevant discourses in the historically largest national emitter of greenhouse gases. Also, the UK government department responsible for climate change and energy affairs (DECC) was disbanded, soon after Theresa May became prime minister in July 2016 and absorbed into the business ministry. The focus of energy policy was redirected towards reducing costs for consumers and business rather than 'green' subsidies, technologies and targets. While these developments make for a bleak outlook from the perspective of sustainable consumption and development, other developments serve as beacons of hope for many.

An imperative is to devise effective measures to reduce consumption, for example, but not restricted to, high carbon-emitting sectors such as energy, transport and food (IPPC 2014; Genus and Thorpe 2016). There have been notable policy developments concerning sustainable consumption in the European Union, for example, and some remarkable policies undertaken by and in EU states. For instance, in relation to mobility, one can point to the French 'bonus/malus' private vehicle tax/credit scheme and the city-wide Paris Velib bicycle-sharing initiative, particulates badges and environmental zones banning the biggest polluters from German cities, and in the UK to the national level Carbon Plan of 2011 and the central London congestion charge. In the energy sector, the number of energy cooperatives and other community energy projects aimed at energy sovereignty and sustainability has risen steeply, often benefitting from national subsidy schemes. In the food sector, labelling schemes developed and implemented by public–private, multi-stakeholder platforms seek to address persistent problems with respect to human and animal welfare as well as environmental protection. Next to policy-led or policy-driven developments, interest in sustainable business models is high, with companies and scientists invested in optimising solutions for shared value creation. In addition, 'transformative science' has become a catch phrase for interventions at various levels that aim to test and promote more sustainable ways of living. Last but not least, countless civil society initiatives have sprouted, reviving old or pioneering new approaches to sustainable living, including solidarity, open source or peer-to-peer approaches to production and consumption.

In recent years, EU policy-makers have identified social innovation as a potentially effective approach for tackling grand societal challenges such as those connected to water, climate change and energy as well as to the production of goods (BEPA 2010, 2014; European Commission 2013a, 2013b; Science Communication Unit 2014): social innovation 'can provide local answers to complex social and societal challenges mobilising local actors' (European Commission 2013b: 10). The EU can be considered to have followed in the footsteps of Latin America, which has a much longer tradition of fostering social innovation to address policy problems and market failures (Rey de Marulanda and Tancredi 2010). In European policy circles, social innovation emerged as a potential solution to the needs of citizens at the local level and to challenges for which conventional markets are ill-adapted (Mulgan *et al.* 2007). In line with this reasoning, the European Commission has allocated an increasing budget to researching and understanding social innovation in Europe (see European Commission 2013a; n.d.).

One of these research projects is TRANSIT (Transformative Social Innovation Theory). In collaboration with SCORAI Europe (Sustainable Consumption Research and Action Initiative Europe – which is a body with roots in an earlier EU-funded project known as SCORE! and closely connected with the North American SCORAI network). TRANSIT jointly organised a workshop where most of the contributions to this book were presented and discussed. The workshop was inspired by the intriguing nexus between social innovation, sustainable consumption and societal transformation. It built on theoretical considerations, such as the current pervasiveness of the notion of 'transition' and what moving 'beyond transition' could bring to the study of past or ongoing changes and to influencing current practices, ideas and actors. The workshop also explored this nexus through case studies of social innovation and sustainable consumption as well as of policies which influence these at different sub-national, national and international scales. Through contributions, presentations and discussions, participants scrutinised the practice and relevance of social innovation and sustainable consumption initiatives and whether they have some transformative and widely beneficial real-world consequences.

2 Aims

Building on the workshop contributions, this book provides timely coverage of the nexus between social innovation, sustainable consumption and societal transformation. It explores this nexus through discussion of cornerstone concepts as well as providing empirical observation and critical reflections on developments in practice. It brings together theoretical and empirical contributions on questions such as: What is social innovation and how can it contribute to sustainable consumption or societal transformation? What is the transformative potential of social innovation initiatives vis-á-vis incumbent institutions and dominant practices? How might societies unlock the full potential of social innovation for sustainable consumption?

The book provides a space for developing a better understanding of the merits of different perspectives on societal change in relation to social innovation which can both positively and negatively contribute to sustainable or reduced consumption in defined sectors or across social practices, space and time. The discussions are enriched by contributions from academic researchers, practitioners and 'pracademics' bringing diverse knowledge and experience to bear on issues of concern. Empirical contributions focus on disentangling, and thereby contributing to a further understanding of, the relation between social innovation, sustainable consumption and societal change. The case studies show the various ways in which 'social innovation', 'transition', 'transformation' and 'sustainable consumption' are understood or practised across several European countries. Through these empirical cases, authors probe the possibility and the difficulty inherent in 'doing things differently' from business-as-usual. These also highlight the point that practitioners in social innovation initiatives challenge yet at the same time are subject to prevailing, dominant institutions, which they reproduce.

The core aims of the book are:

- to analyse the relations between social innovation(s) and sustainable consumption and to identify ways in which social innovation in practice can contribute effectively to sustainable consumption;

- to critically reflect on the relations between social innovation(s) and societal transformation and to assess the transformative potential of social innovation initiatives vis-á-vis incumbent institutions and dominant practices.

3 The nexus of social innovation, sustainable consumption and societal transformation

The book revolves around the three key themes of social innovation, sustainable consumption and societal transformation and their nexus (see Figure 1.1). The following paragraphs introduce each key theme to stimulate thinking about them individually and interrelatedly, and to articulate their salience to the work and concerns of the book. In the further course of the book, each contributory chapter positions itself in relation to these three elements. The contributions come from diverse disciplinary backgrounds, including amongst others innovation studies, sociology and geography, and employ a range of methodological approaches, sometimes in a cross- or trans-disciplinary way.

3.1 Social innovation

Research on social innovation is not coherent in terms of disciplinary focus or approach. Rather the phenomenon is approached from different perspectives and therefore also defined in different ways. Sociological contributions most often identify social innovations as new practices or new combinations of practices (e.g. Howaldt and Kopp 2012). Approaching the phenomenon from urban

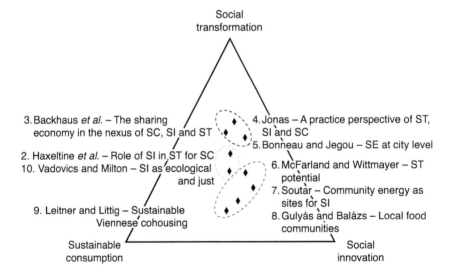

Figure 1.1 Positioning of chapter contributions in relation to the nexus of social innovation, sustainable consumption and societal transformation.

studies, Moulaert and colleagues (2005) distinguish between three dimensions of social innovation such as (1) satisfaction of human needs presently unmet, (2) changes in social relations and (3) empowerment. A recent review identified changing social relations or systems as well as the goal of addressing or solving a socially relevant problem as common themes across distinct bodies of literatures grappling with this topic (Van der Have and Rubalcaba 2016). Relevant to the themes of the book are certainly those authors who connect social innovation to social change (Cajaiba-Santana 2014) or more specifically to societal transformations (Haxeltine *et al.* 2016; Avelino *et al.* 2017; Pel and Bauler 2014). The latter authors (as part of the TRANSIT research project) approach social innovations as changes in social relations, involving new ways of doing, organising, knowing and framing and consider transformative social innovations as those that challenge, alter or replace dominant institutions.

3.2 Sustainable consumption

Current lifestyles in the Western world and among the affluent everywhere are based on patterns of overproduction and overconsumption, already exceeding several of the physical boundaries of our planetary system (Rockström *et al.* 2009) and leading to the exhaustion of natural resources and climate change. While the global, capitalist economy is facing several systemic, interrelated crises, research and action on more sustainable consumption patterns and lifestyles aims to explore and experience what it means to live a happy, healthy and sustainable life (Backhaus *et al.* 2011). Recurring themes are 'one planet living', 'a footprint of 1.0' or 'a good life', and points of attention include infrastructures, policy frameworks, governance approaches, business models and communities that foster or achieve more sustainable – or reduced – consumption (Genus and Thorpe 2016). In recent years, sustainable consumption research has increasingly concerned itself with social inequalities and the identification and creation of sustainable consumption 'corridors' (Di Giulio and Fuchs 2014) or of a 'safe and just operating space for humanity' (Raworth 2012). Another central theme has been to challenge the notion that (un)sustainable consumption – and related policies – should be focused on the attitudes, behaviour, and choices of the individual consumer, the so-called 'ABC' approach (Shove *et al.* 2012; Shove and Walker 2014). Rather, it is argued that a focus on unsustainable practices should be adopted, drawing attention to collective conventions and cultures of practice in everyday living, in which complexes of related practices are recognised (e.g. working in an office, using a computer and automobile transport), each comprising material, symbolic and knowledge elements. How and to what extent these may be undone and more sustainable practices embedded are questions which demand much of institutional entrepreneurs – whether these be policy-makers, social movements or businesses, currently mainstreaming or operating on its fringes or in its basement (Genus 2016).

3.3 *Societal transformation*

Societal transformations can be conceptualised as fundamental, persistent and irreversible change across society (Avelino *et al.* 2014). The use of the term 'transformation' draws on the work of Karl Polanyi (1944) who described the rise of the market economy and the ideology of economic liberalism as the 'great transformation'. As such, societal transformation exceeds radical change in individual societal or socio-technical sub-systems, which are commonly referred to as system innovation or transition. While some scholars have discussed transitions at a more aggregated level (Rotmans and Loorbach 2010), others suggest that transition thinking encapsulates the (illusion of) intentional societal change (Stirling 2014). In relating societal transformation to sustainable consumption, several of the book's chapters reflect on questions related to intentionality, empowerment and the intended and unintended (side-)effects of social innovations. To be transformative, these kinds of innovations should enable or bring about new relations between politics, society, science and the economy (WBGU 2011), globally and in people's everyday lives. This may sound highly visionary and universal. However, the tension between local innovations and such grand ambitions calls into question the boundaries of effective putative societal change and the means by which it is to be achieved. Moreover, the question is posed as to the possible political purposes of utopian 'imaginaries' (Jasanoff and Kim, 2013), for example, employed as persuasive or coercive co-opting devices and of the nature and distribution of often unacknowledged potential 'bads' of transformation. A more rounded view appreciates that there may be losers as well as winners in the new society/economy, as it may well (re)produce injustices, unfairnesses and inequities.

4 The structure of the book

The chapters offer theoretical–conceptual advancements in the understanding of social innovation and its potential contribution to sustainable consumption and societal transformation. They also present case studies situated in a range of sites, for example in relation to food, housing, energy and policy, and geographical locations, mostly in Europe. Analytically, the case studies focus on actors, discourses or practices and illustrate recent research and practice on the relation between social innovation, societal change and sustainable or reduced consumption. This includes processes of institutionalisation at different scales, and invites questions about the roles of different actors, such as city administrators or local food activists and thinking about the roles of narratives in societal transformations. There is analysis and reflection on the normative direction of a desired societal transformation towards sustainability.

The order in which chapter contributions appear in the book mirrors the positioning depicted in Figure 1.1. Working in a (roughly) clockwise direction around Figure 1.1, the book proceeds with one of the contributions positioned most centrally in the diagram (Chapter 2), which most clearly addresses the interrelationship of social innovation, societal transformation and sustainable consumption. Chapters 3–5 are more directly concerned with social innovation and its relation with societal transformation. Chapters 6–9 are more explicitly concerned with sustainable consumption as they address issues connected with the role of social innovation within societal transformation. Chapter 10 completes the (not quite) circle, to consider the framing and mapping of social innovation initiatives and their potential contribution to societal transformation and sustainable consumption. A summary of each chapter contribution is given below.

The following chapter (Chapter 2), by Haxeltine and colleagues, explores the nexus of social innovation and societal transformation, which they conceive of as 'sustainability transformations'. The authors draw on the cases of the Transition Network, Global Ecovillage Network, Slow Food and credit unions. They argue that potentially transformative social innovations such as these require explicit political strategies to challenge, reshape and ultimately supplant prevailing institutional arrangements which reproduce extant unsustainable practices, systems and modes of organisation and governance.

Chapter 3, by Backhaus and colleagues, explores insights that conceptual tools, rooted in different yet complementary understandings of the world, may be able to offer to sharing economy initiatives to help navigate the sustainable consumption, societal transformation and social innovation nexus in practice. Based on theoretical and empirical analysis, several intuitive challenges for sharing schemes to be successful and sustainable are identified and a set of guiding principles is suggested to enhance the successful interlocking of old and new practices and to foster sectoral and cross-sectoral transformation towards sustainability.

The chapter by Michael Jonas (Chapter 4) considers the view that grand societal challenges fundamentally require processes capable of transforming social practices. Accordingly, Jonas explores connections among sustainable consumption, social innovation and societal transformation taking a position rooted in practice theory. Centrally, the argument is made that transformation may be manifest in the emergence of frugal practices which engender wellbeing, and which may entail social innovations which are but one element of a more equal and sustainable social order.

The chapter co-authored by Marcelline Bonneau and François Jégou (Chapter 5) addresses institutional transformation as contributing to societal transformations drawing on the examples of the cities of Amersfoort (the Netherlands) and Gdańsk (Poland). In searching for new ways to interact with citizens, public administrations adopt social innovation as a way of experimenting with new governance models. These new practices also translate into changes within the public administration, with changing internal processes, attitudes and procedures as a consequence.

In Chapter 6, Keighley McFarland and Julia M. Wittmayer show that consumption practices are 'only one part of the problem'. Thus it is unwise to focus interventions on 'consuming better', without reshaping underlying policy processes and institutions which govern market and social relations. Their analysis is informed by a case study of food systems in Germany, focusing on the Food Assembly (FA), an example of community pick-up point schemes, which are in turn a kind of alternative food network. Critically, in the authors' view the case represents a social innovation which challenges certain dominant institutions but not others. Thus it partially reproduces prevailing approaches to sustainable consumption (of food) based upon political consumerism, rather than any more fundamental rethinking of policy, and economic and social organisation around food.

Iain Soutar's contribution (Chapter 7) examines community energy in the UK as a site for social innovation. For Soutar, social and technological innovations connected with community energy are able to challenge dominant institutions to effect and realise energy systems transformation. A vital role is played by discourse and experimentation regarding what the relation between energy systems and communities should be and in constituting this relation. It is argued that community energy discourse and experiments as social innovation embrace much more than the conventional preoccupations of policy, connected with objectives of decarbonisation, security and affordability. Indeed, they take in a far broader range of concerns, including societal objectives pertaining to health and wellbeing, economics, fairness and democracy.

The chapter by Emese Gulyás and Balint Balázs (Chapter 8) scrutinises the role of consumers in social innovation; namely in community-supported agriculture and direct food-purchasing groups in Hungary. Employing a 'narrative of change' framework, they show that consumers participate because they consider dominant market structures as failing: they want to take an active role and regain power. They also show that those participating in the initiatives have strong social capital and links to other initiatives. Finally, in line with the motivations for participating, they scrutinise how change is thought to come about through bottom-up initiatives rather than by established institutions and is closely related to levels of trust and distrust.

Chapter 9, by Michaela Leitner and Beate Littig, examines the transformative potential of cohousing, focusing on a case study of its emergence in Austria and possible limitations thereto. Leitner and Littig see cohousing – including the Viennese case they analyse – as social experimentation, which may engender novel patterns of intentional communal everyday living. In this context, residents collectively may adopt more sustainable practices across a range of domains of their daily lives and work. However, whilst voluntary and collective initiatives such as cohousing may not be driven by external pressure (e.g. from policy-makers), those who participate or might do so will be subject to conditions in wider society. Cultures of individualism and gendering may complicate well-meaning attempts at living communally and sustainably in socially innovative arrangements.

In Chapter 10, Edina Vadovics and Simon Milton present a tool for 'convergence mapping', which might allow for comparison among social innovation initiatives in relation to their potential to contribute to greater sustainability and societal transformation based on ecological principles and social equity. The work they present is founded on research undertaken as part of the CONVERGE project, funded under the European Union Seventh Framework programme, a project which aimed to 'rethink globalisation' based on considerations of fair access to planetary resources and respect for ecological limits. The authors illustrate the use of the tool with three examples: a carbon-reduction action group in the UK; a transition town initiative located in Hungary; and a not-for-profit poverty alleviation organisation based in Tamil Nadu, India.

Much of the empirical material presented in the chapters below is situated in a European context. To transcend this geographical focus and to acknowledge the global scope and scale required for meaningful transformations towards more sustainable levels and patterns of consumption, two of the chapters appearing near the end of the book (Chapters 11 and 12) take the form of commentaries as reflections. There is one commentary from Philip Vergragt, a senior researcher at the Tellus Institute and Clark University in the USA, and one from Satoru Mizuguchi, chair of the Japanese Forum of Environmental Journalists, both of whose work is closely connected with the themes and concerns of the book. The concluding chapter (Chapter 13), is written by Sylvia Lorek and Edina Vadovics, two members of the editorial team. It analyses and synthesises the different chapters with regard to their contribution to the guiding questions of the book, as well as proposing ways for taking the issues raised in them further.

Note

1 Names of co-authors of this chapter are listed alphabetically.

References

Avelino, F., Wittmayer, J.M., Haxeltine, A., Kemp, R., O'Riordan, T., Weaver, P., Loorbach, D., and Rotmans, J. (2014) 'Game changers and transformative social innovation: the case of the economic crisis and the new economy' (TRANSIT working paper 1) TRANSIT: EU SSH.2013.3.2-1 Grant agreement no. 613169.

Avelino, F., Wittmayer, J.M., Pel, B., Weaver, P., Dumitru, A., Haxeltine, A., Kemp, R., Jørgensen, M.S., Bauler, T., Ruijsink, S., and O'Riordan, T. (2017) 'Transformative social innovation and (dis)empowerment: towards a heuristic' *Technological Forecasting and Social Change*. Online first: http://dx.doi.org/10.1016/j.techfore.2017.05.002.

Backhaus, J., Breukers, S., Mont, O., Paukovic, M., Mourik, R., and SPREAD Sustainable Lifestyles 2050 consortium (2011) *Sustainable Lifestyles: Today's Facts and Tomorrow's Trends* (SPREAD Sustainable Lifestyles 2050 project deliverable 1.1), www.sustainablelifestyles.eu/fileadmin/images/content/D1.1_Baseline_Report.pdf (accessed 5 May 2017).

BEPA (Bureau of European Policy Advisors) (2010) *Empowering People, Driving Change: Social Innovation in the European Union* European Commission: Brussels.

BEPA (Bureau of European Policy Advisors) (2014) 'Social innovation: a decade of changes', www.transitsocialinnovation.eu/resource-hub/social-innovation-a-decade-of-changes-a-bepa-report (accessed 5 May 2017).

Cajaiba-Santana, G. (2014) 'Social innovation: moving the field forward: a conceptual framework' *Technological Forecasting and Social Change* 82: 42–51.

Di Giulio, A., and Fuchs, D. (2014) 'Sustainable consumption corridors: concept, objections, and responses' GAIA – *Ecological Perspectives for Science and Society* 23: 184–192.

European Commission (n.d.) 'Research on social innovation' (inventory of projects funded under the EU Research Framework Programmes), https://ec.europa.eu/research/social-sciences/pdf/project_synopses/ssh-projects-fp7-5-6-social-innovation_en.pdf#view=fit&pagemode=none (accessed 5 May 2017).

European Commission (2013a) *Social Innovation Research in the European Union. Approaches, Findings and Future Directions* (policy review EUR 25996 EN) Directorate-General for Research and Innovation Socio-Economic Sciences and Humanities, European Commission: Brussels.

European Commission (2013b) 'Guide to social innovation', http://s3platform.jrc.ec.europa.eu/documents/20182/84453/Guide_to_Social_Innovation.pdf (accessed 5 May 2017).

Genus, A. (2016) 'Sustainability transitions: a discourse-institutional perspective' in Brauch, H., Oswald Spring, Ú., Grin, J., and Scheffran, J. (eds) *Handbook on Sustainability Transition and Sustainable Peace* Springer: Berlin, 527–541.

Genus, A., and Thorpe, A. (2016) 'Introduction' in Genus, A. (ed.) *Sustainable Consumption: Design, Innovation and Practice* Springer: Dordrecht, 1–15.

Haxeltine, A., Avelino, F., Pel, B., Dumitru, A., Kemp, R., Longhurst, N., Chilvers, J., and Wittmayer, J.M. (2016) 'A framework for transformative social innovation' (TRANSIT working paper 5) TRANSIT: EU SSH.2013.3.2–1 Grant agreement no. 61316.

Howaldt, J., and Kopp, R. (2012) 'Shaping social innovation by social research' in Franz, H.W., Hochgerner, J., and Howaldt, J. (eds) *Challenge Social Innovation: Potentials for Business, Social Entrepreneurship, Welfare and Civil Society* Springer: Berlin and Heidelberg, 43–56.

IPPC (2014) 'Drivers, trends and mitigation' in *Climate Change 2014: Mitigation of Climate Change* (Contribution of Working Group III to the Fifth Assessment Report of the Intergovernmental Panel on Climate Change) Cambridge University Press: Cambridge and New York.

Jasanoff, S., and Kim, S-H. (2013) 'Sociotechnical imaginaries and national energy policies' *Science as Culture* 22(2): 189–196.

Lundvall, B-A. (forthcoming) 'Is there a technological fix for the current global stagnation? A response to Daniele Archibugi, Blade Runner economics: will innovation lead the economic recovery?' *Research Policy*.

Moulaert, F., Martinelli, F., Syngedouw, E., and Gonzalez, S. (2005) 'Towards alternative model(s) of local innovation' *Urban Studies* 42: 1969–1990.

Mulgan, G., Tucker, S., Ali, R., and Sanders, B. (2007) 'Social innovation: what it is, why it matters and how it can be accelerated' (working paper, Skoll Centre for Social Entrepreneurship, Saïd Business School, Oxford).

Pel, B., and Bauler, T. (2014) 'The institutionalization of social innovation: between transformation and capture' (TRANSIT working paper 2) TRANSIT: EU SSH.2013.3.2–1 Grant agreement no. 613169.

Polanyi, K. (1944 [1997]) *The Great Transformation: Politische und ökonomische Ursprünge von Gesellschaften und Wirtschaftssystemen* Suhrkamp: Frankfurt.

Raworth, K. (2012) *A safe and just space for humanity: can we live within the doughnut?* (Oxfam discussion paper) Oxfam: Oxford.

Rey de Marulanda, N., and Tancredi, F.B. (2010) 'From social innovation to public policy: success stories in Latin America and the Caribbean' UN Economic Commission for Latin America and the Caribbean LC/W.351, http://repositorio.cepal.org/bitstream/handle/11362/3795/lcw351.pdf?sequence=1&isAllowed=y (accessed 5 May 2017).

Rockström, J., Steffen, W., Noone, K., Persson, Å., Chapin, F.S., III, Lambin, E., Lenton, T.M., Scheffer, M., Folke, C., Schellnhuber, H., Nykvist, B., De Wit, C.A., Hughes, T., Van der Leeuw, S., Rodhe, H., Sörlin, S., Snyder, P.K., Costanza, R., Svedin, U., Falkenmark, M., Karlberg, L., Corell, R.W., Fabry, V.J., Hansen, J., Walker, B., Liverman, D., Richardson, K., Crutzen, P., and Foley, J. (2009) 'Planetary boundaries: exploring the safe operating space for humanity' *Ecology and Society* 14(2): 32, www.ecologyandsociety.org/vol. 14/iss2/art32 (accessed 5 May 2017).

Rotmans, J., and Loorbach, D. (2010) 'Towards a better understanding of transitions and their governance: a systemic and reflexive approach, part II' in Grin, J., Rotmans, J., and Schot, J. (eds) *Transitions to Sustainable Development: New Directions in the Study of Long Term Transformative Change* Routledge: New York.

Science Communication Unit, University of the West of England, Bristol (2014) *Science for Environment Policy In-Depth Report: Social Innovation and the Environment* (report produced for the European Commission DG Environment, February), http://ec.europa.eu/science-environment-policy (accessed 5 May 2017).

Shove, E., and Walker, G. (2014) 'What is energy for? Social practice and energy demand' *Theory, Culture and Society* 3(5): 41–58.

Shove, E., Pantzar, M., and Watson, M. (2012) *The Dynamics of Social Practice: Everyday Life and How It Changes* Sage: London.

Stirling, A. (2014) 'Transforming power: social science and the politics of energy choices' *Energy Research and Social Science* 1: 83–95.

Van der Have, R.P., and Rubalcaba, L. (2016) 'Social innovation research: an emerging area of innovation studies?' *Research Policy* 45: 1923–1935.

WBGU (German Advisory Council on Global Change) (2011) *World in Transition: A Social Contract for Sustainability Flagship Report 2011* WBGU: Berlin.

2 Conceptualising the role of social innovation in sustainability transformations

Alex Haxeltine, Flor Avelino, Julia M. Wittmayer, Iris Kunze, Noel Longhurst, Adina Dumitru and Tim O'Riordan

1 Introduction

This chapter argues that current attempts to integrate sustainability goals into a social innovation context must avoid being overly instrumental and focusing only on indicators and valuation metrics that do not capture the complex and systemic nature of the couplings between social innovation processes on the one hand and (processes of) sustainability transformation on the other hand. We introduce the concept of 'transformative social innovation' as a suitable way of analysing the interactions of social innovation initiatives with the dynamics of sustainability transformations. Using this concept, this chapter explores the nexus of social innovation and societal transformation, conceptualised specifically in terms of sustainability transformations.

We use a dynamic framing of sustainability, as processes of sustainability transformation, conceptualised as broad systemic shifts in the dominant structures and institutions of a given societal context that result in a transformation from an unsustainable state of affairs to one in which both environmental limits and goals for human well-being are addressed. We draw upon insights from the transitions research field (Grin *et al.* 2010; Markard *et al.* 2012; Rotmans 2005; Van den Bergh *et al.* 2011) as a basis for conceptualising a sustainability transformation as a dynamic, systemic and contested change process that involves systemic changes in the dominant institutional arrangements within a particular societal context. Sustainable consumption is implicit in the framing of social innovation and sustainability transformation developed here, and is observed in the cases we present as one type of activity that is engaged with as sustainability ambitions are put into practice.

'Bottom-up' or 'grassroots' social innovations in particular may provide a means by which actors who are not situated in powerful positions can still influence transformative change in dominant social structures and institutions. In a situation, where the current system of arrangements is 'locked-in' to unsustainable patterns, the potential for social innovation to manifest in different 'places' in the system (e.g. policy, civil society, markets), can be of great importance.

Social innovation also has great potential for adaptation and evolution in a wider context of a changing set of political and social values. A key to bringing knowledge, values and technological innovations into action can be found in the social dimension of sustainability. Beyond innovations in ecological techno-logy, the challenge lies in exploring social principles for more appropriate and sustainable forms of economy, organisation and living. We argue that, despite the potential of social innovation to contribute to sustainability, our under-standing of both phenomena and their relations needs to be better developed.

We argue that, because of the systemic nature of the challenge, social innovation that contributes to sustainability transformations must take the form of transformative social innovation. The main argument can be summarised as follows: (i) Social innovation initiatives attempt to contribute to sustainability transformation processes by innovating new ways of doing, organising, framing and knowing. Our empirical case studies emphasise that this is an essential feature of social innovations that have the potential to contribute to sustain-ability transformations. (ii) However, because of the persistence of unsustain-ability, social innovation might be a necessary condition, but it is not a sufficient condition, we need rather transformative social innovation that also challenges, alters, replaces or supplements the dominant institutions that are reproducing the 'unsustainability' dynamic in the societal context. (iii) To do so, social innovation initiatives need explicit political tactics and strategies to deal with the challenge of institutionalising social innovation for sustainability, in doing so they must navigate between achieving transformative change on the one hand versus being influenced, even captured, by currently dominant institu-tions on the other hand.

The structure of the remainder of this chapter is as follows. Section 2 pro-vides a brief framing of the role of social innovation in sustainability transfor-mations. Section 3 then applies this framing to four social innovation initiatives that have both a civil society orientation and a sustainability focus. Building on this, Section 4 discusses the role of social innovation in sustainability transfor-mations, and concludes by outlining some implications for practice.

2 Conceptualising the role of social innovation in sustainability transformations

We conceptualise social innovation processes as potentially contributing to sustainability transformations but note that care is needed to avoid the trap of assuming that successful social innovation will necessarily have beneficial impacts in terms of sustainability goals. Such a perspective has hitherto been widespread in the policy discourse on social innovation (e.g. BEPA 2010) and to a certain extent also in the social innovation research literature (Avelino *et al*. forthcoming). Contrary to this widespread argumentation, we suggest that a social innovation developed to address a local problem framing often ends up having unforeseen impacts as it develops and expands, and it can happen that not all of these impacts are seen as beneficial for society at large.

Building on insights from research on social innovation, sustainable development and sustainability transitions, as well as several other areas of social theory, a theoretical and conceptual framework for transformative social innovation has been developed (Haxeltine *et al.* 2016). In this section, we draw upon this framework to briefly outline a framing of the role of social innovation in sustainability transformations, as the basis for a further empirical exploration in Section 3 and a discussion in Section 4.

2.1 Social innovation

A key starting point is to conceptualise social innovation in terms of changing social relations. Social innovation is defined as a process that involves a change in social relations, involving new ways of doing, organising, framing and/or knowing (Haxeltine *et al.* 2016). We approach social innovation as a process and as a qualitative property of ideas, objects, activities and/or (groups of) people. Recognising the dispersed nature of agency characterising social innovation phenomena (Scott Cato and Hillier 2010), all of these can be (or become) socially innovative to the extent that they engage in and/or contribute to a change in social relations, involving new ways of doing, organising, framing and/or knowing. Combinations of ideas, objects and activities that are considered socially innovative can be referred to as 'social innovations'. (Groups of) people that are considered socially innovative can be referred to as 'social innovators' or 'social innovation actors'. Any particular social innovation initiative is always embedded in complex webs of social relations. Changes in social relations will also usually be associated with changing social-ecological relations, and social-material relations more generally. The sustainability impacts of a social innovation (initiative) are bound up with how it brings about changes in social relations and institutions and cannot be measured only in terms of material outcomes, such as reductions in ecological footprints or carbon emissions.

2.2 Sustainability transformations

For conceptualising the systemic and dynamic nature of the challenge of achieving a more sustainable society, we turn to the field of sustainability transitions (Grin *et al.* 2010; Markard *et al.* 2012; Van den Bergh *et al.* 2011). Informed by transitions scholarship, we start from the contention that sustainable development must now be characterised as a response to the problems of late modernity that itself has become part of the problem (Loorbach 2014, 32) as environmental policies and sustainable development discourse have become part of dominant regimes and have primarily served to make them a bit less unsustainable:

> The currently dominant regimes based on the foundations of modernity are systemically unsustainable in a fundamental way. Besides the fact that their designs are based on historical societal problems and are therefore not adequate for today's societal challenges. They are unsustainable because the foundations upon which they are built are eroding rapidly: in terms of the

resources they use, the underlying financial models, the power relationships and their performance.

(Ibid., 32–33)

We argue that social innovation initiatives with sustainability goals are increasingly grappling with this type of systemic and fundamental diagnosis of the nature of the challenge presented by the sustainability imperative. One of the central premises in transition studies is that persistent problems are symptoms of unsustainable societies, and that dealing with these persistent problems requires sustainability transitions: "radical transformation[s] towards a sustainable society" (Grin *et al.* 2010, 1).

In this chapter we conceptualise sustainability transformations as processes of institutional transformation that involve broad structural changes in the institutional arrangements and the social relations of a society towards more sustainable arrangements and patterns across multiple parts of that society. A sustainability transformation can be understood as involving a persistent adjustment in societal values, outlooks and behaviours of sufficient 'width and depth' to alter any preceding situation in the societal context, and these adjustments in turn imply transformed social-ecological relations (Haxeltine *et al.* 2016). Change in only one 'part' of the societal context is not considered to be a sustainability transformation. There have to be related changes in several parts, and they have to happen simultaneously and across an array of places.

2.3 The role of (transformative) social innovation in sustainability transformations

Social innovation may include impacts on material, ecological and financial resources, as well as impacts on the nature and quality of social relations. Assessments and evaluations can then be made about whether, how and to what extent specific changes in social relations contribute to a specific sustainability transformation process. Actors who come together to form a new social innovation initiative often do so in response to some local or global problem framing and/or an articulated tension between the needs of participants and their perceptions of whether current institutional arrangements satisfy those needs and/or an aim to realise some inspiring vision (Dumitru *et al.* 2016b).

We define transformative social innovation as a specific type of social innovation process that challenges, alters, replaces or supplements dominant institutions in a specific societal context (Haxeltine *et al.* 2016). We frame a concept of institutions, starting from the observation that 'structures can be viewed as a set of institutionalized traditions or forms that enable and constrain action' (Cajaiba-Santana 2014, 47) and adopting a working definition of institutions as 'norms, rules, conventions and values' (ibid., 46) that both constrain and enable social relations and dominant patterns of doing, organising, framing and knowing. Dominant institutions can be viewed as the dominant ways of doing, organising, framing and knowing in the societal context. Transformative social innovation is a process that challenges, alters, replaces or supplements existing patterns in the 'structuring' of local practices, resulting in varying degrees of institutionalisation as the transformative social innovation unfolds across time and space.

The relations between social innovation and sustainability transformations can be framed in terms of the following four analytical questions:

a   *What are the (transformative) sustainability ambitions of the social innovation initiative?* Transformative ambitions are understood as a vision or ambition held by an initiative to catalyse or contribute to an identified sustainability transformation. Social innovation actors formulate such sustainability ambitions as 'narratives of change', taking the form/s of sets of ideas, concepts, metaphors, discourses or story-lines about change and innovation (Wittmayer *et al.* 2015a). These reveal, amongst other things, ideas about why the world needs to change, who has the power to do so and how this can be done. By developing and sharing their narratives of change, social innovation actors connect with the broader societal context and, if successful, help to co-create new societal narratives.

b   *Which social innovations does the initiative employ to achieve its sustainability ambitions?* New ways of doing, organising, framing and knowing are understood here in terms of the social innovations that an initiative adopts, adapts or develops in pursuit of its sustainability ambitions. This question in turn leads to a set of related questions about how, why and in what combinations different social innovations are adopted, adapted and further developed.

c   *What are the specific strategies and tactics that the social innovation initiative employs in attempting to increase its (transformative) sustainability impacts?* A specific social innovation initiative must find strategies and tactics that allow it to model and then spread the social innovations which it promotes in line with its sustainability ambitions. At the same time, existing dominant institutions will both enable and constrain (structure) the processes by which strategies are formulated and selected. As the social innovation initiative implements strategies, it will encounter responses from other actors: both from supporters and, possibly negative ones, from actors associated with the currently dominant institutional arrangements.

d   *How and to what extent does the social innovation initiative challenge, alter, replace or supplement dominant institutions?* Ultimately to advance a sustainability transformation process, the initiative must have an impact in terms of transforming current institutional arrangements, by challenging, altering, replacing or supplementing dominant institutions towards more sustainable solutions. This question explores the fit or mismatch between transformative ambitions and the actual processes of institutional change being engaged with and the actual transformative impacts being achieved.

In the next section, we apply this framing to four empirical case studies to develop a synthesis of observations about the role of social innovation in sustainability transformations.

3 Four empirical cases of social innovation networks with sustainability ambitions

In this section, we apply the four questions outlined above to four social innovation networks (networks of multiple social innovation initiatives) studied using an embedded case-study approach (Yin 2003). We chose social innovation networks which are explicitly aiming for sustainability but that do so in distinctly different ways. For the empirical analysis, we relied on secondary material from full case-study reports (Longhurst and Pataki 2015; Kunze and Avelino 2015; Dumitru *et al.* 2015, 2016a) as well as on the original data gathered through interviews, participant observation and document review (for the methodological guidelines, see Jørgensen *et al.* 2014; Wittmayer *et al.* 2015b). The four social innovation networks are:

The Transition Network is a social movement consisting of individuals who come together voluntarily in place-based communities (transition initiatives) to work on projects and activities that relate to the broad goal of achieving a 'transition', understood as 'changes we need to make to get to a low-carbon, socially-just, healthier and happier future, which is more enriching and more gentle on the earth than the way most of us live today' (Transition Network 2016; see Longhurst and Pataki 2015).

The Global Ecovillage Network (GEN) is a network of sustainable communities and initiatives that bridge different cultures, countries and continents (GEN 2016). An ecovillage is understood as an intentional community that is consciously designed through locally owned, participatory processes to regenerate social and natural environments: the ambition is that the multiple dimensions of sustainability can in this way be integrated into a holistic approach to sustainability (see Kunze and Avelino 2015).

Slow Food is a 'global, grassroots movement with thousands of members around the world that links the pleasure of food with a commitment to community and the environment' (Slow Food UK 2016). It was founded in 1989 in Italy and has been defined as a 'culture movement' based on the intrinsic cultural value of local production and a critique of the increasingly globalised food system (see Dumitru *et al.* 2016a).

Credit unions are organisations that aim to provide financial intermediation services guided by a set of ethical principles focusing on social and environmental goals. They aim to transform the economy through switching the focus of economic activity from financial gains and profit-making to sustainable livelihoods (see Dumitru *et al.* 2015).

Both GEN and the Transition Network have an explicit focus around 'relocalisation' and community-level initiatives. Both networks encompass a great diversity of attitudes towards sustainability amongst participants. These two networks are also in fact quite intertwined through, for example, the permaculture movement and common participants and so on. Slow Food directly addresses the challenge of sustainability transformations in food systems. Credit unions have a long history of ethical concerns around social issues with a more recent emphasis also on environmental issues and 'financing for sustainability'. Table 2.1 summarises

Table 2.1 Social innovation in relation to sustainability transformations, for four empirical case studies

	Transition Towns	Global Ecovillage Network	Slow Food Movement	Credit Unions
Sustainability ambitions framed	Initial framing in terms of notion of 'energy descent' and addressing climate change and peak oil; more recently the focus has shifted towards 'local economic resilience'. Deliberate framing in terms of building 'local resilience' rather than sustainable development, on the basis that it had been 'sold out'.	Holistic vision of sustainability: economic, social, ecological but also cultural, spiritual ('worldview'). Saving energy and resources through sharing, commons and living in community as a starting point for sustainability. Self-sufficiency and growing own food is often the initial guiding vision.	Transformation of 'food cultures' towards 'clean and fair food'; ideal of enjoying food-based social relations. Protecting traditional food stuffs, and food-related natural resources (e.g. a landscape with olive groves). Creating economic sustainability, especially for producers that can't access mainstream markets.	Transform the economy through switching the focus of economic activity from financial gains and profit-making, to positive social and environmental outcomes and impacts. Vision of finance as embedded in communities; facilitating both the marginalised and environmental protection/restoration goals.
Social innovations manifested	Predominately promotes and adapts pre-existing SIs around local food (e.g. community supported agriculture schemes), community energy, new ways of networking and organising, etc. The 'innovation' is in how these elements are brought together with the narrative.	Living in an intentional community. Elaborated culture, system and practices of communal ownership, decision making and conflict resolution; spirituality and love. New forms of doing: local economy, community food systems, cooking together, car sharing systems; low-tech innovation e.g. permaculture gardens, regenerating the natural environments, eco-housing.	New social relations between food producers, distributors and consumers. A new culture and new practices in (mainly local) food systems, based on trust relations between food producers and consumers. (Re-)claiming the experience of enjoying food in community.	Provides financial intermediation services guided by a set of ethical principles, focusing on social and environmental goals. New forms of governance and organisational model. New social relations; CU as partner in communities and actively helps to promote social/environmental goals.

Strategies and tactics employed	Aims to be 'apolitical' and inclusive; non-confrontational strategy while also proposing radical changes in production and consumption systems. Model of local initiatives linked in to global 'learning network'. Strong international networking strategy, which led to rapid spread of TTs initiatives in many countries. Focus on building local parallel infrastructure (e.g. food and energy systems). Working at local community level to build local resilience through the localisation of social-material relations. Dual focus on personal/cultural change and practical experiments. An easy to implement twelve-step plan for starting a 'transition town', which was later updated to a more ingredient based approach. (Perhaps non-intentional) tactic of Totnes becoming the iconic example for the movement.	Applying and further development of community building which includes trust building, communication tools, group processes and conflict resolution. Differences between ecovillages in terms of types of ownership model, importance of eco-technologies, and concerning political activities engaged in. Capacity building through learning by doing. A lot of attention to networking, education (GAIA/EDE), sharing knowledge (e.g. Solution Library); professional education centres. Applying for funding for practical research of sustainable technologies. Strategies and practices for shared ownership: cooperative ownership of land and building properties, from gift economy through collective economy to complementary currencies.	Re-claim 'the right to the pleasure of food'; emphasis on 'conviviality', tradition, family and cultural roots. Strategies of new (traditional) food practices in 'dialogue' with a new (reframed) food narrative. A new way of classifying traditional products and ways of producing; a system for international labelling. Slow Food university and other educational innovations such as bringing SF into schools (esp. in US). 'Kilometre zero restaurants', networks of chefs who bring SF principles to their restaurants. International networking strategy: connect different areas of the world; bring together in different events. Lobbying of EU and national governments to promote Slow Food vision and principles. Principle of maintaining coherence and credibility of SF vision, especially when interacting with governments.	Embedding of financial relations based on trust and cooperation in the web of activities and social relations in a community. Being close to projects and embedded in community; emphasis on in-depth relationships and knowledge (negating the need for conventional risk guarantees). Promote activities that provide opportunities for marginalised groups and environmental projects. Creating a parallel finance system within which new social relations are possible; but also a longer-term vision of a radically transformed financial system. Promote a culture of responsibility concerning where your money goes. Strategy of expanding to places where CUs don't yet exist. Developing indicators of the social impacts of finance (working with academics, EU, and governments).
Institutional arrangements to be transformed	Initial focus on need for radically new localised systems of production and consumption in a post-oil world. Initially at least posited the need to build new local institutions and structures in face of 'energy descent'.	Ecovillages challenge infrastructure and planning regulations when they implement sustainable features. In developing 'alternatives' they must confront existing regulations around e.g. schooling or employment.	A change in market relations, from competition to collaboration and the sharing of knowledge. Aims to transform food cultures, but also, to change food production, distribution and consumption systems.	A vision of creating a parallel finance system within which new, more sustainable, social and financial relations are possible; but also a longer-term vision of a radically transformed financial system.

the findings of confronting each of the four empirical cases with the framing developed above.

4 Discussion of the main findings

The following subsections respond to each of the analytical questions framed in Section 2.

4.1 Sustainability ambitions framed by the social innovation initiatives studied

All four networks have developed novel narratives of change that link discourses and concerns in society more generally to a particular vision and set of proposed solutions. None of the initiatives have simply adopted an existing sustainability discourse:

- The Transition Network was initially framed deliberately in terms of the goal of building 'local resilience', as a response to a perceived 'corporate capture' of the narrative of change around sustainable development.
- Ecovillages explicitly build on a holistic concept of sustainability – aiming to connect the social, economic, ecological and cultural dimensions of sustainability through common activities in a defined location.
- Slow Food has a distinct focus on sustainability as the re-claiming of traditional culture, practices and landscapes around food, with an emphasis on conviviality, lifestyle and improving the quality of social relations.
- Credit unions emphasise economy activity as an entry point for addressing environmental and social sustainability, with an emphasis on inclusivity and helping marginalised groups in society.

The narratives of change that express an initiative's transformative ambitions are themselves subject to change as the initiative develops, this can be based on strategic considerations (in response to external developments) or on a reflexive feedback loop concerning the working out of ambitious social innovation practices in the context of real-world dynamics. In the Transition Network case, for example, the original narrative of change was developed around 'localisation' as a means to build resilience in the face of peak oil and climate change. After the financial crisis of 2008 (and subsequent austerity measures) and the receding of peak oil as a compelling narrative in public discourse, there was a shift to an emphasis on 'local economic resilience'. Thus, the narrative was, to a certain extent, adapted to continue to justify a preferred 'solution'.

Social innovation initiatives make use of and draw upon existing societal discourses and over time even come to play a role in shaping these wider discourses. The Transition Network, started by drawing on discourses of peak oil and climate change and developing a narrative that made a connection to a discourse on localisation' The GEN draws on discourses concerning self-sufficiency, commons and spiritual development, while Slow Food tapped into a focus on traditions and critiques of industrial agriculture. Each of the four narratives of change make a different fundamental critique of the currently dominant institutions and structures. Such narratives of change, which emphasise that the current set-up just cannot be continued and that fundamental change is therefore required, are increasingly emerging from civil-society-led initiatives and movements. Being able to learn across social innovation networks about the changing nature of sustainability challenges and update narratives, mental models and theories of change accordingly then becomes a significant factor in the ability of initiatives to generate a sustained influence in transformation processes.

4.2 Social innovations employed by the initiatives studied

All four cases aim to change social relations: the Transition Network broadly between people and their local community; the GEN between people, community and land; the Slow Food movement between food producers, distributors and consumers; and credit unions between financial institutions and communities. These new social relations are in all cases also associated with new ways of doing, organising, framing and knowing. For example, new ways of doing can involve engaging in local food schemes or community energy projects (Transition Network), living in an intentional community, taking part in car-sharing systems and community food systems or regenerating natural environments (GEN), sourcing food locally and preparing it according to different ideas (Slow Food),or providing financial intermediation services (credit unions). However, it may sometimes be the specific combinations of new ways of doing, organising, framing and knowing, which make for the real novelty and therefore the potential to contribute to societal transformations.

4.3 Strategies and tactics employed by the initiatives studied

A key strategy observed in all cases was the provision of 'alternative' arrangements, in effect providing a localised response to certain dominant institutions. The Slow Food movement for example promotes traditional food practices and aims to re-claim 'the right to the pleasure of food', emphasising conviviality and the importance of food to tradition, family and cultural roots. Credit unions provide alternative forms of finance, which differ from the mainstream not in only in technique but also in the ethics and values they imply. The ecovillages perhaps most obviously provide alternatives, usually with a degree of independence in terms of social–ecological relations and energy and material flows. Transition initiatives also strive to provide alternative forms of, for example, food and energy production but always in the context of existing local communities. In doing so each has to work within the limitations of what is permitted by dominant institutions.

The Slow Food movement does not only engage in the provision of alternatives however, it also engages in lobbying the EU and national governments, international networking to connect supporters in different parts of the world, engaging with education through establishing a Slow Food university and by bringing Slow Food to the school curriculum, working on new systems for food labelling and generally emphasising the importance of traditional values. Our findings illustrate how, as well as directly providing alternatives, the initiatives also engage in activities of building a movement or platform for change, including growing their membership and access to resources, in part by connecting up with other similar initiatives.

Social innovation initiatives furthermore need to continuously update and adapt their vision and strategies, in response to broader societal developments and the direct actions of supporters of dominant institutions. As they update and adapt their vision and strategies, they need to hold true to the original core motivations which caused them to start the initiative in the first place. The latter holds especially when dominant institutions are taking up (some of) the initiative's practices or vision. In such situations social innovation initiatives need to maintain their radical core while translating and adapting to changing circumstances.

4.4 Dominant institutions that the initiatives are attempting to challenge, alter or replace

The four initiatives all have the ambition to replace specific dominant institutions: the consumption and production of food (Slow Food), the current financial system (credit unions), the way we work, relate and live (GEN) and the shift from a global to a local economy and social relations (Transition Network). They challenge these through their vision and narrative of change and through the novel practices that they promote. The GEN, for example, challenges amongst others planning, construction and schooling regulations. There are localised examples where this challenge leads to the altering of a regulation, such as the example of the approval of own schools. The Slow Food movement challenges current food consumption practices including the underlying norms and values and provides alternatives. This also translates into localised examples, where 'slow' has become the new normal, such as at the level of households, restaurants or festivals. The current organisations belonging to the credit union movement to date are arguably challenging the financial system through their very existence, however they currently supplement dominant institutions rather than representing an existential threat to the existing system.

5 Conclusion

The enabling conditions that support transformative social innovations in contributing to sustainability transformations, can be unpacked using the insights from the four empirical cases and with reference to the four questions articulated in Section 2.

- First, by positively engaging with and supporting social innovation initiatives to develop new narratives of change around what needs to be transformed (and by supporting learning across social innovation networks about the changing nature of sustainability challenges, etc.); such support could involve ensuring that the required knowledge base is available to social innovation initiatives and that available sources of knowledge and framings have credibility and are trusted.
- Second, by generating awareness of and learning on existing relevant social innovations and removing institutional barriers to their uptake and diffusion, one of the important functions of the social innovation networks explored in this chapter has been to facilitate the exchange of social innovations across diverse regional contexts.
- Third, by supporting initiatives in implementing strategies to further develop and diffuse social innovations, by acknowledging that they contribute to 'diverse transformations' (Stirling 2011), and, by providing guidance on potential and realised sustainability impacts; evaluating actual sustainability impacts is a key challenge given the complex and systemic nature of the dynamic between social innovation and sustainability transformations that has been outlined in this chapter.
- Fourth, by acknowledging and acting on the insight that sustainability transformations require that certain dominant institutional arrangements are to be transformed and that social innovation initiatives can play an important role in such transformation processes.

However, the framing presented in this chapter also points to a basic tension inherent in the idea that policy-makers associated with currently dominant (and deeply unsustainable) institutions might support transformative social innovations that contribute to transformations to sustainability. Social innovation initiatives have a two-way relationship with dominant institutions: they challenge them but also reproduce them. The founders of a new social innovation initiative will recruit members and supporters and engage them in co-productive activities of doing, framing, organising and knowing. If successful, they will find strategies and tactics that facilitate the diffusion of specific social innovations, in line with their sustainability ambitions. Dominant institutions (as norms, rules, conventions and values) will inevitably also influence the processes by which strategies are formulated and selected. As strategies are implemented, they will encounter negative reactions from actors associated with dominant institutions. It can be that the very processes that leads to success in the form of the more widespread uptake of the innovation, can also lead to a loss or dilution of the core vision and values. In terms of sustainability goals, the risk might be either that the initiative morphs into something which is helping to sustain fundamentally unsustainable dominant regimes, or that it refuses to change and remains as an isolated local manifestation.

If the sustainability imperative is understood as representing an existential challenge to the foundational regimes of late modernity, as argued in Section 2 of this chapter, then the size of the challenge becomes apparent. The dominant institutions and worldview of late modernity enter the social innovation process as dominant norms, rules, conventions and values, including the dominant ways of organising and governing. This can be through formal laws and regulations, but also in far more subtle ways such as through the micro-level dynamics of interpersonal relations between participants in a specific social innovation initiative. To succeed they need to not only address specific environmental and social problems but must do so in ways that navigate and transform the systemic patterns of unsustainability that dominant institutions are currently locked into.

Acknowledgements

This chapter is based on research carried out as part of the Transformative Social Innovation Theory (TRANSIT) project which is funded by the European Union's Seventh Framework Programme (FP7) under grant agreement 613169. The views expressed in this chapter are the sole responsibility of the authors and do not necessarily reflect the views of the European Union.

References

Avelino, F., Wittmayer, J.M., Pel, B., Weaver, P., Dumitru, A., Haxeltine, A., Kemp, R., Jørgensen, M.S., Bauler, T., Ruijsink, S., and O'Riordan, T. (forthcoming) 'Transformative social innovation and (dis)empowerment: towards a heuristic' *Technological Forecasting and Social Change*.

BEPA (Bureau of European Policy Advisors) (2010) *Empowering People, Driving Change: Social Innovation in the European Union* European Commission: Brussels.

Cajaiba-Santana, G. (2014) 'Social innovation: moving the field forward. A conceptual framework' *Technological Forecasting and Social Change* 82: 42–51.

Dumitru, A., Lema-Blanco, I., García-Mira, R., Haxeltine, A., and Frances, A. (2015) 'Credit unions' (WP4 case study report) TRANSIT: EU SSH.2013.3.2–1 Grant agreement no: 613169.

Dumitru, A., Lema-Blanco, I., Kunze, I., and García-Mira, R. (2016a) 'Slow Food Movement' (case-study report) TRANSIT: EU SSH.2013.3.2–1 Grant agreement no: 613169.

Dumitru, A., Lema-Blanco, I., Mira, R-C., Kunze, I., Strasser, T., and Kemp, R. (2016b) 'Social learning for transformative social innovation' (TRANSIT deliverable 2.3) TRANSIT:EU SSH.2003.3.2–1 Grant Agreement no. 61316.

GEN (2016) http://gen.ecovillage.org/en/page/what-gen.

Grin, J., Rotmans, J., Schot, J., Loorbach, D., and Geels, F.W. (2010) *Transitions to Sustainable Development: New Directions in the Study of Long Term Transformative Change* Routledge: New York.

Haxeltine, A., Avelino, F., Pel, B., Dumitru, A., Kemp, R., Longhurst, N., Chilvers, J. and Wittmayer, J.M. (2016) 'A framework for transformative social innovation' (TRANSIT working paper 5) TRANSIT: EU SSH.2013.3.2–1 Grant agreement no. 613169.

Jørgensen, M.S., Wittmayer, J.M., Avelino, F., Elle, M., Pel, B., Bauler, T., Kunze, I., and Longhurst, N. (2014) 'Methodological guidelines for case studies Batch I' (TRANSIT deliverable 4.1) EU SSH.2013.3.2-1 Grant agreement no. 613169.

Kunze, I., and Avelino, F. (2015) 'Social innovation and the Global Ecovillage Network' (TRANSIT research report) TRANSIT: EU SSH.2013.32–1 Grant agreement no: 613169.

Longhurst, N., and Pataki, G. (2015) 'The Transition Movement' (WP4 case study report) TRANSIT: EU SSH.2013.3.2–1 Grant agreement no. 613169.

Loorbach, D. (2014) 'To transition! Governance panarchy in the new transformation' (inaugural address, DRIFT/Erasmus University Rotterdam).

Markard, J., Raven, R., and Truffer, B. (2012) 'Sustainability transitions: an emerging field of research and its prospects' *Research Policy* 41(6): 955–967.

Rotmans, J. (2005) 'Societal innovation: between dream and reality lies complexity' (shortened inaugural speech, Rotterdam School of Management, ERIM, Erasmus University Rotterdam).

Scott-Cato, M., and Hillier, J. (2010) 'How could we study climate-related social innovation? Applying Deleuzean philosophy to transition towns' *Environmental Politics* 19(6): 869–887.

Slow Food UK (2016) www.slowfood.org.uk.

Stirling, A. (2011) 'Pluralising progress: from integrative transitions to transformative diversity' *Journal of Environmental Innovation and Societal Transitions* 1(1): 82–88.

Transition Network (2016) https://transitionnetwork.org/about-the-movement/the-charity/purpose.

Van den Bergh, J., Truffer, B., and Kallisa, G. (2011) 'Environmental innovation and societal transitions: introduction and overview' *Environmental Innovation and Societal Transitions* 1(1): 1–23.

Wittmayer, J.M., Backhaus, J., Avelino, F., Pel, B., Strasser, T. and Kunze, I. (2015a) 'Narratives of change: how social innovation initiatives engage with their transformative ambitions' (TRANSIT working paper 4) TRANSIT: EU SSH.2013.3.2–1 Grant agreement no. 613169.

Wittmayer, J.M., Avelino, F., Dorland, J. Pel, B. and Jørgensen, M.S. (2015b) 'Methodological guidelines Batch 2' (TRANSIT deliverable 4.3) TRANSIT: EU SSH.2013.3.2–1 Grant agreement no: 613169.

Yin, R.K. (2003) *Case Study Research, Design and Methods* 3rd edn Sage Publications: Newbury Park, CA.

3 The idea(l) of a 'sustainable sharing economy'

Four social science perspectives on transformative change

Julia Backhaus, Harro van Lente and René Kemp

1 Introduction: the sharing economy in the sustainable consumption, social innovation and societal transformation nexus

The sharing economy has received much attention in recent years by practition-ers, policy-makers, researchers and businesses alike. Across the globe, inter-national corporations and small, local initiatives have sprung up to support the sharing of, for example, rooms, rides, books or bikes – for profit, pleasure or both. New social relations underpin these novel connections of supply and demand or forms of (collective) ownership that have been conceptualised as 'social innova-tions' without losing sight of the oftentimes central and crucial role that techno-logy may play as an enabler or facilitator (Haxeltine *et al.* 2016).

While there appears to be widespread agreement that sharing platforms and initiatives imply a shift away from ownership towards more collaborative con-sumption patterns, disagreement prevails with respect to sustainability effects and potentials. A focus on the social innovation, sustainable consumption and societal transformation nexus draws attention to two crucial issues in this regard: (i) the extent to which a sharing platform or initiative subverts and transforms existing social structures and (ii) the extent to which a sharing platform or initi-ative contributes to more sustainable consumption patterns. In exploring these issues, this chapter seeks to help initiators, practitioners, researchers and policy-makers navigating the social innovation, sustainable consumption and societal transformation nexus in relation to the sharing economy. Following a review of scientific publications on the sharing economy (Section 2), four theories of change that feature prominently in current social scientific discourse, including social practice theories, socio-technical transitions, institutional theories and Karl Polanyi's *The Great Transformation* are consulted separately with respect to ideas and principles for a 'sustainable sharing economy' (Section 3). The discus-sion (Section 4) teases out conflicting and complementary notions across these four bodies of literature and is followed by concluding remarks on sustainable consumption and societal transformation effects and potentials of the sharing economy (Section 5).

2 Questioning sustainability and transformative potentials of the sharing economy: towards a definition of a sustainable sharing economy

Amidst the plethora of publications on the sharing economy, Belk (2014) offers succinct definitions of sharing and collaborative consumption that allow a clear delineation of the sharing economy from conventional marketplace exchange involving the transferal of ownership of new or second-hand products. Belk applauds Benkler (2004) for a concise statement capturing the essence of sharing as 'nonreciprocal pro-social behaviour', comprising 'demand sharing' and 'open sharing' (Belk 2010) and the 'borderline cases': borrowing and lending (Belk 2014, 1596). Freely shared, user-generated content on the Internet (like on YouTube or Wikipedia) as well as traditional sharing, even if web-facilitated (as in the case of CouchSurfing) are also comprised in Belk's understanding of sharing. In fact, online platforms support 'stranger sharing' (Schor 2014) by means of features such as rating and commenting.

Belk (2014) usefully demarcates collaborative consumption as involving the '[coordinated] acquisition and distribution of a resource for a fee or other compensation', thus including reciprocal exchange on bartering or swapping platforms as well as business models granting access to a product or service in exchange for money (including Airbnb and car- or ride-sharing schemes). In short, the sharing economy is often understood as people conceding access to goods and services for free, for a fee or for another compensation. While Frenken and colleagues (2015) appear to concur with these definitions, they diverge in one relevant respect: for them, the sharing economy only includes cases of people 'granting each other temporary access to under-utilized physical assets ("idle capacity"), possibly for money', thus excluding Uber and similar ride-hailing platforms and even those offers on Airbnb that have been specifically appropriated to be rented out.

Following their definition of the sharing economy, Frenken and Schor (2017) embark on assessing its sustainability impacts and arrive at rather disenchanting conclusions. While economic benefits are undeniable, their distribution is skewed, favouring the 'haves' (granting access) over the 'have nots' (seeking access) (Frenken and Schor 2017). Moreover, many sharing platforms negatively affect businesses offering similar services, often at higher cost (see e.g. Zervas *et al.* 2017 on the case of Airbnb). Positive social effects have been found in the form of new and sometimes lasting social connections, yet there are indications of economic interest superseding social benefits (Schor 2015). Finally, environmental benefits have been proven for car and ride sharing (Chen and Kockelman 2016), but, overall, environmental effects elude comprehensive assessment and are likely to be 'small' due to complex rebound effects (Frenken and Schor 2017).

A more comprehensive analysis by Schmitt and colleagues (2017) identifies best resource-efficiency gains for items whose production and disposal is comparatively more resource-intensive than their actual use and that are, as also noted by Frenken and Schor (2017), underutilised. Schmitt and co-authors (2017) also highlight the need for further research to better assess sustainability potentials, specifically to gain insight into negative or rebound effects due to increased packaging and transport (Schmitt *et al.* 2017). Following similar musings, Frenken and Schor (2017) suggest that, in the future, small, local sharing platforms that are owned and governed by their users and that reap the benefits of open-source software and blockchain technology open 'possibilities for a fully socialized sharing sector'. While this rosy vision is desirable from a sustainability perspective, it warrants scrutiny.

A classic definition of sustainable development takes a needs-based approach and demands inter- and intra-generational equity in the pursuit of meeting the needs of every person on this planet, especially the needs of the disadvantaged (World Commission on Environment and Development 1987). This notion appears to reverberate in more recent work on a 'just transition' towards sustainability that discusses solidarity, equity, common property, cooperation and sharing when calling for, for instance, climate or energy justice in the political and economic changes that are necessary from an environmental and sustainability perspective (Newell and Mulvaney 2013; Swilling and Annecke 2012; Vadovics and Milton in this volume). In the following, we explore conceptual and practical opportunities and challenges for a sustainable sharing economy based on four theoretical perspectives. In so doing, we tread in the footsteps of those before us who have stipulated sustainability as a normative concept based on equity and justice (Agyeman *et al.* 2002; Schneider *et al.* 2010) and take a sustainable sharing economy to denote sharing practices and platforms that are based on equity and efficiency. In our understanding, sustainable sharing economy initiatives are thus aimed at wellbeing, social cohesion and resource efficiency or even sufficiency, instead of buying into all-pervasive marketisation in the pursuit of generating financial revenues and outperforming competitors (Slee 2016). Following the idea that highest efficiency gains exist for local sharing schemes, this chapter specifically focuses on the more efficient and equitable sharing of resources on a local scale: in cities, quarters and communities. Local sharing initiatives can be understood as transformative social innovations (De Majo *et al.* 2016), involving new social relations that challenge, alter or replace existing institutions (Haxeltine *et al.* 2016).

3 Four theoretical perspectives on advancing towards a sustainable sharing economy

Following the premise that a sustainable sharing economy implies a shift away from all-pervasive marketisation and could help realise many sustainability potentials based on a self-governed and more equitable and efficient sharing of resources, four prominent social scientific theories of stability and change are scrutinised for insights on how such a transformation may unfold or be hampered. Social science theories of stability and change are typically grounded in different assumptions about reality (ontology) and thus about how change may unfold or can perhaps even be intentionally brought about. To profit from a rich range of perspectives, we selected four bodies of literature that differ on two basic dimensions: (i) whether they highlight structure or agency in their analysis of change and (ii) whether they analyse change as a long-term or as a continuous process. Figure 3.1 shows our categorisation of the selected literature which comprises readings on socio-technical transitions, social practice theories, institutionalism, and Karl Polanyi's *The Great Transformation*.

It is worth noting that the four conceptual perspectives addressed conflict in their view of the world in a number of ways. Practice theories, for example, assume a 'flat ontology' that does away with scale and solely considers sociospatial relations. Socio-technical transitions, on the other hand, are thought to unfold over – and to some extent even be steerable – at three different levels of scale. Neo-institutionalism and Karl Polanyi as a representative of 'old institutionalism' could be considered to reside in-between these views by accepting the duality of structure and agency that practice-theoretical approaches reject. While literature in the tradition of social practice theories is saturated with accounts of individual actions, transformative change is mostly thought to emerge from institutional or infrastructural change. Conversely, neo-institutional theorists have a rather structuralist view of the world but transformative agency is assigned to individuals and groups (institutional entrepreneurs). In addition, socio-technical transitions and the great transformation are described as temporally confined phenomena, while neo-institutionalism and social practice theories view change as continuously occurring. These differences allow for a rich discussion of a sustainable sharing

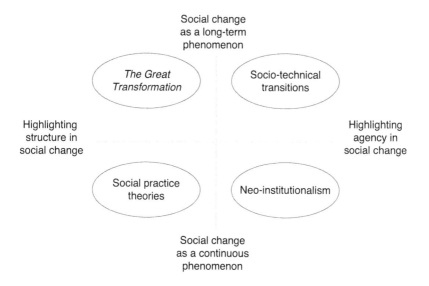

Figure 3.1 Categorisation of the four bodies of literature reviewed for insights on transformative change.

economy as a case of social change and, by drawing attention to different actors and processes, give rise to a range of conceptual and practical insights.

3.1 Changing elements of social practices in a sustainable sharing economy

Practice theories provide powerful conceptual tools to trace and discuss changes in people's everyday lives that an increase in local sharing schemes, mediated by online platforms or otherwise, would entail. For example, practice-theoretical approaches to pondering the possible success of local, community-based sharing schemes would draw attention to the necessity of recruiting a sufficiently large group of practice carriers. It has been rightly pointed out that the critical mass to make a platform a success is much lower at a local, than on a national or global scale (Frenken and Schor 2017). However, many sharing initiatives, especially more principled ones adhering to ideals such as equality and reciprocity, struggle to enrol and maintain a large membership base and therefore achieve a rather low number of transactions (Schor *et al.* 2016).

It has already been noted that the renting or otherwise organised access to items and services will have to match and interlock well with people's existent practices if 'entry barriers' are to be kept low (Schmitt *et al.* 2017). An added challenge in this respect is the rhythm of social life and the associated interlocking of practices. For example, while during the week many household items lie idle, their use peaks on Saturdays (on the difficulty of synchronising work schedules with communal activities in a co-housing environment, see Leitner and Littig in this volume). It is therefore questionable how far the more flexible use of resources across a larger number of users could be organised amidst rigid work hours. Another issue arises with respect to social norms and the sharing of personal possessions with others. Although online sharing platforms and their rating and commenting features facilitate 'stranger sharing' (Schor 2014), not everyone will share everything with everyone, even if people are known and part of one's social network. Social norms pertaining to hygiene or status may prevent the sharing of certain items (such as clothes or cars) or skills (such as those valued and remunerated highly on the market, see Schor *et al.* 2016).

Practice-theoretically inspired reflections on possibilities for local sharing schemes to emerge and thrive also call into question the successfulness of overcoming the 'paradigm of ownership' that prevails in current arrangements. Central to the notion of practices is a focus on meaning and the understanding of practices as social conversations, most notably involving the displaying of objects (Røpke 2009). If sharing is pervasive and it is less clear whether what is on display is borrowed or owned, ownership may lose some of its relevance – as it arguably already has for some things, including cars. It would, however, be naïve to believe that access trumps ownership, also from a sustainability perspective. For example, easy access to previously unknown or unused items may even spark a desire of ownership (Schmitt *et al.* 2017). What has been criticised in this regard with respect to the sharing economy in general, namely the accumulation of wealth by some by granting temporary access to products or services to others would thus continue, independent from the scale of a sharing network. Even if temporary access did not require paying a monetary fee but another type of compensation (such as swapping or a Time Bank hour) people who offer items or services that are of higher demand are and will continue to be better off and might leave even further behind those who cannot afford possession or who only offer less-sought-after services. Bearing in mind that social sustainability remains a challenge, the following section addresses the question whether and how local initiatives bearing environmental and economic benefits may gain a foothold and thereby transform existing systems.

3.2 Socio-technical transitions towards a sustainable sharing economy

Until now, transition scholars have not engaged with the study of economy-wide pervasive changes[1] while this would present an interesting endeavour in relation to the sharing economy. Instead, the multi-level perspective on socio-technical transitions (Geels 2002) more immediately lends itself to an analysis of sectoral changes that take place, for example, in the transport or tourism sector when sharing initiatives emerge, initially at a niche level only. Transition scholars have proposed goal-oriented modulation on the niche and regime levels to effect change (Rip and Kemp 1998; Kemp *et al.* 2001, 2007). This focus on niche-level innovation and experimentation resonates well with the suggestion that sustainability gains are highest for local-level initiatives (Frenken and Schor 2017) and ties into global trends of devolution (Rodríguez-Pose and Gill 2003). Advice for local governments on how to best engage with the sharing economy tends to follow the logics of transition thinking by taking a sectoral approach (energy, mobility, food) and by suggesting investment and policy support for specific types of initiatives.

Starting points for strategic consideration and evaluation to ensure, trace and enhance the sustainability effects of local sharing schemes have been proposed with respect to seven focal areas: absolute reductions in energy and material flows, climate change adaptation, environmental protection or restoration, social equity and inclusion, connectivity and well-being as well as economic prosperity (Cooper *et al.* 2015). Elsewhere, fiscal, social and environmental regulation has been suggested for commercial platforms like Uber and Airbnb that offer transport or accommodation services at cheaper rates than traditional providers, occasionally by exploiting legislative loopholes (Haucap 2015). The complete banning of certain platforms and initiatives has, however, been criticised on the grounds of risking backwardness and losing out on positive effects of innovation, such as increased efficiency and usability (Belk 2014; Haucap 2015). Empirical evidence appears to suggest the opposite, however, with more innovative and transformative initiatives, organised on a peer-to-peer, non-profit or cooperative basis, emerging after regulation sought to improve the security of drivers and customers and ended up driving out two major ride-hailing platforms in the city of Austin (Sutton 2016).

Although transition dynamics, including 'the importance of building networks, managing expectations and the significance of external "landscape" pressures, particularly at the level of national-type' (Seyfang and Longhurst 2013: 881) have been found for grassroots innovations, including sharing economy initiatives, theorising entirely based on transition thinking has been found to be useful 'only up to a point' (Smith and Seyfang 2013). Research on sharing initiatives as diverse as community currencies (Seyfang and Longhurst 2013), car sharing (Ornetzeder and Rohracher 2013), communal food growing (White and Stirling 2013), community energy (Hargreaves *et al.* 2013) and commons-based peer-learning and production (Smith *et al.* 2013) highlights the diversity of individual and organisational actors involved, the increasing fragmentation, the absence of formalised learning, the cross-sectorial spaces they occupy and their synergetic or antagonistic entanglement. Thereby, these studies show empirically the challenge of achieving sustainability vis-à-vis the complex systems of production and consumption that these initiatives are embedded in and, at the same time, transform. These studies thus substantiate the question of how civil-society-led sharing initiatives could and, even, ought to be governed in a quest for sustainability. This question is further explored in the following section.

3.3 Institutional changes for a sustainable sharing economy

Different typologies of institutions exist, including formal versus informal institutions, institutions as entities or elements or, the commonly used distinction of institutions as regulative, normative or cultural-cognitive rules, constituted and carried by routines, artefacts, symbolic or relational systems (Scott 1995). Neo-institutional theories offer conceptual tools to better understand the stabilising role institutions play in current, ownership-based consumption patterns, including, first and foremost, the capitalist economy that connects supply and demand globally and is firmly embedded in national policies and international trade agreements. So far, the sharing economy has progressed most swiftly in instances yielding promising business models, including bike, car or tool rental schemes as well as product-service systems. While these developments suggest more efficient usage of longer-lasting products, as noted in Section 2, actual resource-efficiency gains are difficult to estimate (Schmitt *et al.* 2017). Moreover, following the notion that the joint acquisition and commonly governed use of durable, everyday objects by local communities offer the greatest sustainability gains, including social benefits (Schmitt *et al.* 2017; Frenken and Schor 2017), business-driven initiatives appear as one, yet not the most effective, approach to a 'sustainable sharing economy'. Instead, new forms of local governance supporting changing norms and forms of ownership, product use and access would provide an institutional landscape in which local sharing initiatives could thrive.

A central question, as always, is how some individuals and groups escape the phenomenon of 'path dependence' (Garud *et al.* 2010) and come to question and deviate from certain taken-for-granted social facts, including current norms, customs, habits and even regulation. Neo-institutionalism seeks to understand how individual actors and actor groups as well as exogenous events and developments contribute to institutional change. In this regard, research has shown how language, and more specifically discourse, affects institutional change by sustaining more or less influential discourse coalitions (Hajer 1993) that critique, deliberate and may eventually decide to make changes (Schmidt 2015), all the while following particular ideas and interests (Kern 2011). It has been suggested that a discourse-institutional perspective that pays due attention to the relevant types of institutions as well as to the carriers, mechanisms and processes that underpin their stability, but can also bring about change, may yield a better understanding of how governance and scientific enquiry can contribute to a transition to sustainability (Genus 2016). Following this reasoning, it is notable how the concept of 'sharing' has become ubiquitous since its rise in economy-related discourse about a decade ago. Business, policy and civil-society-led initiatives have transformed policies and practices in the name of the 'sharing economy', oftentimes with little or even negative sustainability effects. The on-demand economy jumped on the bandwagon when disguising flexible and precarious work conditions as 'sharing' (Cockayne 2016), thereby adding a great deal of impetus to debates addressing negative effects on traditional industries and potential remedies in the form of changing policies – or outright banning. Local-level research, in turn, found the concept of 'sharing' laden with different understandings, hopes and practices, proposing local stakeholder-dialogue as a means to develop context-sensitive concepts of and approaches to the 'sharing economy', instead of a universally applicable definition (Gruszka 2017). Guidebooks for local governments have been written in an attempt to support such processes (Cooper *et al.* 2015).

Although critical discourse analysis has been challenged for an over-emphasis of the discursive, ever since Foucault, there has been a focus on the role of bodies, objects, spaces and practices (Hardy and Thomas 2015) and the dialectic relationship between material and discursive reality (Putnam 2015; Fairclough 2012). In addition to revealing ideas and interests that underpin the efforts of different discourse and practice coalitions (while the two are not to be mistaken as perfectly matching, see Gruszka 2017), critical discourse analysis provides ammunition for normative critique, also – or especially – on prevailing institutions (Fairclough 2012). Two schools of thought within neo-institutionalism offer diverging views on how a shift towards a sustainable sharing economy might unfold. On the one hand, scholars committed to the notion of 'embedded agency' (Garud *et al.* 2007) would argue for resourceful institutional entrepreneurs to take the lead (see also Haxeltine *et al.* in this volume). And indeed, a growth of some sharing platforms can currently be observed to an extent that there is talk about (the threat of) global monopolies and 'digital capitalism' which involves a further expansion of capitalist motives into people's private homes and lives (Theurl *et al.* 2015). On the other hand, scholars proclaiming large-scale, wave-like cultural developments behind social change would hold that, to proliferate, the sharing economy can either surf on the wave of increased individual freedom and personal rights (perhaps even freed of some duties usually concomitant of ownership) or form part of a new 'cultural tide', related to collective wellbeing and communal ownership that fosters a sustainable sharing economy. The following section explores reasons that may necessitate and perhaps even drive the hoisting of a different set of values that signposts the way towards a sustainable sharing economy and, generally, a more sustainable future.

3.4 Lessons for a sustainable sharing economy based on K. Polanyi's The Great Transformation

Taking aboard the need for cultural change in developments towards a sustainable sharing economy, effectively carried by changed institutions in the form of communal ownership and commonly governed rules of access, inspiring lessons for a sustainable sharing economy can be drawn from the oldest and conceptually most ambivalent literature (Block 2003; Adler 2015; Dale 2008) consulted here. In *The Great Transformation*, Karl Polanyi discusses the causes for the collapse of nineteenth-century civilisation and the changes this set in motion, including the transformation of land and labour into 'fictitious commodities' and a 'double movement' of international policies facilitating global trade and competition and national policies protecting national industries and citizenries. Polanyi notes that the economy is always embedded in state action and cultural norms and calls a free market society a 'stark utopia' (Polanyi 1944, 3). In his view, an important task to remedy the detrimental social effects of global industrialisation and capitalism is to reconcile the economy with human nature. From today's point of view, this line of argumentation can be extended to comprise a reconciliation of the economy with all nature. Polanyi discusses the de-commodification of land, labour and money as cornerstones of a different world order and muses that this would decrease the importance of financial motives for labour and increase collective or public land ownership as well as public deposits. Current initiatives around collective ownership and governance of the commons, basic income and local currencies that are discussed in relation to the sharing economy resonate well with this line of reasoning.

It has been suggested that Polanyi's notion of a double movement can be usefully extended to a model of three movements comprising marketisation, state-based (social) protection and humanisation. Evidence for the latter can be found in social innovation initiatives that, following principles of conviviality and cooperation, seek to address and to some extent remedy the detrimental effects on nature and society brought about by the other two movements. Modern technologies often play a central role in the institutions, networks and practices of these initiatives, of which sharing initiatives are but one example, that transform social relations in pursuit of greater autonomy and social, political and economic participation (Kemp *et al.* 2016; Schneider *et al.* 2010).

An understanding of societal transformations as the dialectic (Kemp *et al.* 2016) or contingent (Adler 2015) outcome of processes of dis-embedding and re-embedding sees potential for terminating the treatment of natural resources and labour as externalities. However, only a particular form of the sharing economy might deliver on re-embedding. If the sharing economy evolves into or turns out to be an extension of capitalist practices by creating profit from 'sharing' privately owned objects, it represents another manifestation of a disembedded economy. If, however, the sharing economy brings (back) forms of collective ownership and cooperatives that share land, labour and objects for a variety of reasons (one of them potentially being profit), a step towards an embedded, sustainable, sharing economy is made. Arguably, rising costs for scarcer resources will eventually necessitate a re-embedding by demanding sufficiency and sharing. However, perhaps a pre-emptive shift away from a consumerist culture is possible (Assadourian 2010). The following section addresses this issue in an attempt to summarise and synthesise the four conceptual perspectives on a 'sustainable sharing economy'.

4 Overview of challenges and opportunities for a sustainable sharing economy

The above section brought to bear four conceptual perspectives on the notion of a sustainable sharing economy based on core literature for each perspective and recent research on the sharing economy. This approach made apparent several challenges and opportunities (see Table 3.1) for sharing to become the socially just and environmentally sustainable practice it promises to be. While many, especially the currently most successful and best-known examples of sharing initiatives, imply an expansion of capitalist motives and practice, there are innumerable examples of thinkers and practitioners devising alternatives: alternative practices, alternative forms of ownership and governance and an alternative political economy with a changed allocation of costs and benefits (Kemp *et al.* 2016; Schneider *et al.* 2010). The discussion above thus brought to the fore two relevant 'action arenas' that can carry or compromise a transformation towards a sustainable sharing economy: (inter-)national policy-making and activism as setting the scene for economic activity, environmental protection and social equity, and local policy-making and initiatives as building or supporting suitable, meaningful and equitable sharing schemes.

5 Conclusions: a need for local governance and (inter-)national transformative policies

This chapter investigated the idea(l) of a sustainable sharing economy based on a review of literature on the sharing economy and of key readings on four different, theoretical perspectives. In particular, this chapter addressed the social innovation, sustainable consumption and societal transformation nexus and investigated conceptual and practical challenges and opportunities related to (i) more sustainable consumption patterns and (ii) the transformative effects of sustainable sharing economy initiatives. In the literature, sustainability effects are deemed highest for local initiatives that make efficient use of idle capacity, be it

Table 3.1 Views on, challenges to and opportunities for a sustainable sharing economy

Conceptual perspective	View on a sustainable sharing economy	Challenges	Opportunities
Practice theories	People as carriers of practices involving the sharing of tasks or material objects by reciprocally: • offering idle time or items to others, and • accepting idle time or objects from others.	New practices need to replace, co-exist or interlock well with old practices. Recruiting flexible practitioners despite rhythmic, synchronised practice patterns. Social norms may prevent sharing.	Collaboration in cases of synchronous practices. ICT and other tools change norms and practices.
Socio-technical transitions	Niche-level initiatives offer experimental and experiential spaces. Possibly affecting or being supported by regime-level changes. Particularly should landscape pressures demand such change.	Governance for sustainability. Local solutions where national or international schemes are established.	Devolution offers leverage to local policy makers.
Neo-institutionalism	Existing institutions favour less sustainable forms of the sharing economy, but Local initiatives can be tailored to meet local needs and global necessities.	'Sharing' and 'sustainability' take on different meanings. 'Digital capitalism'.	New forms of governance to create and sustain values of collective well-being and communal ownership. Local(ised) sharing schemes.
Karl Polanyi's The Great Transformation	The economy needs to be re-aligned with human nature by fostering collaboration and participation.	Idea that the economic sphere is independent from the political. Commodification of land and labour in the current system.	Alternative ideas on how to de-commodify labour, organise life and govern resources abound.

time or items. Principles for sustainable sharing initiatives recurring in the literature and throughout the analysis presented here include a shift away from market-based organisation towards the joint acquisition of resources and a shared governance of their use, providing equal access rights and opportunities for all.

These aspects tap into the second relevant issue concerning the transformative effects and potentials of sharing initiatives. Practice and discourse related to the sharing economy has already set in motion broader systemic changes in some sectors, particularly those yielding large profits. At the same time, local – not necessarily profit-seeking – initiatives are already offering successful alternatives to their users, often coinciding with regime-level changes on the local scale with respect to policies or infrastructures (De Majo *et al.* 2016; Gruszka 2017). Adding to existing sustainability guidelines for local governments interested in supporting sharing economy initiatives (Cooper *et al.* 2015), this analysis pointed to the importance of public investment in shared infrastructures and resources as well as the development of local capacity for public participation (on related challenges in practice, see Bonneau and Jégou in this volume) if the social justice potential of sharing initiatives is to be realised.

Finally, the analysis brought out the most crucial challenge that is to be addressed if consumerist culture is to be superseded by a more sustainable counterpart, namely that of allowing for change to happen. In line with propositions by theorists and practitioners in the degrowth tradition (Kallis 2011), this analysis points to a number of powerful policies, including for example participatory governance, local currencies, basic income or reduced and more flexible work hours, that can create opportunity and capacity for citizens to 'be the change' and build a sustainable sharing economy.

Note

1 Pervasive changes have been studied in the tradition of techno-economic paradigms (Freeman and Perez 1988).

References

Adler, P. S. (2015) 'Book review essay: the environmental crisis and its capitalist roots: reading Naomi Klein with Karl Polanyi – Naomi Klein: This Changes Everything: Capitalism vs. the Climate' *Administrative Science Quarterly* 60(2): NP13–NP25.

Agyeman, J., Bullard, R. D., and Evans, B. (2002) 'Exploring the nexus: bringing together sustainability, environmental justice and equity' *Space and Polity* 6: 77–90.

Assadourian, E. (2010) 'The rise and fall of consumer cultures' in Worldwatch Institute, *State of the World* W. W. Norton: London and New York.

Belk, R. (2014) 'You are what you can access: sharing and collaborative consumption online' *Journal of Business Research* 67: 1595–1600.

Benkler, Y. (2004) 'Sharing nicely: on shareable goods and the emergence of sharing as a modality of economic production' *Yale Law Journal* 114: 273–358.

Block, F. (2003) 'Karl Polanyi and the writing of the Great Transformation' *Theory and Society* 32: 275–306.

Chen, T. D., and Kockelman, K. M. (2016) 'Carsharing's life-cycle impacts on energy use and greenhouse gas emissions' *Transportation Research Part D: Transport and Environment* 47: 276–284.

Cockayne, D. G. (2016) 'Sharing and neoliberal discourse: the economic function of sharing in the digital on-demand economy' *Geoforum* 77: 73–82.

Cooper, R., Timmer, V., Ardis, L., Appleby, D., and Hallsworth, C. (2015) 'Local governments and the sharing economy', www.localgovsharingecon.com/uploads/2/1/3/3/21333498/localgovsharingecon_report_full_oct2015.pdf.

Dale, G. (2008) 'Karl Polanyi's the Great Transformation: perverse effects, protectionism and Gemeinschaft' *Economy and Society* 37: 495–524.

De Majo, C., Morten, E., Hagelskjær Lauridsen, E., and Zuijderwijk, L. (2016) 'Shareable's sharing cities' (WP4 case study report) TRANSIT: EU SSH.2013.3.2–1 Grant agreement no: 613169.

Fairclough, N. (2012) 'Critical discourse analysis', www.academia.edu/3791325/Critical_discourse_analysis_2012.

Freeman, C., and Perez, C. (1988) 'Structural crises of adjustment, business cycles and investment behaviour' in Dosi, G., Freeman, C., Nelson, R., Silverberg, G., and Soete, L. (eds) *Technical Change and Economic Theory* Pinter Publishers: London.

Frenken, K., and Schor, J. (2017) 'Putting the sharing economy into perspective' *Environmental Innovation and Societal Transitions* 23: 3–10.

Frenken, K., Meelen, T., Arets, M., and Van de Glind, P. (2015) 'Smarter regulation for the sharing economy' *Guardian* 20 May.

Garud, R., Hardy, C., and Maguire, S. (2007) 'Institutional entrepreneurship as embedded agency: an introduction to the special issue' *Organization Studies*, 28: 957–969.

Garud, R., Kumaraswamy, A., and Karnøe, P. (2010) 'Path dependence or path creation?' *Journal of Management Studies* 47: 760–774.

Geels, F. W. (2002) 'Technological transitions as evolutionary reconfiguration processes: a multi-level perspective and a case-study' *Research Policy* 31: 1257–1274.

Genus, A. (2016) 'Sustainability transitions: a discourse-institutional perspective' in Brauch, H. G., Oswald Spring, Ú., Grin, J., and Scheffran, J. (eds) *Handbook on Sustainability Transitions and Sustainable Peace* Springer: Cham.

Gruszka, K. (2017) 'Framing the collaborative economy: voices of contestation' *Environmental Innovation and Societal Transitions* 23: 92–104.

Hajer, M. A. (1993) 'Discourse coalitions and the institutionalization of practice: the case of acid rain in Britain' in Fischer, F., and Forester, J. (eds) *The Argumentative Turn in Policy Analysis and Planning* Duke University Press: Durham, NC, and London.

Hardy, C., and Thomas, R. (2015) 'Discourse in a material world' *Journal of Management Studies* 52: 680–696.

Hargreaves, T., Hielscher, S., Seyfang, G., and Smith, A. (2013) 'Grassroots innovations in community energy: the role of intermediaries in niche development' *Global Environmental Change* 23: 868–880.

Haucap, J. (2015) 'Die Chancen der Sharing Economy und ihre möglichen Risiken und Nebenwirkungen' *Wirtschaftsdienst* 2: 87–105.

Haxeltine, A., Avelino, F., Pel, B., Kemp, R., Dumitru, A., Longhurst, N., Chilvers, J., Jørgensen, M. S., Wittmayer, J. M., Seyfang, G., Kunze, I. Dorland, J., and Strasser, T. (2016) 'A second prototype of TSI theory' (TRANSIT deliverable 3.3) TRANSIT: EU SSH.2013.3.2–1 Grant agreement no. 613169.

Kallis, G. (2011) 'In defence of degrowth' *Ecological Economics* 70: 873–880.

Kemp, R., Rip, A., and Schot, J. (2001) 'Constructing transition paths through the management of niches' in Garud, R., and Karnøe, P. (eds) *Path Dependence and Creation* Lawrence Erlbaum: Mahwah, NJ, and London.

Kemp, R., Loorbach, D., and Rotmans, J. (2007) 'Transition management as a model for managing processes of co-evolution towards sustainable development' *International Journal of Sustainable Development and World Ecology* 14: 78–91.

Kemp, R., Strasser, T., Davidson, M., Avelino, F., Pel, B., Dumitru, A., Kunze, I., Backhaus, J., O'Riordan, T., Haxeltine, A., and Weaver, P. M. (2016) 'The humanization of the economy through social innovation' (paper presented at SPRU 50th Anniversary Conference, University of Sussex, 7–9 Sept.).

Kern, F. (2011) 'Ideas, institutions, and interests: explaining policy divergence in fostering "system innovations" towards sustainability' *Environment and Planning C: Government and Policy* 29: 1116–1134.

Newell, P., and Mulvaney, D. (2013) 'The political economy of the "just transition"' *Geographical Journal* 179: 132–140.

Ornetzeder, M., and Rohracher, H. (2013) 'Of solar collectors, wind power, and car sharing: comparing and understanding successful cases of grassroots innovations' *Global Environmental Change* 23: 856–867.

Polanyi, K. (1944) *The Great Transformation: The Political and Economic Origins of Our Time* Farrar and Reinhart: New York.

Putnam, L. L. (2015) 'Unpacking the dialectic: alternative views on the discourse–materiality relationship' *Journal of Management Studies* 52: 706–716.

Rip, A., and Kemp, R. (1998) 'Technological change' in Rayner, S., and Malone, L. (eds) *Human Choice and Climate Change* Batelle Press: Washington DC.

Rodríguez-Pose, A., and Gill, N. (2003) 'The global trend towards devolution and its implications' *Environment and Planning C: Government and Policy* 21: 333–351.

Røpke, I. (2009) 'Theories of practice: new inspiration for ecological economic studies on consumption' *Ecological Economics* 68: 2490–2497.

Schmidt, V. A. (2015) 'Discursive institutionalism: understanding policy in context' in Fischer, F., Torgerson, D., Durnová, A., and Orsini, M. (eds) *Handbook of Critical Policy Studies* Edward Elgar Publishing: Cheltenham.

Schmitt, M., Leismann, K., Baedeker, C., and Rohn, H. (2017) 'Sharing: eine innovative, soziale Praktik fuer einen ressourcenschonenden, nachhaltigeren Konsum?' in Jaeger-Erben, M., Rueckert-John, J., and Schaefer, M. (eds) *Soziale Innovationen fuer nachhaltigen Konsum: Wissenschaftliche Perspektiven, Strategien der Foerderung und gelebte Praxis* Springer: Wiesbaden.

Schneider, F., Kallis, G., and Martinez-Alier, J. (2010) 'Crisis or opportunity? Economic degrowth for social equity and ecological sustainability. Introduction to this special issue' *Journal of Cleaner Production* 18: 511–518.

Schor, J. B. (2014) 'Debating the sharing economy', www.greattransition.org/publication/debating-the-sharing-economy (accessed 15 May 2017).

Schor, J. B. (2015). 'Getting sharing right' *Contexts* 14(1): 14–15.

Schor, J. B., Fitzmaurice, C., Carfagna, L. B., Attwood-Charles, W., and Dubois Poteat, E. (2016) 'Paradoxes of openness and distinction in the sharing economy' *Poetics* 54: 66–81.

Scott, W. R. (1995) *Institutions and Organizations* Sage: Thousand Oaks, CA.

Seyfang, G., and Longhurst, N. (2013) 'Desperately seeking niches: grassroots innovations and niche development in the community currency field' *Global Environmental Change* 23: 881–891.

Slee, T. (2016) *What's Yours is Mine: Against the Sharing Economy* OR Books: New York.

Smith, A., and Seyfang, G. (2013) 'Constructing grassroots innovations for sustainability' *Global Environmental Change* 23: 827–829.

Smith, A., Hielscher, S., Dickel, S., Soederberg, J., and Van Ost, E. (2013) 'Grassroots digital fabrication and makerspaces: reconfiguring, relocating and recalibrating innovation.' (SPRU working paper, University of Sussex), http://sro.sussex.ac.uk/49317.

Sutton, M. (2016) 'New ridesharing alternatives thrive after Uber leaves Austin', www.shareable.net/blog/new-ridesharing-alternatives-thrive-after-uber-leaves-austin (accessed 6 June 2017).

Swilling, M., and Annecke, E. (2012) *Just Transitions: Explorations of Sustainability in an Unfair World* United Nations University Press: Tokyo.

Theurl, T., Haucap, J., Demary, V., Priddat, B. P., and Paech, N. (2015) 'Ökonomie des Teilens: nachhaltig und innovativ?' *Wirtschaftsdienst* 95: 87–105.

White, R., and Stirling, A. (2013) 'Sustaining trajectories towards sustainability: dynamics and diversity in UK communal growing activities' *Global Environmental Change* 23: 838–846.

World Commission on Environment and Development (1987) *Our Common Future* Oxford University Press: Oxford.

Zervas, G., Proserpio, D., and Byers, J. W. (2017) 'The rise of the sharing economy: estimating the impact of Airbnb on the hotel industry' *Journal of Marketing Research*, https://doi.org/10.1509/jmr.15.0204.

4 Societal transformation, social innovations and sustainable consumption in an era of metamorphosis

Michael Jonas

1 Introduction

In current political debates about the necessity for change in industrial and post-industrial societies in Europe and elsewhere, the need for societal transformations, social innovations and sustainable consumption to counteract the risks of the present multiple crises is often stressed. However, in political as well as in scientific discourse these terms are oftentimes used as catchwords and are not precisely defined. Moreover, in many cases, the relationships between them are unclear, if not contradictory. Should they, for instance, be used as central concepts in a general theory of change? If so, should they be treated as being on a par, or would it be more plausible to favour one of them? How do they relate to the conceptualisation of change processes in world society? What are the important and pressing problems and change processes for societies?

Against this background, my aim in this chapter is to take up the questions of whether and, if so, how the above-mentioned concepts of societal transformation, social innovation and sustainable consumption can serve as keywords in a practice-theory-based analysis of societal change in an era of metamorphosis. In doing so, I approach these questions in several steps. First, I delve into the respective debates on innovations, transformation and consumption. I then explain the core aspects of a practice-theory perspective. Following this, I clarify the concept of societal transformation, discuss central aspects of the term "social innovation" and focus on the concept of sustainable consumption. As I summarise in a concluding step, a well-balanced frame for these terms is needed for a socio-critical analysis of current societal crises.

2 Central themes in innovation, transformation and sustainability discourses

In an ongoing debate in the well-known journal *Research Policy* about current changes in the relationship between innovations and the development of world society (Archibugi forthcoming), Lundvall argues that the "combination of the global rule of financial capital, economic globalization and neoliberal austerity has led to increasing inequality" (Lundvall 2017) and that we now can see "the social and political impact in terms of growing emigration from poor countries and growing nationalism in several high-income countries" (ibid.). In the same discussion, Steinmueller states that the "threat of climate change means that most of the world's agricultural and industrial systems ... need a massive retrofit to avoid catastrophic changes in the earth's environment" (Steinmueller forthcoming). According to Lundvall, the main questions here are whether important political meetings like the Marrakech Climate Change Conference (in 2016) will be "followed up by action" (Lundvall 2017) and whether people around the world will be able "to form movements that oppose the current tendency toward inequality" and create "unity across national borders on such a scale that it truly makes a difference" (ibid.).

In a similar way, advocates of the transformation concept stress the necessity of fundamental change processes in world society in light of the current societal crises, such as the crisis in the financial sector or the environmental, the economic and the refugee crises: "Business as usual can only deliver more of the same, which means more crises and increasing environmental and economic problems" (Smart 2011, 146). Instead, a multiplicity "of material transformations, constituting novel forms of 'object-oriented' ecocitizenship practices" (Blok 2012, 2341) is required. In this regard, Brand observes that "discussions about transformation have a similar function to those around sustainable development in the 1990s, putting the ecological crisis into a larger context and uniting different fields of thinking" (Brand 2016, 23). While sustainability initiatives "grow and spread by the many of thousands", the ongoing change processes take place "in the context of established social structures and power configurations ... and the elaborated institutional arrangements of what in many ways has been a historically successful industrialization/modernization paradigm" (Burns 2016, 893). However, the established structures and power configurations are in no fit state to elaborate adequate solutions to the actual problems. As a consequence, they should be treated as parts of the problems to be solved rather than as drivers of possible solutions that would include their fundamental reconfiguration (ibid.).

Criticising the dominance of sociotechnical transitions and their governance in the respective discourses on societal change, it is pointed out that the focus of ongoing debates should be more on the "central role that practitioners themselves play in generating, sustaining and overthrowing everyday practices" (Shove and Walker 2010, 476) in relation to sustainable production and consumption. Sen contended that "many consumption habits would have to be changed because they would interfere with the requirements of sustainable development" (Sen 2013, 12). In the sustainability discourse, it is stressed that national states have at the same time "enabled the valorisation of individualism through the promise of individual freedom and choices" (Barr and Pollard 2017, 50). Here, citizens are primarily treated as individuals "who make consumption choices and it is on them that responsibility lies for making ... 'better choices'" (ibid.). As a consequence, "the political framing of the citizen has radically shifted from one dominated by collective activism to a situation where behavioural change has pacified the majority of citizens into belief" (ibid., 51) that multiple crises and their related impacts can primarily be resolved through individualised changes in behaviour. In contrast, Urry maintains that everyday life goods and services are embedded in and parts of social worlds and that a change towards sustainability "requires changing such embedded and embodied social worlds" (Urry 2011, 4).

Against the background of these statements in the respective discourses, it is also useful to refer to Beck's attempt to grasp ongoing change processes in world society. In his last (and unfinished) book *The Metamorphosis of the World* (Beck 2016), he questions the usability and plausibility of concepts like "change" or "transformation" to capture the ongoing transfiguration of world society. In his view, current world society is not changing (in the sense that some things change but others remain the same), it is "metamorphosing". The concept of metamorphosis signifies "a mode of changing the nature of human existence" (ibid., 20), "a much more radical transformation in which the old certainties of modern society are falling away" (ibid., 3) and in which "spaces of action are cosmopolitized, which means that the frame of action is no longer only national and integrated but global and disintegrated" (ibid., 10). Treated in this way, the metamorphosis of the world is seen not as a normative but as a descriptive expression that "refers to an unprecedented historical form of global change" (ibid., 51) in which "the deconstructive externalities of industrial production cannot be externalized forever" (ibid., 63) and the inequality between the rich members of society and the rest of world is no longer accepted. While metamorphosis does not mean "a change for the better" (ibid., 19), "it might bring a cosmopolitan turn into our contemporary life and the world might be changed for the better" (ibid., 35). In short, metamorphosis

> affects not only a political regime but also the understanding, the concept of the political and of society itself. It is not just a temporally, spatially and socially limited exception (like revolution or war) but progresses ever further, and even escalates with the escalation of risk capitalism. It is not intentional, programmatic and ideological … but, rather, kept going by political inaction.
>
> (Ibid., 56)

3 Core aspects of a practice theory perspective

It has already been pointed out (Schatzki 2002) that practice-theory approaches are characterised by family resemblances, which can be taken as evidence of heterogeneity and multiplicity. However, practice-theory approaches can be split into two basic – and different – groups. The first, more general, group includes those approaches which treat sociality as a praxis which encompasses the whole of human activity and its entanglement with its socio-material contexts. The second, and more specific, variant contains those approaches which assume that praxis consists of the enactment of various bundles and complexes of practices in which individual actors are involved (Reckwitz 2002; Schatzki

2017). Common to both variants is the focus on the praxis and on the goal of understanding the praxis as praxis (Bourdieu 1977). However, in the more specific version preferred here, central importance is accorded from a theory perspective to the concept of "the practice". Unlike the singular term "praxis", the term "practice" is generally defined as a specific bundle of activities.

In line with the influential definition proposed by Schatzki (2002), a practice is understood as a nexus of doings and sayings that brings the individuals involved into contact with people, creatures and objects in their everyday life. A practice can be studied by directing the attention towards the performance of the respective activities by the individuals involved or by focusing on its constitutive organising aspects. These aspects are specific understandings (how to say or do something), rules (implicit or explicit) and leitmotifs in which individuals engage according to the situation and in particular societal contexts. Such contexts are grasped as socio-material arrangements in various societal spheres, which are constituted from the relationships between the activities of the individuals, artefacts and material spaces involved. In addition, consideration has to be given to the fact that individuals are generally involved in many different practices, which may or may not complement, overlap or exclude each other. As a result, the focus moves towards various configurations of practices (e.g. randomly ordered ensembles, webs, closely linked networks and stable complexes) and how the practices in these configurations interrelate, erode and reinforce each other. Additionally, the focus shifts to how these configurations are connected with each other and associated arrangements as well as what this means (for instance, with regard to solutions to environmental problems, "for the use of energy, water and other natural resources" (Shove and Spurling 2013, 3)).

Further, a practice-theory view assumes that the world is flat. In contrast to multi-level approaches that grasp social sites as something that is constituted on different societal levels (distinguishing, for instance, between a micro-, a meso- and a macro-level), sites are understood in practice theory as plane milieus "where the dynamic properties of matter produce a multiplicity of complex relations and singularities that sometimes lead to the creation of new, unique events and entities" (Marston *et al.* 2005, 422), but more often to relatively redundant practice/arrangement configurations. Consequently, the quasi-natural niches, regimes and landscapes proposed by transition research (Geels and Schot 2007) are not located at different levels but are instead grasped as pure differences in spatial extension (Schatzki 2016) and as parts of various networks of practices/arrangement configurations with different levels of stability. Highlighting the central role of activities in the reproduction and change of practice/arrangement configurations, a practice-theory perspective endeavours to capture a change or continuation in practices and related socio-material arrangements with recourse to the respective activities and competences of the individual actors involved (Alkemeyer *et al.* 2017).

Based on these central aspects, a discussion grounded in practice theory asks if the concepts of societal transformation, social innovation and sustainable consumption could be grasped as structures or actions (or their results), or if it makes more sense to conceptualise them as practices, practice/arrangement bundles or complex configurations thereof.

4 Societal transformation

A practice-theory understanding of the transformation concept (Polanyi 1997) encompasses not only a technology- and innovation-induced transition from one societal formation to another but also the effects, reshapings and changes of all affected practices and arrangements. It thus addresses a radical change of hegemonic practice/arrangement configurations. In this respect, a transformation represents a particular type of social change process. Whereas the transition concept can be used to signify an intentional political means of control that represents a structured, national, political intervention in development paths and logics in order to steer dominant developments in another direction, a critical interpretation of the term "transformation" focusses on comprehensive socio-economic, political and socio-cultural change processes. While these can be based in part on steering and innovation technology strategies, as emphasised in transition research, they cannot be simply reduced to them (Jonas 2017).

At first glance, this would seem to be in line with the suggestion made by Avelino and colleagues (2014, 17), who define societal transformation "as fundamental, persistent and irreversible change across society". However, they treat societal transformation as the outcome of a process but not as a change process in itself, arguing "that societal transformation results from a specific interaction between game-changers, narratives of change, system innovation, and social innovation, as distinct but intertwined dimensions of innovation and change" (ibid., 18), which they refer to as "transformative social innovation". To avoid a re-conceptualisation of the term "transformation" in innovation theory terminology – where economic theory approaches dominate – it makes sense to follow Brand (2016), who advocates the use of the term transformation in a specific analytical sense:

> An analytical concept of transformation points to the highly asymmetric and hierarchical characteristics of societies where social and power positions are constituted in line with social relations of class, gender and race and are inscribed in economic, political and cultural relations.
>
> (Ibid., 25)

Such a perspective then focuses on "a clearer understanding of different transformative dynamics" (ibid.) and "involves analysing the context and barriers" (ibid.) of fundamental change processes as well as the configuration of the social relations: that is, the practices and socio-material arrangement configurations in various societal spheres that are seen as the cause of the diagnosed multiple crises. This also implies what Beck refers to as "a reverse valuation of naturally given asymmetries" (Beck 2016, 59) into "political bads" as well as the need to include in particular the post-colonially excluded in the negotiation of world affairs.

Additionally, and related, for instance, to the environmental crises, this view then requires us to focus on the question of whether practices "might develop in directions that lead, en masse, to a spectacular reduction in collective ecological and carbon footprints" (Shove and Spurling 2013, 2). Taking this seriously, the transformation concept can only be used in conjunction with an absolute, and not relative, reduction of emissions. "Relativist conceptions give the appearance of traveling toward low-carbon societies even while absolute increases of emissions push societies toward a hyper-carbon world" (Murphy 2015, 321). Thus, seen from a practice-theory perspective, the societal transformation concept signifies radical change processes of hegemonic practice/arrangement configurations towards a more sustainable, just and equal world society. Grasped in this way, the transformation concept should not only be used to criticise existing practice/arrangement complexes in various societal spheres. To avoid being negatively critical and instead expose "the positive and the possibilities of change" (Marcuse 2009, 185), it is advisable to look for central aspects of utopian concepts to catch a glimpse of a radical remodelling of existing practices and arrangements. Of central relevance here are the debates on far-sighted development visions, which fundamentally question the hegemonic exploitation of nature by mankind (as a species) as the purported natural ruler of the planet. Based on the assumption that an end must be put to our domination of nature (Horkheimer and Adorno 1982), we need to comprehend and figure out what form societal practices and arrangements would need to take if, for example, the unsustainable utilisation of natural resources and exploitation of other creatures were to be stopped (Joy 2010) and unjust economic relationships were to be transfigured in a way that would enable all actors to recognise themselves as cooperative members of society (Honneth 2011). Only then would we have the necessary and adequate starting point to "sense the benefits of a global project that tries to provide a good life for all" (Jonas 2017, 128).

5 Social innovations

Given the observations of the need for change processes encountered in the discourse on innovation research, the diagnosis (in this discourse) that social innovation research can be labelled as an emerging area of innovation studies (Have and Rubalcaba 2016) should come as no surprise. Aside from the acknowledgement of diverse social innovation concepts (from economic to sociological variations), sociological conceptualisations often treat social innovations as "new ways of creating and implementing social change" (ibid. 1924) or more precisely – and at first glance well in line with the practice-theory approach used in this chapter – as new practices or new combinations of practices for resolving societal challenges (Avelino et al. 2014).

In a recent book, Howaldt and colleagues (2015) have tried to concretise what it means to treat social innovations as practices. Developing a theory-based concept, they use Tarde's sociological approach (1899, 1903) to grasp "social innovation as a social mechanism of change" (Howaldt *et al.* 2015, 11). Stressing that invention and innovation are the two key elements of societal development in Tarde's approach, they adopt his view in a first step to treat invention and imitation as basic social mechanisms. They explicate that an "invention, through imitation, becomes an innovation, and only then a social fact" (ibid.). Consequently, imitation is seen as "central mechanism of social reproduction *and* of social change" (ibid., 29) bringing "innovations into social structures and practices" (ibid.). In a second step, they combine this notion with practice-theory approaches and suggest avoiding the term "social innovation" as an analytical concept that is intended to be normative. Instead, they argue, the term should denote "the result of intentional and targeted action to establish new social practices" (ibid., 21), or, more precisely, should be grasped "as new social practice" (ibid., 34) or targeted new combinations or con-figurations of practices (Howaldt and Schwarz 2010, 10). This allows them to demarcate social innovations from techno-economic innovations with the argu-ment that the new manifests itself neither "in the medium of technological arte-facts" (Howaldt *et al.* 2015, 17) nor primarily in (the form of) products or processes in the economy, but in practices (ibid., 78) in various societal spheres. Following the multi-level approach developed in transition research (see above), the authors argue that "new practices … would first be discovered and invented at the micro level, in social niches and (protected) action contexts, and from there be imitated and spread by particular actors or networks of actors" (ibid., 56). This conception clearly stresses "the benefit of a micro-foundation of the social realm" (ibid., 32) in which social change – but also social reproduc-tion – is explained by imitated individual initiatives and which "directs atten-tion to the importance of acts of imitation as the central mechanism for the spread and institutionalisation of social innovation" (ibid., 79). It likewise high-lights the benefits and potentials of a creative reconfiguration of existing inven-tions instead of celebrating a constant "producing [of] new individual inventions" (ibid., 72). However, the authors stress that if their social innova-tion concept is linked to socio-ecological transformation processes, civil society engagement or a necessary empowerment of citizens must also be considered because a "change in the direction of social change which is aimed for in trans-formation research is one possible, but not exclusive, 'option' for social innova-tions" (ibid., 55). Consequently, this concept of social innovation is not linked to any particular goal of a socio-ecological transformation of society.

A further weak point is that the authors treat new practices (or social innova-tions) as mechanisms, yet avoid clarifying what they mean when they use this term (or what Tarde had meant by using it). In the ongoing debate on social mechanisms, protagonists claim that the "mechanism" concept is generally used to signify recurring processes in which certain causes are connected with certain outcomes or mark a specific class of real phenomena. To this effect, mechanisms "mediate between cause and effect" (Gross 2009, 362). Thus, a social mechanism is grasped as a process which has provable effects and consequences for something else. Mayntz argues that mechanisms represent generalised effect relationships. In her view, they "*are* such and such" and "they *do* such and such" (Mayntz 2004, 239). She further argues that the mechanism concept should generally be connected with other concepts. In this sense, statements "about mechanisms are *links* in theory; they are causal propositions that explain specific outcomes by identifying the generative process that ... produces them" (ibid., 253). However, following this concept, it is highly questionable to equate mechanisms with practices because the former explicitly exclude the centrality of activities and of the competences of the individuals involved that is stressed by the latter. In addition, putting Tarde's mechanisms on a level with practices is problematic because Tarde uses his concepts of invention and imitation to signify series of activities or events, which – from a practice-theory perspective – are not practices but are embedded in or parts of practices. According to Schatzki, this means "that a general understanding of the nature, trajectories, and effects of these series requires grasping (1) the relations of event series to practices ... and (2) how practices compose social phenomena" (Schatzki 2014, 2).

As such, Howaldt and colleagues' concept (of social innovation) only seems to be usable as a sub-concept in the analysis of societal practice/arrangement configurations, a sub-concept which can be used to study event series dominated by intentional and targeted activities which (might) have a specific impact on transformative social change as defined above from a practice theory perspective. It then makes sense to follow the suggestion that a social innovation "refers to those changes in agendas, agency and institutions that lead to a better inclusion of excluded groups and individuals in various spheres of society" (Moulaert *et al.* 2005, 1978). Similar to Howaldt and colleagues, Moulaert and co-authors stress "that such changes do not necessarily refer to something 'new' .... Social innovation in the sense of changes in institutions can, therefore, also mean a return to 'old' institutional forms" (ibid.). In addition, this would allow us to accept the advice from innovation researchers "that to understand the sources of innovation we need to understand the milieu in which *creativity* takes part ... [and which] should not be an integral part of the definition of social innovations" (Pol and Ville 2009, 884).

6 Sustainable consumption

Following Beck's diagnosis, the multiple societal crises and the conflicts they evoke are

> taking place *not* in the "environment" but in institutions, political parties, trade unions and global corporations, within and between governments and international organizations, or at the breakfast table, where everything turns on the legitimacy of lifestyles, of breakfast and of consumption.
>
> (Beck 2016, 64)

If we now ask ourselves what the term "sustainable consumption" actually means and how its relevance can be elaborated in conjunction with the concepts of societal transformation, social innovations and metamorphosis discussed above, we would be well advised to consider that all consumption processes (and production processes) require resources such as energy, materials, land and human (and often non-human) labour. Additionally, we should bear in mind that consumption and production generally generate waste and emissions. Consequently, a societal transformation (process) towards a more sustainable, just and equal world society in which both social innovations (in various societal spheres) and sustainable consumption are and will be of central relevance "entails the clear recognition that there is limited capability to supply resources and to absorb pollution" (Urry 2011, 119). Discussing the term "sustainable consumption" might then tackle several pressing questions, namely how "do different economic activities influence the use of natural resources" (ibid.), how "could low carbon lives be innovated, generalized and sustained as a practical, desirable and fashionable set of alternatives" (ibid., 122) especially in the Global North, and how could those low carbon forms of life at the same time make a contribution to transfiguring unjust and unsustainable economic relationships.

Bearing in mind that consumption is a means to an end and that the concept of sustainable consumption is at risk of lacking "the evaluative force that the idea of 'sustainable development' enjoys" (Sen 2013, 12), the term contains a broad range of practices in which individual actors participate to perceive, acquire, use, exploit and dispose of both market-brokered and non-market-brokered entities without damaging themselves, their environment or the need to satisfy future generations (Jonas and Littig 2015; Jonas 2016). It thus becomes clear that, strictly speaking, there is no such thing as a sustainable consumption practice per se. Instead, consumption can be seen as a key aspect of many very different configurations of practices (Warde 2005) that trigger distinction effects in the social space.

In this regard, practice theories "have asserted the commingling of the material and the symbolic with what users know, do and say in relation to consumption, and whether and how these are transformed" (Genus and Thorpe 2016, 8). It also becomes clear that "consumption is connected to individuals' ideas of what their lives should look like" (Di Giulo and Fuchs 2014, 187). Seen from this point of view, "consumers and practitioners are as central and vital to change as promoters of any kind or another" (Shove and Walker 2010, 475), although it has to be pointed out that the governance of sustainability emphasises "individualism, the primacy of market relations and consumer choice over collectivism" (Genus 2014, 299) as well as "non-market relations and citizens as active shapers of a 'better' society" (ibid.). In this context, Sen raises the question of whether a required "behavioural change that makes people less inclined towards massive – and massively resource-depleting – consumption" (Sen 2013, 13) can indeed happen voluntarily. He goes on to argue that if there should be a need for coercion "something important would have to be sustained – in particular, a crucial freedom to decide how to live and what to consume, without being ordered around by some 'big brother'" (ibid.).

However, to foster their chances of success, realisation or dispersion, discussions about sustainable consumption practices, sustainable forms of life (Jaeggi 2014) or sustainable labour (Littig forthcoming) should not be restricted merely to the sphere of politics, the economic sphere or the breakfast table: they should also be part of vivid debates in the public sphere. It is worth remembering that the concept of the public sphere has become a keyword in a critical and democratic perspective through the work of Habermas (1989). This concept emphasises in particular the relevance of the formation of a public body which anyone can join without restriction. This body serves as the forum in which the public can deliberate aspects of public interest in an unrestricted manner, aspects which can then have an impact on politics or the economy. However, given the observed unsustainability of most consumption practices and forms of life, for instance in European countries or in the USA, it makes sense to adapt Frasers' plea to focus on those "nonliberal, nonbourgeois, competing public spheres" (Fraser 1990, 60–1) or counter-publics in which more sustainable practices and forms of life are debated, developed further and tested. The public sphere in this sense is constituted of various arenas, namely hegemonial bourgeois publics on the one hand, and corresponding counter-publics on the other, which "emerge in response to exclusions within dominant publics" (ibid., 67).

In light of the advancing pace of globalisation processes, Fraser (2007) stresses the need for cosmopolitan public spheres. In these spheres, public opinion can only be seen as legitimate when it is the result of a negotiation process in which all those affected can participate as equals. This also requires specific socio-material spaces and "powerful forms of self-restraint anchored in emotional identification with 'distant strangers'" (Linklater 2007, 35). This is important irrespective of the question of whether sustainable practices in everyday life are or should be spatially restricted (for instance, in the cases of local do-it-yourself initiatives, refugee relief networks or alternative food networks), or whether they are or can frequently only be enacted in wide-ranging, often global networks (as is the case, for instance, in some, albeit few, fair-trade value chains, sustainable and just financing practices, various vegan or vegetarian food practices or global mobility practices), because even the most local consumption practices are linked to and embedded in global labour and value chain processes, whose effects and consequences have to be taken into consideration.

7 Conclusions

As I have shown in the above, the concepts of societal transformation, social innovations and sustainable consumption can be of central relevance in a practice-theory-based analysis of the current, pressing and multiple socio-economic and environmental crises as well as the ongoing change processes. Indeed, they are particularly relevant in light of the metamorphosis of the world society in which the politics of invisibility is an important strategy to stabilize state authority and the reproduction of social and political order by denying the existence of global risks and their effects of "ecological and risk appropriation" and health effects to large parts of the population.

(Beck 2016, 101)

In contradiction to Beck's diagnosis especially, the transformation concept is suitable to act as a central term in a practice-theory-based analysis of the ongoing multiple crises as well as of the political strategies and visions which may be used to change societies towards sustainability. Such an analysis allows us to highlight the necessary substantial change processes – especially in those countries in world society in which an imperial, unjust and unsustainable mode of living (Brand and Wissen, 2012) is performed and reproduced in various societal milieus and forms of life. It is more than questionable if it is really the case that "it is not individuals who have to change" (Urry 2011, 156). What is needed are more individuals who engage themselves in more sustainable forms of life. What is also needed are frugal practices "that enhance and contribute to well-being" (Shove and Spurling 2013, 11) – not only of the individuals involved but also of the other creatures and other entities that are likewise included. Sustainable consumption practices that often entail social innovations as important ingredients can then be grasped as necessary, but not sufficient, parts or aspects of the cosmopolitan practice/arrangement configurations of societal transformation that are needed to create a more equal and sustainable world society, the realisation of which remains open and contested.

Acknowledgement

This chapter is based on the project Moralization of the Market Sphere: The Fairtrade Case, which was co-funded by the Jubiläumsfonds der Oestereichischen Nationalbank (project no. 15216).

References

Alkemeyer, T., Buschmann, N. and Michaeler, M. (2017) "Critique in praxis: arguments for a subjectivation theoretical expansion on practice theory" in Jonas, M., and Littig, B. (eds) *Praxeological Political Analysis* Routledge: London, 67–83.

Archibugi, D. (forthcoming) "Blade Runner economics: will innovation lead the economic recovery?" *Research Policy* 46.

Avelino, F., Wittmayer, J.M., Haxeltine, A., Kemp, R., O'Riordan, T., Weaver, P., Loorbach, D., and Rotmans, J. (2014) "Game-changers and transformative social innovation: the case of the economic crisis and the new economy" (TRANSIT working paper 1) TRANSIT: EU SSH.2013.3.2–1 Grant agreement no. 613169.

Barr, S., and Pollard, J. (2017) "Geographies of transition: narrating environmental activism in an age of climate change and 'peak oil'" *Environment and Planning A* 49: 47–64.

Beck, U. (2016) *The Metamorphosis of the World* Polity: Cambridge.

Blok, A. (2012) "Greening cosmopolitan urbanism? On the transnational mobility of low-carbon formats in Northern European and East Asian Cities" *Environment and Planning A* 44: 2327–43.

Bourdieu, P. (1977) *Outline of a Theory of Practice* Cambridge University Press: Cambridge.

Brand, U. (2016) "'Transformation' as a new critical orthodoxy: the strategic use of the term 'transformation' does not prevent multiple crises" *GAIA – Ecological Perspectives for Science and Society* 25: 23–7.

Brand, U., and Wissen, M. (2012) "Global environmental politics and the imperial mode of living: articulations of state–capital relations in the multiple crisis" *Globalizations* 9: 547–60.

Burns, T.R. (2016) "Sustainable development: agents, systems and the environment" *Current Sociology Review* 64: 875–906.

Di Giulio, A., and Fuchs, D. (2014) "Sustainable consumption corridors: concept, objections, and responses" *GAIA – Ecological Perspectives for Science and Society* 23: 184–92.

Fraser, N. (1990) "Rethinking the public sphere: a contribution to the critique of actually existing democracy" *Social Text* 25/26: 56–80.

Fraser, N. (2007) "Transnationalizing the public sphere: on the legitimacy and efficacy of public opinion in a post-Westphalian world" *Theory, Culture and Society* 24: 7–30.

Geels, F.W., and Schot, J. (2007) "Typology of sociotechnical transition pathways" *Research Policy* 36: 399–417.

Genus, A. (2014) "Governing sustainability: a discourse-institutional approach" *Sustainability* 6: 283–305.

Genus, A., and Thorpe, A. (2016) "Introduction" in Genus, A. (ed.) *Sustainable Consumption: Design, Innovation and Practice* Springer: Dordrecht, 1–15.

Gross, N. (2009) "A pragmatist theory of social mechanisms" *American Sociological Review* 74: 358–79.

Habermas, J. (1989) *The Structural Transformation of the Public Sphere: An Inquiry into a Category of Bourgeois Society* Polity Press: Cambridge.

Have, R.P.v.d. and Rubalca, L. (2016) "Social innovation research: an emerging area of innovation studies" *Research Policy* 45: 1923–35.

Honneth, A. (2011) *Das Recht der Freiheit: Grundriß einer demokratischen Sittlichkeit* Suhrkamp: Frankfurt a. M.

Horkheimer, M., and Adorno, T.W. (1982) *Dialektik der Aufklärung* Fischer: Frankfurt a. M.

Howaldt, J., and Schwarz, M. (2010) *Soziale Innovation im Fokus: Skizze eines gesellschaftstheoretisch inspirierten Forschungskonzepts* Transcript: Bielefeld.

Howaldt, J., Kopp, R., and Schwarz, M. (2015) *On the Theory of Social Innovations: Tarde's Neglected Contribution to the Development of a Sociological Innovation Theory* Beltz Juventa: Weinheim.

Jaeggi, R. (2014) *Kritik von Lebensformen* Suhrkamp: Berlin.

Jonas, M. (2016) "Nachhaltigkeit und Konsum: Eine praxissoziologische Kritik" in Schäfer, H. (ed.) *Praxistheorie: Ein Forschungsprogramm* Transcript: Bielefeld, 341–61.

Jonas, M. (2017) "Transition or transformation? A plea for the praxeological approach of radical socio-ecological change" in Jonas, M., and Littig, B. (eds) *Praxeological Political Analysis* Routledge: London, 116–33.

Jonas, M. and Littig, B. (2015) "Sustainable practices" in Wright, J.D. (ed.) *The International Encyclopedia of the Social and Behavioral Sciences* 2nd edn Elsevier: Oxford, vol. 23, 834–38.

Joy, M. (2010) *Why We Love Dogs, Eat Pigs and Wear Cows: An Introduction to Carnism* Conari: San Francisco.

Linklater, A. (2007) "Public spheres and civilizing processes" *Theory, Culture and Society* 24: 31–7.

Littig, B. (forthcoming) "Good 'green jobs' for whom? A feminist critique of the 'green economy'" in MacGregor, S. (ed.), *Routledge International Handbook of Gender and Environment* Taylor & Francis: Abingdon.

Lundvall, B.-A. (2017) "Is there a technological fix for the current global stagnation? A response to Daniele Archibugi, Blade Runner economics: will innovation lead the economic recovery?" *Research Policy* 46: 544–9.

Marcuse, P. (2009) "From critical urban theory to the right to the city" *City* 13: 185–97.

Marston, S.A., Jones, P.J., III and Woodward, K. (2005) "Human geography without scale" *Transactions of the Institute of British Geography* 30: 416–32.

Mayntz, R. (2004) "Mechanisms in the analysis of social macro phenomena" *Philosophy of the Social Sciences* 34: 237–59.

Moulaert, F., Martinelli, F., Syngedouw, E., and Gonzalez, S. (2005) "Towards alternative model(s) of local innovation" *Urban Studies* 42: 1969–90.

Murphy, R. (2015) "The emerging hypercarbon reality, technological and post-carbon utopias, and social innovation to low carbon societies" *Current Sociology* 63: 317–38.

Pol, E., and Ville, S. (2009) "Social innovation: buzz word or enduring term?" *Journal of Socio-Economics* 38: 878–85.

Polanyi, K. (1997 [1944]) *The Great Transformation: Politische und ökonomische Ursprünge von Gesellschaften und Wirtschaftssystemen* Suhrkamp: Frankfurt a. M.

Reckwitz, A. (2002) "Toward a theory of social practices: a development in culturalist theorizing" *European Journal of Social Theory* 3: 243–63.

Schatzki, T. (2002) *The Site of the Social: A Philosophical Account of the Constitution of Social Life and Change* Pennsylvania State University Press: University Park.

Schatzki, T. (2014) "Larger scales" (DEMAND Research Centre working paper 5).

Schatzki, T. (2016) "Practice theory as flat ontology" in Schäfer, H. (ed.) *Praxistheorie: Ein Forschungsprogramm* Transcript: Bielefeld, 27–42.

Schatzki, T. (2017) "Multiplicity in social theory and practice ontology" in Jonas, M., and Littig, B. (eds) *Praxeological Political Analysis* Routledge: London, 17–34.

Sen, A. (2013) "The ends and means of sustainability" *Journal of Human Development and Capabilities* 14: 6–20.

Shove, E., and Spurling, N. (2013) "Sustainable practices: social theory and climate change" in Shove, E., and Spurling, N. (eds) *Sustainable Practices: Social Theory and Climate Change* Routledge: London, 1–13.

Shove, E. and Walker, G. (2010) "Governing transitions in the sustainability of everyday life" *Research Policy* 39: 471–6.

Smart, B. (2011) "Another 'great transformation' or common ruin?" *Theory, Culture and Society* 28: 131–51.

Steinmueller, W.E. (forthcoming) "Science fiction and innovation: a response" *Research Policy* 46.

Tarde, G. (1899) *Social Laws: An Outline of Sociology* Macmillan: New York.

Tarde, G. (1903) *The Laws of Imitation* Henry Holt: New York.

Urry, J. (2011) *Climate Change and Society* Polity: Cambridge.

Warde, A. (2005) "Consumption and theories of practice" *Journal of Consumer Culture* 5: 131–53.

5 Local authorities and their development of new governance approaches

Distilling lessons from a social innovation project

Marcelline Bonneau and François Jégou

1 The impact of social innovation uptake on developing new governance approaches

Both science and policy are interested in improving our understanding of the raison d'être and the evolution of citizen-led creative initiatives. Such initiatives appear to be playing an increasingly active role in public and social life (Meroni 2007). Their emergence is explained against the background of an increasing number of inadequately addressed public problems. Whether supported by public authorities or not, many initiatives seem to share the "wish to fill the incapacity of existing institutions to fight efficiently against terrible injustice that characterizes today's world" (Boulanger 2015, 3). Such injustice can be social (inequality, unemployment), intergenerational (legacy to new generations), geographical (pillaging of resources in the South) and environmental (Boulanger 2015).

The above-mentioned citizens' initiatives have been identified as having the potential to support local authorities not only in solving problems, but also in improving – for instance – the resilience of cities (Carton *et al.* 2013). Arguably, one of the recurring domains for their engagement in cities is related to sustainable consumption (Jaeger-Erben *et al.* 2015; Martin and Upham 2016). Simultaneously, the focus on city-level dynamics is based on relatively well-known proximity effects (Wittmayer and Loorbach 2016): we know a city's "history, its streets, its geography, its shops, its issues at stake … sometimes the elected representatives personally!" (Servigne 2011, 3: trans. from French). In addition, social innovation, including citizens-led initiatives, are by configuration very deeply anchored in their territory (Van Dyck and Van den Broeck 2013).

In response to such collective action, public authorities also seek to position themselves to support societal transformation. Some cities have found that they cannot address this by doing what they have done so far through traditional governance approaches. The reliance on the deployment of resources over which leaders and managers have direct authority and the rigidity of this top-down governance approach have had their limits exposed (Jégou and Bonneau

2015). Consequently, a growing number of cities are developing new approaches for identifying issues and finding solutions. Some turn to the use of social innovation as a way of experimenting with new governance approaches. Such innovations

> are social in both their ends and their means. Specifically, we define social innovations as new ideas (products, services and models) that simultaneously meet social needs (more effectively than alternatives) and create new social relationships or collaborations. In other words, they are innovations that are not only good for society but also enhance society's capacity to act.
>
> (BEPA 2011, 33)

As a result, innovations vary widely in terms of the actors involved, infrastructures used, funding procedures, processes developed, and platforms tested. Innovations also include initiatives that connect different levels of formal institutional governance and informal governance arrangements. City administrations are at least partially facing a new challenge: to rethink their mandate, their skills and their relationship with citizens. Against this background, some city administrations have started to engage in co-creation exercises to reconfigure governance structures with the aim of redefining and deepening the role of citizens as well as their own. The present chapter addresses this shift and advances the understanding of administration-led changes in governance.

Our assumption was that, due to the fact that public institutions adopt a new paradigm – i.e. social innovation – as a yardstick to reconfigure their internal processes, they also play an important role in societal transformation. The relevance of our work is twofold: on the one hand, it relies on our long-standing engagement with theories and approaches in public administration, which we use to further concrete institutional transformative processes. On the other hand, it seeks to contribute to the academic literature by providing in-depth empirical examples to increase the dataset available for further conceptualisation of institutional and societal transformation.

This chapter begins by presenting a brief literature review. This is followed by an outline of our conceptual lenses, and our methodology. We then present two cases, Amersfoort (Netherlands) and Gdańsk (Poland) followed by a discussion of a series of elements which appear to be enablers of institutional and societal transformations.

2 Frameworks for understanding changing governance approaches in city administrations

New strategies for city administrations to interact with citizens have been covered in a wide range of literatures. For example, in the literature relating to participatory governance[1] (Coenen 2008; Torfing *et al.* 2012) or to citizen participation (Bifulco 2013; Hurard 2011). Alternatively, there are authors who envision citizens' innovations as a driver for societal transformation (Bauler and Pel 2014; Bauler et al. 2016).

For analysing these administration-led governance shifts, two different lenses have been chosen to research and explore the particular cases. Taking these complementary lenses helps us to understand the role of city administrations in changing the governance of their city towards co-creation with citizens and the enabling elements for such a process. Combining these approaches further enables us to investigate both systemic and individual processes, shedding light on two complementary processes: on the one hand the methodologies and approaches for change in governance, on the other, the individual postures and roles of the people involved in such a change.

First, we build upon ideas of reflexive governance (Marsden 2013; Voß and Bornemann 2011) or one of its applications, transition management practiced by public administrations (Roorda et al. 2014). This framework enables us to focus on the self-critical and self-conscious co-evolution of the interaction between the structure (the regime level) and the agency (innovative practices, such as "transition experiments"), where sustainable development is a normative orientation (Grin 2012). Some authors have designed a grid that is particularly useful to understand some of the strategic requirements for innovation in governance and to look for their (lack of) implementation in city strategies (Voß and Kemp 2006):

- **transdisciplinary knowledge production** sheds lights on the need to develop an inter- and transdisciplinary problem-solving strategy to support an integrated approach which would encompass the complexity of the issues at stake;
- **adaptive strategies and institutions** relates to the need to monitor closely policies and their implementation in order to adjust them according to experience and learning throughout the ongoing socio-ecological transformations;
- **anticipation of long-term system effects** of action strategies refers to the need to account for the wider side – and indirect or even undesired – effects of dynamics that could occur in the long-term;
- **iterative participatory goal formulation** backs up the need to re-evaluate regularly the goals based on the evolution of socio-ecological systems and values in involving the range of concerned actors; and
- **interactive strategy development** brings up the need to interact with relevant stakeholders across institutional political fields and functional domains which enable socio-ecological transformation to become an outcome of social interaction.

Such an approach also stresses the side – and wider societal – effects of the changes induced in governance: "the reflexivity of governance also includes the possibility that certain governance patterns undermine themselves by inducing changes in the world that then affect their own working" (Voß and Kemp 2006, 4).

Inspired by writings on reflective governance, we formulate the following questions to guide the analysis of our case material: Which form(s) did participation and collective learning take to support the reflexivity of governance (Voß and Bornemann 2011)? What type of new institutional and procedural arrangements have enabled more efficient problem-solving (Marsden 2013)? How do our examples support (or not) the role of niches to experiment and the focus on bottom-up framework for policy development (Hendriks and Grin 2007)?

Second, looking at innovation in the public sector, "public innovation" sheds light on the meaning and importance of public innovation in a more linear and causal way: going from the objectives of the innovation (its rationale) to its effects looking at the factors that hamper or stimulate the innovation process (De Vries *et al.* 2014). Such a lens distinguishes between the stages "before" and "after" innovation has taken place – i.e. the generating and the adopting phases – making it possible to distinguish the key innovation-triggering individual and institutional features. Such features can be part of the policy processes or the policy actors. The public innovation approach has identified drivers and barriers to changes within the administration that can support grounding our cases in their individual contexts (Bekkers *et al.* 2013, 5). These drivers and barriers correspond mainly to the social, political and legal cultures of the cities: it can be the complexity and characteristic of such cultures, the type of governance and state tradition or the relation with stakeholders throughout the networks, and the related resource availability and resource dependency coming out of it.

Also based on these writings in public administration and public innovation, we formulate the following questions to guide the analysis of our case material: How has the faith of public authorities in citizens enabled innovation (Moyson *et al.* 2016)? Did leadership support public innovation (Bason 2010)? What was the role of internal political and administrative actors in creating a climate that could support innovation (Borins 2000)? How could street-level bureaucrats make city administrations adjust the way they solve problems (Agger and Poulsen 2017)?

3 On methodology

The overall research design combined and confronted empirical explorations on the ground with academic literature. As such, the research was based on principles inspired by inductively-led grounded-theory approaches. We identified and discussed empirical evidence of changing governance approaches, while using the data collected to gain new insights which led to further iterations of empirical explorations (Punch 2005). Some form of generalisation of our results was subsequently operated, notably with the prospect to discuss the relevance of results for other city administrations.

3.1 Selecting the case studies

Case studies provide an in-depth exploratory research approach (Gerring 2004; Yin 2014). Notwithstanding some inevitable bias (about the lack of generalisability or their specific cultural, geographical and economic contexts), this approach enabled us to compare the mechanisms related to the governance shifts in detail (Gerring 2004; Yin 2014).

We selected two distinct cities: the more distinct they were – and thus the greater insights we could get of particular individual cases – the better for our purposes. The following criteria were used to assure case distinctiveness: geographical location, size, culture of citizens' participation, EU membership, market economy, advanced versus in transition. In addition, selected cities should show evidence of proactive initiatives led by their respective city administration. The choice for Amersfoort (in the Netherlands) and Gdańsk (in Poland) as contrasting examples was also mediated by project considerations. The activities formed part of a capitalisation exercise for the URBACT programme.[2] While the public administration of Amersfoort already has advanced collaboration practices with its citizens, Gdańsk is taking initial steps towards sharing governance responsibilities.

3.2 Compiling, comparing and analysing the case studies

We visited the two cities in the autumn of 2014. We interviewed a wide variety of stakeholders involved in the change of the administration including the municipality level (elected officials, heads of departments/units, civil servants), civil society (NGOs), (individual) citizens and others such as facilitators of the process (consultants). The selection of the sample was based on availability during the visits. This resulted in 34 interviews in Amersfoort and 13 in Gdańsk. This material was compiled in detailed case study reports (Bonneau 2015; Jégou 2015). This chapter is based on these interviews and secondary documents, as well as the analysis carried out for the case study reports along the lines of the conceptual lenses outlined above.

4 Two examples of cities developing new approaches to governance

4.1 Amersfoort, Netherlands: designing a collaborative city administration

In Amersfoort, a city of 160,000 inhabitants, city leaders used social innovation as an opportunity to initiate a complete process of experimentation and change of their administration's practices. The goal was to build collaboration with citizens and deliver better-designed and more-cost-efficient public services. This initiative was a reaction to budget shortages, to the transfer of some administrative competences from the national to the city level and to the wish for deeper involvement of citizens in city governance. The citizens selected to participate were engaged in grassroots initiatives. The institutional transformation started in 2012 through three parallel processes: collaborative experiments, ad hoc initiatives implemented by citizens, and the institutionalisation of a new governance paradigm; i.e. social innovation. The complexity and overlap of the initiatives undertaken since 2012 is presented in Figure 5.1.

The New Collaboration, which took place in 2012, is an example of a collaborative experiment, which brought together citizens, council members and civil servants in a large public conference to discuss the democratic system and explore how to organise new modes of collaboration between citizens and the city administration. The G1000, organised in 2014, was another experiment based on Brussels' first experience, where citizens as well as civil servants and elected representatives (in their function as citizens) discussed perspectives for the city and developed ten project plans from more than 100 ideas. This process was considered innovative because the participants were randomly invited, and out of the 1,000 invitees 650 turned up.

One of the first initiatives implemented by citizens was the creation of a green area at an abandoned site. Due to the citizens' interest and passion for expressing their new park design ideas, the administration gave a group of citizens the mandate to redesign it. Subsequently, the Elisabeth Project was submitted to the city council, who approved it. Following this success, the administration started a reflective process with citizens asking how they wanted their city to be governed. In 2013, they promoted Samen-Foort (Forward Together), a year of reflection with multiple experiments in participation and bottom-up pilot projects including collective innovation forums, exchange initiatives between citizens and the city

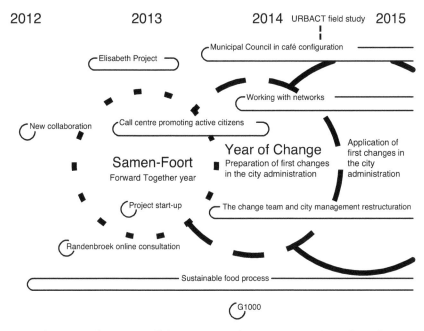

Figure 5.1 Towards a more collaborative city administration in Amersfoort: key experiments, projects and practices.

Source: Jégou and Bonneau 2015.

administration and new participative processes. The success of all these initiatives and the growing recognition and interest by all stakeholders in the city pushed Amersfoort's city leaders to declare 2014 as the Year of Change. The Year of Change was a year of collective rethinking and preparation resulting in the reorganisation of the city administration's practices and management structure. This change was implemented from 2015 onwards in order to facilitate this new approach to collaboration between the city's population and its administration. The administration also developed the role of "free-range civil servants", who spend time meeting and interacting with citizens in their daily settings before bringing back their insights and sharing them with their colleagues inside the administration.

4.2 Gdańsk: initial steps towards responsibility sharing

Gdańsk is a city of 462,000 inhabitants in the Baltic region of Poland. Its geographical and historical position played an important role throughout Poland's economic and political history. More recently, in 1980, it was the cradle of the country's first free trade-union movement led by Solidarność. As in many other European cities, the administration of the city has been traditionally perceived as being closed and isolated from its citizens. Citizens did not have faith in the city council's decisions nor did they have faith in the channels they could use to communicate with the administration. The administration was not familiar with the issues faced by citizens which could not be tackled with routine procedures. As such, an incremental and unplanned process started to take place as of 2007 as presented in Figure 5.2.

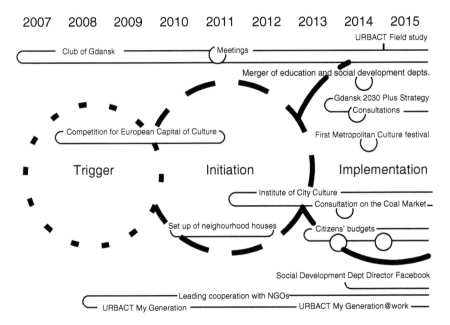

Figure 5.2 Initial steps towards responsibility sharing in Gdańsk.

The change started with the work of a so-called "internal think tank", the Club of Gdańsk: administrators gathered with the support of an external moderator in order to reflect on their city's present and desired future. After a series of meetings, some key values were defined, which were meant to provide the conceptual basis for the strategic work of the city. These were, amongst others, trust, participation, honesty, responsibility, being closer to the citizen, individual and institutional openness, harmonisation, social cohesion and long-term perspectives. Although this work was not translated into any strategic document, it was the baseline for Gdańsk, My City, a programme on citizenship and social policy. More importantly, it nurtured the vision of a participatory process, which was carried out in order to design the new city strategy, Gdańsk 2030 Plus. Through a mix of online consultation, drawing contests and workshops, citizens were given *carte blanche* to express their needs and wishes. The administration could then assess the expectations of the citizens and combine them to form the city strategy. The administration is now operationalising each point of the citizen-made strategy. At the same time, Gdańsk joined two URBACT networks, one after the other: My Generation and My Generation@work.

In parallel, the mayor realised the need to change the way the city was being governed. He appointed high-level officials from non-administrative backgrounds. They included former psychologists, journalists and NGO activists. Through these appointments and the creation of a unit dedicated to cooperating with NGOs, the administration started to work outside of its traditional silos. As a result, departments started to interact, expertise from the ground was being integrated and responsibility started to be shared with street-level actors. This cross-fertilisation among departments also shed light on the need to be more efficient and effective at problem-solving. This lead to the merging of the Department of Social Development with the Department of Education.

In addition, the city administration created the Institute of City Culture: its purpose was to use culture as a vector for citizens' empowerment and to instil feelings of belonging. The institute was also responsible for setting up projects with citizens, such as the improvement of the centrally located Coal Market. This was used as a lighthouse project to showcase the results of joining forces.

Finally, the city administration worked on increasing its visibility, communication and transparency, based on the observation that "the most important part of the process has been the meetings where we got to know the citizens and the citizens got to know us" (see Figure 5.3) as Żaneta Kucharska, involved in the participatory processes of the Gdańsk 2030 Plus Strategy, stated. This included the creation of a Facebook page for the city and a personal one for the directors of the Social Development Department, which made the administration more accessible and more "human".

Figure 5.3 The participatory process of the Gdańsk 2030 Plus Strategy.
Source: © Żaneta Kucharska and Jacek Zabłotny, City Hall of Gdańsk.

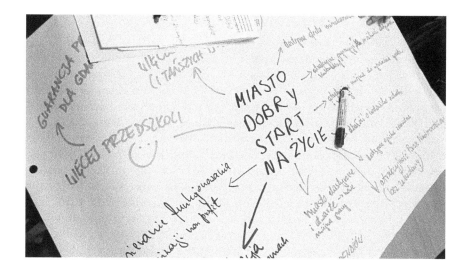

Figure 5.3 Continued

5 A discussion of the elements required for institutional and societal transformation

How can we better understand the shift borne by the new challenges of city administrations and the increasing role of citizens in the reconfiguration of governance structures, and how can we enhance our comprehension of administration-led changes in governance? From our two cases we can see a contrast in the cultures of governance, which have grown amid different historical backgrounds and citizenship cultures, each of these providing specific contexts enabling (or preventing) innovation (Bekkers *et al.* 2013): a more bottom-up and participative one in Western Europe (the Netherlands) contrasting with a more top-down command-and-control one in Eastern Europe (Poland). The former is based on a progressive design process of a collaborative city administration, and the latter starts from a repositioning of the city administration. However, both highlight the need to take action in order to initiate collaboration with citizens. This must include as starting point, accessible initiatives and less risky experiments to document and demonstrate first results and raise trust among stakeholders. The remainder of this section discusses our key findings related to the two conceptual lenses taken: reflexive governance and public innovation, summarised in Table 5.1.

5.1 From a reflexive governance perspective

We observed that both city administrations followed paths which are echoed in other European cities and that similar key characteristics of governance change are found in the two cities. We found that the change processes from one governance approach to another echoed insights from the literature on reflexive governance. Such processes can be defined as: "although acknowledging a fundamental ambivalence of goals, uncertainty of knowledge, and distribution of power, [the new governance designs] all emphasise participation, experimentation, and collective learning as key elements of governance" (Voß and Bornemann 2011, 9). Indeed, the process was triggered by the city administrations' recognition of the limits of their knowledge in designing and delivering the most suitable and effective public policies and switching to a more user-centred perspective. Moreover, they recognised their limits to develop and/or acquire this knowledge. As such, they sought to **build capacity**. Civil servants

Table 5.1 Findings of our case studies along our two analytical frameworks

Reflexive governance	Public administration
Capacity-building	Strong leadership
Multi-stakeholder approach	Internal disruption
Co-production beyond bottom-up and top-down	Brokers and matchmakers
Small steps	Conversation through social media

received training in new skills and competences, especially regarding providing advice, guiding processes and networking. In Amersfoort, specific trainings were organised, where civil servants and elected representatives together with citizens learned about integrated problem-solving, working with networks, collaboration and fluid communication. In Gdańsk, the competences – for example, for moderating participatory processes and co-creating projects such as the Gdańsk 2030 Plus Strategy or the refurbishment of the Coal Market – came from experts outside the administration, combined with training received in the framework of the URBACT programme.

A shift in governance can occur when various actors (varied by their levels of governance and/or their epistemic backgrounds) are involved in new institutional and procedural arrangements (Marsden 2013). Actors involved in such new arrangements seek to adjust their cognitive and normative beliefs. They take into account and acknowledge alternative understanding and framings of the problem and attempt to integrate multiple approaches to problem solutions (ibid.). In Amersfoort and Gdańsk, the city administrations developed new ways of designing public services, based on a **multi-stakeholder approach**. Mapping and connecting existing actors and initiatives from different backgrounds and with different interests was key to the start of each new project led by the city. These included elected members, active citizens, entrepreneurs, civil servants, large and small organisations, commercial firms, NGOs and so on, all treated equally. In Amersfoort, systematic stakeholder mapping before starting projects has been developed as a good practice, referred to as a "project start-up". It is considered a prerequisite for any new project. In Gdańsk, such a mapping was carried out within two URBACT network projects, My Generation and My Generation@work. Through direct involvement in these two networks, the stakeholders got to know each other, tested working together and initiated new modalities of interaction and collaboration among each other. Simultaneously, the power of the administration was distributed through this more transversal way of working. Also, the roles of citizens and NGOs changed as they acquired important responsibilities and mandates. What was quite new and innovative in Gdańsk was that for the first time the processes involved people with various background (journalists, psychologists) and occupations (administration, NGOs).

The transition approach provides a bottom-up framework for policy development through its focus on experimentation in niches (Hendriks and Grin 2007; Smith *et al.* 2010). In our cases, we observed that cities sought to **co-produce beyond the traditional bottom-up or top-down divide**. We identified areas where citizens are involved in the collaborative design of public services, and where there is ongoing communication and exchange. In Amersfoort, citizens acted beyond the remits of the administration: "We, as citizens, got the assignment from the administration. But we did not do it their way. We did it our way", said Lia Bouma, one of the key citizens engaged in the Elisabeth Project. In Gdańsk, the administration was leading the consultations for the renovation of the Coal Market and also coordinated the participatory process for the

Gdańsk 2030 Plus Strategy. However, they engaged an external moderator to ensure openness and freedom of speech for the engaged citizens.

One of the principles of the transition management approach is to develop **"small but radical steps** ... guided by a long-term perspective, which can be acquired by questioning mind-sets and being open to unorthodox ideas and actions" (Roorda *et al.* 2014, 10). Similarly, we found in our cases that experimentation was first initiated with "low hanging fruits": focusing on projects which would raise little political or controversial issues, quick results could be expected. These first achievements ensured visibility to the overall process and helped to understand possible outcomes, both to the administration and to the general public. In Amersfoort, the New Collaboration was a "light" start towards engaging citizens more structurally in a public conference. This lead towards a consensus between citizens, city administration and city council regarding writing a new policy on how the city administration should facilitate citizens' initiatives. In Gdańsk, an internal think tank, in the form of regular meetings during five years, together with closer collaboration with NGOs enabled the following steps of the process. In our two cases, these small steps had systemic impact and are comparable to a process of acupuncture.[3] A series of new practices emerged progressively in the city and in the administration leading to systemic change in the city (Jégou 2010).

5.2 *From a public administration perspective*

As a starting point, it is crucial to stress the (change of) attitude of public authorities towards citizens and their initiatives. Of note is the evolution of their trust and trustworthiness (Moyson *et al.* 2016) which we observed in our cases by the increased faith in the initiative of citizens. City administrations **changed their posture** from doing *for* citizens to doing *with* citizens, positioning themselves on equal footing (e.g. enabling a multi-stakeholder approach).

Whether it comes from the administration or from the political level, innovation in the public sector is strongly connected to **strong leadership** (Bason 2010), and this is in line with our observations. In our cases, changes that occurred in the city administrations have emerged from various levels of hierarchy: city mayors, other city leaders, front-line civil servants and external actors to the institution. These de facto leaders of the process appeared to be the carrier of the vision or the coordinator of activities, and were in both cases embedded within the city-level governance institutions. Their activities were guided by a strategic vision. In Amersfoort, notwithstanding the role of the mayor, the initiatives came from the different heads of department who identified the need to mobilise and take advantage of citizens' resources. In Gdańsk, the mayor, on the basis of his observations and knowledge of societal evolutions, was strongly supportive of the vision – and need – for a change within the administration structure. This vision was supported by a series of high-level civil servants who launched the reflexions upon changes in the city governance at the level of the internal think tank, the Club of Gdańsk. All these steps were possible thanks to the individual ambitions of those involved and from getting to know each other: "the most important part of the process has been the meetings where we got to know the citizens and the citizens got to know us" (Żaneta Kucharska, coordinator of the Gdańsk 2030 Plus Strategy).

The literature also points to **internal disruption** in the administration which can serve as driver for innovation. This confirms the role of internal political and administrative actors in creating a climate that can support innovation (Borins 2000). In our cases, civil servants launched micro-initiatives without the formal approval or commitment of their line managers. However, these initiatives were stepping stones in gaining the trust of and persuading those responsible to get involved in new experiments, addressing more difficult problems and trying more risky solutions. In Amersfoort, civil servants organised simple inter-departmental lunches inviting colleagues to explore opportunities for collaboration between their respective departments. In Gdańsk, the flagship initiative was the Club of Gdańsk, in its entirety organised by civil servants and employees who acknowledged the need to start working differently.

Stepping down from their management role, city administrations made room for important innovative roles, such as that of **brokers** and **matchmakers**. The literature refers to these as street-level bureaucrats (Agger and Poulsen 2017). They bring interests and parties together in order to find solutions to issues in a more efficient way (Bonneau 2017). In Amersfoort in particular, civil servants spend more time in the city, interacting with citizens, rather than behind their desks (see Figure 5.4). In Gdańsk, the role of coordinator and matchmaker are still in their infancy, supported by the two above-mentioned URBACT projects. As put by Magdalena Skiba from the unit of cooperation with NGOs in Gdańsk: "The structures are changing: we have a spirit of openness and are able to assess what there is outside, take it on board and implement it."

Figure 5.4 In Amersfoort, civil servants are encouraged to work more in the field and get in contact with the citizens, as free-range civil servants

Source: © City of Amersfoort (left), Cor Holtackers (right).

Finally, another key element enabling change in governance approaches was the use of information and communication technology (ICT) and more specifically **interaction through social media**. Although the literature stresses, that social media can be the origin of all sorts of innovation (Bekkers *et al.* 2013), our cases showed that their innovation was mostly in their use. They provide spaces for people to exchange their opinions through dedicated platforms. In Gdańsk, in particular, one of the key successes was the personal Facebook page of the director of the Social Development Department: he was responsible for it, used his own name and shared personal as well as professional posts. He would reply directly to the messages addressed to him in an informal way, which allowed for direct discussion and sharing.

6 Conclusions

Amersfoort and Gdańsk work strongly on changing their governance for the improved well-being of their citizens and for a more efficient management of local societal issues. By changing their governance approaches and possibly paradigms, the cities are supporting a needed societal transformation. We based our research on empirical work in those cities, directly interacting with city administrations while conducting in parallel an analysis of the transformative processes at stake. As such, we compared the two cases focusing on analysing and reflecting on the enabling processes for institutional and societal transformation. Our analysis is in line with findings from the literature on reflexive governance, whereas the literature on the interaction between public administration and citizens helped us shed light on some of the attitudes and roles that enable transformation.

The BEPA definition introduced earlier stresses the role of social innovation as both a process and an end. In our chapter, we focused on the internal process of city administrations. We assumed that if public institutions develop a new governance approach based on social innovation, their internal process will play an important role in broader societal transformation and, as such, can lead to societal change. Developing a new governance approach and possibly paradigm goes hand in hand with the creation of new opportunities for experimentation. Cities increasingly take the opportunity to brainstorm, co-create and experiment with possible solutions, often supported by external experts. However, municipalities and local authorities could also facilitate the creation of public innovation labs within their own administration to change the way they make policies and provide public services. These could be more bottom-up, usage-based and community-centred approaches, which renew public participation and policy design (Jégou and Bonneau 2014). The societal transformations at the local level can benefit from the role of the institutions and vice versa. The analysis of transformations of public administration institutions are a case of societal transformation and at the same time act for societal transformation. As Paweł Adamowicz, mayor of Gdańsk concluded: "in order to innovate, a city should start by innovating in its own administration". Following their institutional transformations, it would now be time to harvest the societal transformation of Amersfoort and Gdańsk.

Acknowledgements

We would like to thank the URBACT programme for the support received in the frame of its capitalisation exercises, as well as Anne de Feijter and Piotr Wolkowinski for the organisation of our study visits. All the data comes from the publication *Social Innovation in Cities* from URBACT II (Jégou and Bonneau 2015). We would also like to thank Tom Bauler and Carolyn Quick for their review.

Notes

1 This chapter refers alternatively "collaborative" and "participatory". Although there are nuances in these two concepts, these were used interchangeably by the interviewees and more widely in our professional experience.
2 In 2014, the URBACT programme launched a process of capitalising on experiences from the projects it had funded and beyond. This was the second round of such an exercise and it focused on four topics ("Sustainable regeneration in urban areas", "Job generation for a jobless generation", "New urban economies" and "Social innovation in cities"). This research (methodology and findings) relate to the latter and lasted from May 2014 to May 2015.
3 Acupuncture refers to the following:

> the points in acupuncture are part of the patient body and needles pricking them act as an activator of a latent energy self-contained in the body. In the same way, the projects pre-exist disseminated in the urban place or regional land: they have to be identified and activated in order to act in synergy.
>
> The points of acupuncture are very precise points situated on meridian along which life energy is supposed to flow. In our case, not any kind of local projects are suitable for our purpose of transformative change toward a more sustainable region: only the ones that activated in synergy, have a chance to provoke a systemic change. The design of the intervention in a region consists then in identifying these apparently invisible links between projects that prior ignored themselves and could gain in efficiency and visibility through networking and cross-fertilization.
>
> (Jégou 2010, 6)

References

Agger, A., and Poulsen, B. (2017) "Street-level bureaucrats coping with conflicts in area-based initiatives in Copenhagen and Malmö" *Scandinavian Political Studies*, DOI:10.1111/1467–9477.12093.

Bason, C. (2010) *Leading Public Sector Innovation* Bristol: Policy Press.

Bauler, T., and Pel, B. (2014) "The institutionalization of social innovation: between transformation and capture" (TRANSIT working paper 2) TRANSIT: EU SSH.2013.3.2–1 Grant agreement no. 613169.

Bauler, T., Pel, B., and Wallenborn, G. (2016). "Emergent transformation games: exploring social innovation agency and activation through the case of the Belgian electricity blackout threat" *Ecology and Society* 21(2), www.ecologyandsociety.org/vol. 21/iss2/art17.

Bekkers, V. J. J., Tummers, L., and Voorberg, W. H. (2013) *From Public Innovation to Social Innovation in the Public Sector: A Literature Review of Relevant Drivers and Barriers* Erasmus University: Rotterdam, http://lipse.org/userfiles/uploads/From public innovation to social innovation in the public sector.pdf.

BEPA (Bureau of European Policy Advisors) (2011) *Empowering People, Driving Change: Social Innovation in the European Union* European Commission: Brussels.

Bifulco, L. (2013) "Citizen participation, agency and voice" *European Journal of Social Theory* 16(2): 174–187.

Bonneau, M. (2015) *Gdańsk: Initial Steps towards Responsibility Sharing (Case Study)* URBACT Publishing, http://urbact.eu/sites/default/files/cs-03b_si-Gdańsk-f3.pdf.

Bonneau, M. (2017) "How can city administrations better cooperate with citizens? A case for in-house intermediaries", http://resilia-solutions.eu/2017/04/how-can-city-administrations-better-cooperate-with-citizens-a-case-for-in-house-intermediaries.

Borins, S. (2000) "Loose cannons and rule breakers, or enterprising leaders? Some evidence about innovative public managers" *Public Administration Review* 60(6): 498–507.

Boulanger, P.-M. (2015) "Les initiatives citoyennes de transition: significations et perspectives politiques", www.iddweb.eu/docs/Inittrans.pdf.

Carton, H., Stevens, R., and Servigne, P. (2013) "Faut-il sauver le concept de résilience?" (Institut Momentum Workshop, 20 Sept.), www.institutmomentum.org/wp-content/uploads/2013/12/Faut-il-sauver-le-concept-de-r%C3%A9silience.pdf.

Coenen, F. H. J. M. (ed.) (2008) *Public Participation and Better Environmental Decisions: The Promise and Limits of Participatory Processes for the Quality of Environmentally Related Decision-Making* Springer: Dordrecht.

De Vries, H. A., Bekkers, V. J. J. M., and Tummers, L. G. (2014) "Innovation in the public sector: a systematic review and future research agenda" (paper presented at Speyer: EGPA conference), www.lipse.org/userfiles/uploads/Innovation in the public sector – De Vries Bekkers Tummers.pdf.

Gerring, J. (2004) "What is a case study and what is it good for?" *American Political Science Review* 98(2) 341.

Grin, J. (2012) "The politics of transition governance in Dutch agriculture: conceptual understanding and implications for transition management" *International Journal of Sustainable Development* 15(1/2): 72–89.

Hendriks, C., and Grin, J. (2007) "Contextualizing reflexive governance: the politics of Dutch transitions to sustainability" *Journal of Environmental Policy and Planning* 9(3–4): 333–350.

Hurard, M. (2011) *La participation citoyenne au développement durable à l'échelle locale en Europe* (collection working paper) Think Tank Européen Pour la Solidarité: Brussels.

Jaeger-Erben, M., Rückert-John, J., and Schäfer, M. (2015) "Sustainable consumption through social innovation: a typology of innovations for sustainable consumption practices" *Journal of Cleaner Production* 108: 784–798.

Jégou, F. (2010) *Social Innovations and Regional Acupuncture towards Sustainability* Zhuang-shi: Beijing.

Jégou, F. (2015) *Amersfoort: Designing a Collaborative City Administration (Case Study)* URBACT Publishing, http://urbact.eu/sites/default/files/cs-03a_si-amersfoort-f4.pdf.

Jégou, F., and Bonneau, M. (2014) *Social Innovation in Cities: State of the Art* URBACT Publishing, http://urbact.eu/sites/default/files/urbact_state_of_the_art_socinn.pdf.

Jégou, F., and Bonneau, M. (2015) *Social Innovation in Cities: Special Edition* URBACT Publishing, http://urbact.eu/sites/default/files/03_socialinn-web.pdf.

Marsden, T. (2013) "From post-productionism to reflexive governance: contested transitions in securing more sustainable food futures" *Journal of Rural Studies* 29 123–134.

Martin, C. J., and Upham, P. (2016) "Grassroots social innovation and the mobilisation of values in collaborative consumption: a conceptual model" *Journal of Cleaner Production* 134: 204–213.

Meroni, A., (2007) *Creative Communities: People Inventing Sustainable Ways of Living* Edizioni POLI.design: Milan.

Moyson, S., Van de Walle, S., and Groeneveld, S. (2016). "What do public officials think about citizens? The role of public officials' trust and their perceptions of citizens' trustworthiness in interactive governance" in Edelenbos, J., and Van Meerkerk, I. (eds) *Critical Reflections on Interactive Governance* Edward Elgar: Cheltenham.

Punch, K. (2005) *Introduction to Social Research Quantitative and Qualitative Approaches* Sage: London.

Roorda, C., Wittmayer, J. M., Henneman, P., Van Steenbergen, F., Frantzeskaki, N., and Loorbach, D. (2014) *Transition Management in the Urban Context: Guidance Manual* DRIFT/Erasmus University: Rotterdam, https://drift.eur.nl/wp-content/uploads/2016/11/DRIFT-Transition_management_in_the_urban_context-guidance_manual.pdf.

Servigne, P. (2011) "Initiatives de transition une manière originale de penser la politique", www.barricade.be/sites/default/files/publications/pdf/pablo_-_maniere_originale_de_penser_la_politique.pdf.

Smith, A., Voß, J.-P., and Grin, J. (2010) "Innovation studies and sustainability transitions: the allure of the multi-level perspective and its challenges" *Research Policy* 39(4): 435–448.

Torfing, J., Peters, B. G., Pierre, J., and Sørensen, E. (2012) *Interactive Governance: Advancing the Paradigm* Oxford University Press: Oxford.

Van Dyck, B., and Van den Broeck, P. (2013) "Social innovation: a territorial process" in Moulaert, F., MacCallum, D., Mehmood, A., and Hamdouch, A. (eds) *International Handbook on Social Innovation* Edward Elgar: Cheltenham.

Voß, Jan-Peter and Bornemann, B. (2011) "The politics of reflexive governance: challenges for designing adaptive management and transition management" *Ecology and Society* 16(2): 9.

Voß, J.-P., and Kemp, R. (2006) "Sustainability and reflexive governance: introduction" in Voß, J.-P., Bauknecht, D., and Kemp, R. (eds) *Reflexive Governance for Sustainable Development* Edward Elgar: Cheltenham.

Wittmayer, J. M., and Loorbach, D. (2016) "Governing transitions in cities: fostering alternative ideas, practices, and social relations through transition management" in Loorbach, D., Wittmayer, J. M., Shiroyama, H., Fujino, J., and Mizuguchi, S. (eds) *Governance of Urban Sustainability Transitions. European and Asian Experiences* (Theory and Practice of Urban Sustainability Transitions Series) Springer Japan: Tokyo.

Yin, R. K. (2014) *Case Study Research* Sage: London.

6 Hitting a policy wall

The transformative potential and limitations of community pick-up point schemes

Keighley McFarland and Julia M. Wittmayer

1 Introduction

The modern food system has brought many benefits for consumers but has also created significant sustainability problems, ranging from environmental degradation and health problems from over- and under-consumption to food safety scares and imbalances of power and justice in the supply chain (Pretty *et al.* 2001; Wekerle 2004; Spaargaren *et al.* 2012a; Fuchs *et al.* 2016). These problems can be considered as 'persistent' or 'wicked' problems which are embedded in societal structures, are valued differently, and involve a multitude of actors (Grin *et al.* 2010; Schuitmaker 2012). Every attempt to solve these problems will transform them and carries different side effects. As such, scholars argue that to address these problems, transitions are needed: 'radical transformation[s] towards a sustainable society' (Grin *et al.* 2010, 1).

Increasingly, new initiatives aim to address these problems through a diversity of approaches. These include organic farming, the Slow Food movement, community supported agriculture (CSA), and a variety of other alternative food networks (AFNs) (Tregear 2011; Spaargaren *et al.* 2012b). They offer a consumer-based approach to solving food-system problems, and, in public debates, influencing food system outcomes is commonly framed as a matter of consumption choices (Klintman and Boström 2012). This chapter introduces a novel type of AFN: the community pick-up point scheme (CPPS). A CPPS allows consumers to order products directly from small-scale producers through an online platform. Subsequently, the purchase is picked-up directly from the producer at a community pick-up point at a set time and date. CPPSs share characteristics with other AFNs, such as food teams/solidarity purchasing groups, food co-ops, and CSAs. However, CPPSs distinguish themselves from all of these in that they do not involve volunteer labour, risk sharing, or long-term commitments for either consumers or producers.

This chapter considers CPPSs as a social innovation and empirically investigates their potential to address persistent problems of the current food system for increasing sustainability. Taking a 'transformative social innovation' perspective (Haxeltine *et al.* 2016), we investigate CPPSs as social innovations, as they change social relations involving new ways of doing, organizing, knowing, and framing. We focus on their transformative potential as they are a relatively new phenomena and have not yet had the time to achieve major transformative impact. Transformative potential is defined as 'when an object, idea, activity or initiative displays inherent and/or intended qualities to challenge, alter and/or replace dominant institutions in a specific social context' (Haxeltine *et al.* 2015, 28). Given this definition, our research question in this chapter is: What is the transformative potential of CPPS: that is, to what extent do CPPS display inherent and/or intended qualities to challenge, alter, and/or replace dominant institutions in a specific social context?

In the following, we first detail the methodology of our investigation. We then briefly outline the food system as the main social context in which CPPSs operate before we introduce a specific CPPS (the Food Assembly) in more detail. We then contrast dominant food-system institutions with innovative institutions of that CPPS and explore how the institutions which govern the CPPS contribute to or limit transformative potential. In the text, we focus on four dominant institutions to illustrate all four instances: a dominant institution being challenged, altered, and replaced, and one that remains. Finally, we conclude by highlighting two caveats related to CPPSs' transformative potential for food systems and policy.

2 Methodology

To answer the research question, we empirically explore the Food Assembly Berlin (FA) as a case study and embed it in literature on transitions in food. Using a case-study approach allows to generate an in-depth, nuanced, and contextualized understanding of a novel phenomenon (Flyvbjerg 2006). Food Assembly Berlin was chosen as an exemplary CPPS because: (a) it is part of the longest-standing CPPS, the French La Ruche Qui Dit Oui; (b) it had a relatively speaking longer time to develop; and (c) of practical considerations: existing relationships between researchers and actors within the initiative meant that a basis of trust existed, which allowed for quick establishment of a cooperative research relationship and access to information. The case study is based on seven semi-structured interviews and 14 hours of participant observation over two months in early 2015. Interviews were conducted with a variety of actors inside and outside FA (see Annex 2). Additionally, we reviewed primary and secondary literature with regard to the initiative – including internal documents as well as importantly their online presence through websites, Facebook and Twitter.

Based on this material and including relevant scientific and grey literature, we established an understanding of dominant institutions and the social context of the food system in which the CPPS operates. For this analytical framework, we build upon the definition of 'social innovation' as changes in social relations involving new ways of doing, organizing, framing, and knowing, to derive an understanding of 'dominant institutions' as dominant ways of doing, organizing, framing, and knowing. This operationalization builds on institutional theory, in which institutions are understood as formal and informal norms, rules, conventions, and values (Cajaiba-Santana 2014; cf. Haxeltine *et al.* 2015).

We then examined the ways in which the CPPS differs from these institutions (i.e. what is innovative about it) and identified activities through which it displays its transformative potential. This chapter focuses on the empirical identification of the transformative potential of the CPPS, which can be determined by analysing whether and to what extent its innovative institutions display qualities that challenge, alter and replace dominant institutions (cf. Haxeltine *et al.* 2015). We operationalize these concepts as follows:

- Challenging: questioning the legitimacy or existence of dominant institutions (i.e. ways of doing, framing).
- Altering: changing (parts of) dominant institutions.
- Replacing: taking the place of (a) dominant institution(s).

Arguably, conclusions drawn from research about FA can be applied to a large extent to CPPSs across Germany, and possibly across Europe, because of (a) their shared basic structure and (b) the shared context defined largely by national and EU policy (see Section 3 and Annex).

3 The food system

In order to understand the transformative potential of CPPSs, it is crucial to establish an understanding of their social context. We chose to focus on their relation to the food system (Pothukuchi and Kaufman 2000; Hinrichs 2003; Ericksen 2008). A food system is a 'chain of activities connecting food production, processing, distribution, consumption, and waste management, as well as all the associated regulatory institutions and activities' (Pothukuchi and Kaufman 2000, 113). Here the focus is on the food system in Germany, which is embedded in European and global food systems.

There are numerous dominant institutions that characterize the German food system, including trends such as upscaling and industrializing or specializing of activities but also a for-profit mentality – see Annex 1 for an overview. In the following, we detail four specific ones, which are closely related to the transformative potential of CPPSs: retail sector market dominance, externalization of environmental impact, internationalization and standardization, and lack of clarity about responsibilities for food issues.

3.1 Retail sector market dominance

The processing and retail sector wields the most power in organization and orchestration of food value chains, agricultural producers have very little power, and consumers hold some power (Brunori *et al.* 2012; Spaargaren *et al.* 2012b; Fuchs *et al.* 2016). In Germany, discounters and supermarkets are the dominant market force and source of food purchases (USDA Foreign Agricultural Service 2012).

3.2 Externalization of environmental impact

Manifold negative environmental impacts are the result of modern food systems. These include significant greenhouse gas emissions, soil and water resource degradation, emissions of toxic substances and antibiotic-resistant microbes, air pollution, and habitat degradation (Pretty *et al.* 2001). Despite their significant impact, these externalities persist because environmental costs and benefits are not integrated into market costs and benefits (UN FAO 2006; Seyfang 2008; Teufel *et al.* 2014). The current policy framework does not internalize external environmental costs of food production and consumption.

3.3 Internationalization and standardization

The expansion of global markets has increased the volume of international agricultural trade, supported by policy frameworks (Spaargaren *et al.* 2012a). Though consumers in Germany express interest in buying local products (USDA Foreign Agricultural Service 2012), there is a gap between consumer attitudes towards local food and consumption behaviour (Feldmann and Hamm 2015), and local value chains represent a niche market (Born and Purcell 2006; Rossi and Brunori 2010; Tregear 2011; Diamond and Barham 2012; Van Gameren *et al.* 2014).

3.4 Lack of clarity about which actors are responsible for food-system issues

Food-related concerns are seen primarily as a matter of individual choice falling under the realm of the private market (Lockie 2009; Klintman and Boström 2012). Planning officials tend not to see food choices as something that public policy and planning should or can influence (Pothukuchi and Kaufman 2000). Rarely are initiatives undertaken by public actors to spur sustainable food consumption (Lorek *et al.* 2008). Yet consumers' ability to enact change in the food system is limited to their ability to choose between existing consumption options: consumers' desire for change (e.g. new products or supply chains) can only be exercised if an upstream actor brings an appropriate option to market (Lockie 2009).

4 CPPS: the Food Assembly

The CPPS investigated here is the German organization Food Assembly, the first CPPS in Germany. It is the daughter company of La Ruche Qui Dit Qui, the longest standing CPPS founded in France in 2011. Food Assembly was founded in Berlin in 2013 and by December 2016 counted 20 FA pick-up points in Berlin and 49 in Germany (Food Assembly n.d.).

The FA's main goal is to create an efficient and fair local food distribution service. A 'Values and Goals' document (Food Assembly 2015) was developed with the participation of producers, community coordinators, staff, and consumers that sets down guidelines for the initiative. Products are required to be sourced and processed within 150 km of a pick-up point, with some exceptions (e.g. directly traded products from further away which are not available in the region, such as olive oil, can be sold once a month). Food Assembly states that its producers produce 'artisanally, seasonally, and sustainably, thereby respecting people, animals, and the environment' (trans. from German), yet does not set out specific sustainability criteria.

Food Assembly functions as follows: as a first step, the initiative's central office advertises the general opportunity for setting up a pick-up point. An individual approaches the initiative's central office and expresses desire to set up a pick-up point as a community coordinator. New pick-up points are established when a community coordinator is able to prove to staff at the central office that they have the ability to successfully organize one, including organizing the location and enough customers. An example of a pick-up point in Berlin is given in Figure 6.1.

Once established, orders are placed individually by customers to a pick-up point without minimum order or subscription requirements via an online platform and are picked up weekly at a designated location and time. Producers receive the orders a few days before the pick-up and bring the products directly to the pick-up point. Orders are picked up from each customer by the individual

Figure 6.1 Food Assembly community pick-up point in Berlin.
Source: Marktschwärmer Deutschland.

producer. Pick-up point coordinators are encouraged to cover a variety of producers, including fresh vegetables and fruit, bread, dairy products, and meat. Usually they also include artisanally processed products such as jams, juices, and oils. The types of locations where pick-up points are hosted include cafes, cultural centres, and co-working spaces. Producers receive the lion's share of the revenue. About 8 per cent each goes to the community coordinator and the central office. Payment occurs with the placement of the order, so no money is exchanged at the pick-up point.

5 Does Food Assembly exhibit transformative potential?

In this section, we discuss how FA displays inherent or intended qualities to challenge, alter, replace, or leave unchanged each of the four above outlined dominant institutions of the food system.

5.1 Challenging the market dominance of the retail sector

Food Assembly empowers producers and consumers. In FA, producers have significantly more power than in traditional supply chains. They have more freedom in setting their prices, choosing their product palate, and deciding which pick-up points to join and whether the weekly orders are sufficient to make delivery worthwhile. The CPPS gives consumers who are dissatisfied with conventional retailers the ability to use their spending power to support an alternative type of product, producer, and value chain. Returning power to producers and consumers is a central stated goal of FA and is framed as an issue of fairness or justice (Food Assembly 2015).

The existence and legitimacy of market dominance by retailers is called into question through the innovative reorganization of relationships and power in the supply chain (a way of organizing). Efforts to shift the balance of power in the supply chain are framed as a political action in FA documents and in respondents' comments. For example, one staff member described FA as a 'tool to give back power to the people who create value' (Interviewee 1, 2015) and a community coordinator claimed that through FA, consumers 'get back some of the ability to choose. They can say … "I am freeing myself from supermarket structures and am doing my own thing"' (Interviewee 5, 2015: trans. from German). This way of organizing is predicated on the idea that conventional systems are, in contrast to CPPS, not fair and action is required to remedy the injustice.

5.2 Altering the externalization of environmental impact

Food Assembly accounts indirectly for environmental impact. Products are required to adhere to a loose set of sustainability criteria. Many producers produce with lower environmental impact or support ecosystem services more holistically than conventional farming. These methods include certified organic and integrated farming, combining farming with nature conservation, and focusing on rare plant varieties and livestock breeds. This type of production incurs costs that are not sufficiently offset by mainstream farming subsidies, which are oriented towards global markets and commodity production. Although there is no mechanism that explicitly internalizes negative externalities of production and consumption (e.g. offsetting), some of the higher direct production costs are passed on to the consumer in higher prices.

This way of establishing prices and distributing costs alters the externalization of environmental impact by enabling value creation based on environmental qualities of a product. However, producers still set their prices primarily based on market prices and direct production costs, rather than fully taking environmental costs into account. The decisions of customers as well are driven by the actual price next to environmental values. The price structure is not radically different enough to truly reflect external costs and benefits of the value chain. Food Assembly innovates a partial solution to the problem of environmental externalities of food production, but does not replace the framework conditions set by markets, policy, and the social context.

5.3 Replacing internationalization and standardization

Food Assembly features short and direct local value chains. In FA, producers bring products directly to consumers. Only local or directly traded products can be sold through FA, both by rule (i.e. geographical boundaries limiting the intake region for products) and by the higher costs of more complicated logistics associated with small orders and intensive communication. The latter deters producers who cannot offer products with valuable intangible qualities. This is both a mechanism to ensure producers adhere to standards, and also may pose limits to growth of the model as the amount of producers willing to produce in this way is relatively small when compared to those who produce for conventional supply chains. The added benefits of selling through FA is not enough to convince most producers to incur the costs associated with changing production, sales, and logistics systems. Such a switch is also not supported by the current agricultural subsidy regime, as adequate financial support is not available.

The initiative creates an innovative infrastructure for viable supply chains for products, which would have difficulty being successful in conventional supply chains. The CPPS purchases replaced rather than augmented the food purchases through conventional outlets of most respondents, or for producers they replaced the need to sell at least a portion of their products through other outlets. The CPPS did not completely replace all use of conventional value chains: consumers who buy through FA usually do not obtain all of their food purchases through the CPPS, and most producers involved in Berlin also have other outlets for their products. The initiative therefore displays qualities, which replace (parts of) dominant institutions (though replacement has not occurred on a large scale).

5.4 *Remaining lack of clarity about responsibilities for food system issues*

Evidence in the interviews, participant observation, and document review indicated that changing the food system was a goal of FA. However, respondents had difficulty connecting specific, concrete activities of the CPPS to systemic changes. No clear vision seemed to exist of the responsibility or power of the initiative to affect change beyond the individual consumer level. Several respondents mentioned that policy was a central determinant of how the food-system works and also a major constraint to their ability to achieve change. Yet the focus of the initiative remains running a business and not exerting political influence. Due to the small size and niche reach of the initiative, respondents did not feel empowered as individuals or as a collective to affect policy-level change.

A sense of empowerment or responsibility to achieve systemic change is missing from FA. The CPPS offers consumers an alternative choice which takes steps to address some problems created by dominant food system institutions. However, the initiative leaves the basic market structure of supply chains intact, while simply reorganizing the relationships within it to create fairer and more sustainable outcomes. Food Assembly does not seek to affect change through channels other than through consumption behaviour. Thereby, political, social, or other solutions to food-system problems are left untouched rather than seeking to expand into such activities. The political and social framework is a key determining factor of the food system: solely consumption-based solutions do not reframe the established responsibilities of individuals and organizations for food system change, but act within them. This issue remains unsolved by Food Assembly.

6 Conclusion

The case of the Food Assembly, exemplary for other CPPSs, shows indications of challenging, altering, or replacing dominant institutions of the German food system. It creates viable local supply chains for sustainable, high-quality products, which the dominant institutions of conventional supply chains systemically disadvantage. The CPPS changes relationships and (infra)structures within the food system and enables changes in ways of doing, knowing, framing, and organizing.

While taking account of an important limitation of our study, namely its reliance on a single case, we argue that it nevertheless provides valuable insights into the potential of such initiatives for transforming the dominant food system. Specifically, two caveats stand out in the discussion. The first is that the transformative potential of FA and CPPSs more generally is predicated on the assumption that political consumerism can bring about societal change. Political consumerism is the notion that consumers use their purchasing behaviour to support types of products, systems, or behaviours in a targeted manner, with the goal of affecting change (Lockie 2009; Klintman and Boström 2012) – often phrased in lay terms as 'voting with your wallet'. However, the Janus face of this approach is that it allows state actors and upstream actors in the value chain to shift responsibility for instigating sustainable change onto consumers when framing the debate about food system problems (DuPuis and Goodman 2005; Spaargaren et al. 2012a). Behaviourist criticisms of neo-liberal economic theory and approaches point out that the reliance on the consumer to follow a socially optimal consumption pattern is unrealistic in practice, as limitations such as bounded rationality, incomplete or overwhelming information, and biases play a major role in economic behaviour (Pike 2008; Van Bavel et al. 2013). Food Assembly specifically and, in line with it, CPPSs do not challenge, alter, or replace those dominant institutions which perpetuate the reliance on political consumerism but instead offer a novel channel through which to follow (and possibly strengthen) this approach.

Food-related policies – especially agriculture policy, but also trade, health, food safety, city and regional planning, and innovation policies – set the framework conditions for activities in the food system, thus also for innovative initiatives like CPPSs in general. The policy framework is designed to support large-scale, export-oriented commodity agriculture. Consequently the type of producers and products that CPPSs target are structurally disadvantaged by the policy framework. Since the CPPS approach focuses on creating markets and does not actively target policy changes, dominant policy-related institutions remain unchallenged and unchanged. This single non-political strategy significantly limits CPPSs' transformative potential. Changes in the markets that drive the development of food systems are closely linked to changes in the policy framework. This suggests two things: first that there is a certain hierarchy in types of dominant institutions, some of which are more necessary to challenge, alter, or replace in order to achieve transformative change. Second, that any one initiative will not be targeting all of these, but that a variety of initiatives is necessary to put pressure on different aspects of the dominant system.

Thus, CPPSs can only be part of the solution, but they are not a panacea. Consumption is only part of the problem, so it is unrealistic to assume that consuming better can be the entire solution. Further research is needed to identify the transformative potential of other initiatives to complement the strengths and weaknesses of Food Assembly. The methodology used in our case study can be a useful tool in such investigations.

When policy plays such a major role in shaping the food system, transformative change cannot occur without a policy transformation. If policy can be redesigned to better support environmentally, socially, and economically sustainable food chains, such as those that CPPSs strive to establish, CPPSs and other innovative initiatives will be able to translate transformative potential into transformative impact and help solve persistent systemic problems.

Annex 1

Table 6.1 List of markers for dominant and innovative institutions

Ways of	Dominant institutions	Institutions of CPPSs (*innovative institutions appear in normal script, instances of non-innovation appear in italics*)
Doing	**Spatio-temporal disconnect from natural systems**: limitations of time and space have been largely eliminated. Variety and choice for consumers are high, especially for processed foods, and major distances are involved in globalized food value chains (Spaargaren *et al.* 2012a, 2).	**Reconnection of food consumption cycles to production cycles and natural systems**: since products in CPPSs cannot be imported (with a few exceptions), the availability and quality of products is dependent on the local natural systems and production cycles. Producers mostly produce under or in ways near to organic production, so there is no use of, e.g. greenhouses, allowing year-round production of vegetables. Instead, the product offering is limited to seasonal food products.
	Lack of action despite increasing public interest in non-nutritional qualities: non-nutritional qualities like environmental and climate impact, animal welfare, and taste have gained importance in the public. Yet major changes in food practices have not resulted (Marsden and Sonnino 2012; Mount 2012, 111; Spaargaren *et al.* 2012a). For example, despite environmental impact of food and agriculture being a frequent topic in public and policy discourses, only about 6% of agricultural area in the EU is used for organic production and in Germany and the Netherlands organic food makes up only 3.7% and 2.4% of total food retail sales respectively.[1]	**Creating value for non-nutritional and intangible qualities**: the storytelling, direct exchange, and highly visual communication style of CPPSs give producers and consumers the opportunity to communicate and understand product qualities which go beyond quantity and nutritional information. This enables consumers and producers who are interested in these qualities to act effectively on their interest, by changing production and consumption habits.
	Trend towards upscaling and industrializing, specializing, or exiting: producers, processors, and retailers are under constant pressure to scale up, specialize, or exit the market; for farmers this means unstable incomes and in many cases reliance on off-farm income (Jarosz 2008; Diamond and Barham 2012; Mount 2012).	**High variability of products**: CPPSs enable consumer acceptance of high product variability. The reconnection to natural systems built into the model imply a high variability of the type and qualities of products, and the communication style makes it possible to build trust and understanding in consumers so that they accept (or even learn to value) this variability. CPPSs also cater to cultural subgroups which value uniqueness and/or exclusivity, as consumption patterns function as a cultural identifier.
Knowing	**Difficulty identifying consumers' preferences**: producers, retailers, and policy-makers have difficulty finding and connecting with an array of diffuse actors, identifying consumer desires, and integrating often contradictory sets of food-related concerns into their decision-making. This presents a major hurdle to addressing food system challenges (Pothukuchi and Kaufman 2000; Lockie 2009).	**Direct exchange and social learning**: social learning, especially through face-to-face exchange, is an essential component of CPPSs. These direct exchanges allow CPPS neighbourhood coordinators, staff, producers, and consumers to learn about product qualities, histories, recipes, etc.), the natural systems which dictate production, and how the CPPS functions or could be improved.
	Elaborate but ineffective food safety regulation: elaborate regulatory regimes for food safety exist, yet risks and scares stemming from the intensified nature of food production persist (Spaargaren *et al.* 2012b, 2).	**New methods of transparency for consumer trust**: transparency in CPPS is established through direct and often personal contact. Storytelling and visual communication with pictures plays an important role. Rather than relying on complex technical systems, transparency is based on short and direct supply chains.

continued

Table 6.1 Continued

Ways of	Dominant institutions	Institutions of CPPSs (innovative institutions appear in normal script, instances of non-innovation appear in italics)
		Reliance on traditional food knowledge: large-scale industrial processing is not accepted in CPPSs. Traditional processing and preserving methods are used to extend the usable life of products and prevent losses at times of harvest abundance. This includes traditional but little known types of sausage, fermented products such as sauerkraut, and jams and syrups.
Framing	**Quantity-focused agriculture policy**: global food and agriculture policies focus primarily on the production of quantity. Issues such as access, nutrition, or health concerns are rarely reflected in policy (Marsden and Sonnino 2012).	**Agriculture policy in conflict with CPPSs' goals**: agriculture policy is perceived to focus on goals which are in conflict with the vision of CPPSs. Because their goals are incongruous with policies, policy limits the development of CPPSs. Respondents felt that policies to support the type of production which they desired were missing.
	Overconsumption as central health problem: concerns over health problems related to under-consumption (e.g. hunger) have been largely replaced by concerns over health problems related to over-consumption (e.g. obesity) (Spaargaren *et al.* 2012a, 2).	**Food safety, synthetic ingredients, and non-transparent supply chains as central health problems**: respondents from FA expressed concern about product contamination and the health risks of synthetic products from conventional supply chains. The radical transparency of FA, based on personal interaction, visual information, and emotional appeals, offers consumers and producers an alternative to conventional food safety systems. Other health issues, such as over- or under-consumption, did not seem to play a major role, and health issues in general seemed to be less important than economic fairness and sustainability.
	Food used as a cultural indicator: the cultural dimension of food has gained social importance, with groups using food practices in different ways to articulate status and taste (Lockie 2009; Rossi and Brunori 2010; Kjaernes and Torjusen 2012; Spaargaren *et al.* 2012b).	*Eschewing of elite image, but no concrete action to counteract it*: *several respondents expressed worries that the initiative could develop into an elite or exclusive phenomenon. No concrete action was taken, however, to counteract this development (e.g. most pick-up points were located in well-off areas or in spaces frequented by a well-educated audience, such as co-working spaces). In this way, no specific effort was made by the initiative to try to work against the use of food consumption choices as a cultural indicator.*
	The 'alternative paradox': socially innovative initiatives such as AFNs develop a variety of innovations to solve food system problems. However, by understanding themselves as 'alternative' food networks, they inherently distinguish themselves from mainstream actors and qualities. As innovative institutions begin to challenge, alter, or replace dominant institutions and become themselves mainstream, they necessarily lose some of their 'alternativeness'. This 'alternative paradox' implies an inescapable exclusivity among innovative institutions (Hinrichs 2000; Smith 2007; Tregear 2011; Kato 2013; Anguelovski 2014).	*The 'alternative paradox'*: *the initiative has yet to demonstrate the ability to reach beyond a niche market. The relatively high prices of many products and time investment required of consumers in adjusting to and using the pick-up system may keep CPPSs exclusive to consumers with available resources to invest. Several respondents expressed the belief that a systemic, political solution was required to change the framework conditions in agriculture and urban food systems in order for CPPSs to grow beyond a niche.*

Note
1 www.fibl.org/fileadmin/documents/shop/1663-organic-world-2015.pdf.

Annex 2

Table 6.2 List of interviewees

Interviewee number	Function/organization	Date
1	Assembly host, Berlin Mitte ACUD, Food Assembly	05.02.2015
2	International coordinator, Food Assembly	11.02.2015
3	Host coordinator, Food Assembly Germany	17.02.2015
4	Managing director, Food Assembly Germany	17.02.2015
5	Assembly host, Berlin Wedding Himmelbeet, Food Assembly	17.02.2015
6	Producer (organic vegetables) for Food Assembly, Luchgärtnerei	18.02.2015
7	Fördergemeinschaft ökologische Landwirtschaft (FA partner organisation)	25.02.2015

Acknowledgements

This chapter is partly based on research carried out as part of the Transformative Social Innovation Theory (TRANSIT) project which is funded by the European Union's Seventh Framework Programme (FP7) under grant agreement 613169. The views expressed in this chapter are the sole responsibility of the authors and do not necessarily reflect the views of the European Union.

References

Anguelovski, I. (2014) 'Alternative food provision conflicts in cities: contesting food privilege, injustice, and whiteness in Jamaica Plain, Boston' *Geoforum* 58: 184–194.

Born, B., and Purcell, M. (2006) 'Avoiding the local trap: scale and food systems in Planning Research' *Journal of Planning Education and Research* 26(2): 195–207.

Brunori, G., Rossi, A., and Guidi, F. (2012) 'On the new social relations around and beyond food: analysing consumers' role and action in gruppi di acquisto solidale (solidarity purchasing groups)' *Sociologia Ruralis* 52(1): 1–30.

Cajaiba-Santana, G. (2014) 'Social innovation: moving the field forward: a conceptual framework' *Technological Forecasting and Social Change* 82: 42–51.

Diamond, A., and Barham, J. (2012) *Moving Food along the Value Chain: Innovations in Regional Food Distribution* USDA, Agricultural Marketing Service.

DuPuis, E. M., and Goodman, D. (2005) 'Should we go "home" to eat? Toward a reflexive politics of localism' *Journal of Rural Studies* 21(3): 359–371.

Ericksen, P. J. (2008) 'Conceptualizing food systems for global environmental change research' *Global Environmental Change* 18(1): 234–245.

Feldmann, C., and Hamm, U. (2015) 'Consumers' perceptions and preferences for local food: a review' *Food Quality and Preference* 40: 152–164.

Flyvbjerg, B. (2006) 'Five misunderstandings about case-study research' *Qualitative Inquiry* 12: 219–245.

Food Assembly (n.d.) https://foodassembly.de/de (accessed 20 December 2016).

Food Assembly (2015) 'Werte und Ziele' (internal document).

Fuchs, D., Di Giulio, A., Glaab, K., Lorek, S., Maniates, M., Princen, T., and Ropke, I. (2016) 'Power: what's missing in consumption and absolute reductions research and action' *Journal of Cleaner Production* 132: 298–307.

Grin, J., Rotmans, J., and Schot, J. (2010) *Transitions to Sustainable Development: New Directions in the Study of Long Term Transformative Change* Routledge.

Haxeltine, A., Kemp, R., Dumitru, A., Avelino, F., Pel, B., and Wittmayer, J. M. (2015) 'A first prototype of TSI theory' (TRANSIT deliverable 3.2) TRANSIT: EU SSH.2013.3.2-1 Grant agreement no. 613169.

Haxeltine, A., Avelino, F., Pel, B., Dumitru, A., Kemp, R., Longhurst, N., Chilvers, J., and Wittmayer, J. M. (2016) 'A framework for transformative social innovation' (TRANSIT working paper 5) TRANSIT: EU SSH.2013.3.2–1 Grant agreement no. 61316.

Hinrichs, C. C. (2000) 'Embeddedness and local food systems: notes on two types of direct agricultural market' *Journal of Rural Studies* 16(3): 295–303.

Hinrichs, C. C. (2003) 'The practice and politics of food system localization' *Journal of Rural Studies* 19(1): 33–45.

Jarosz, L. (2008) 'The city in the country: growing alternative food networks in Metropolitan areas' *Journal of Rural Studies* 24(3): 231–244.

Kato, Y. (2013) 'Not just the price of food: challenges of an urban agriculture organization in engaging local residents' *Sociological Inquiry* 83(3): 369–391.

Kjaernes, U., and Torjusen, H. (2012) 'Beyond the industrial paradigm? Consumers and trust in food' in Spaargaren, G., Oosterveer, P., and Loeber, A. (eds) *Food Practices in Transition: Changing Food Consumption, Retail and Production in the Age of Reflexive Modernity* Routledge.

Klintman, M., and Boström, M. (2012) 'Political consumerism and the transition towards a more sustainable food regime: looking behind and beyond the organic Shelf' in Spaargaren, G., Oosterveer, P., and Loeber, A. (eds) *Food Practices in Transition: Changing Food Consumption, Retail and Production in the Age of Reflexive Modernity* Routledge.

Lockie, S. (2009) 'Responsibility and agency within alternative food networks: assembling the "citizen consumer"' *Agriculture and Human Values* 26(3): 193–201.

Lorek, S., Giljum, S., and Bruckner, M. (2008) *Inventory and Assessment of Policy Instruments: Sustainable Consumption Policies Effectiveness Evaluation (SCOPE2)* SERI.

Marsden, T., and Sonnino, R. (2012) 'Human health and wellbeing and the sustainability of urban–regional food systems' *Current Opinion in Environmental Sustainability* 4(4): 427–430.

Moulaert, F., MacCallum, D., Mehmood, A., and Hamdouch, A. (eds) (2013) *The International Handbook on Social Innovation* Edward Elgar.

Mount, P. (2012) 'Growing local food: scale and local food systems governance' *Agriculture and Human Values* 29(1): 107–121.

Pike, T. (2008) *Understanding Behaviours in a Farming Context: Bringing Theoretical and Applied Evidence together from across Defra and Highlighting Policy Relevance and Implications for Future Research* DEFRA.

Pothukuchi, K., and Kaufman, J. L. (2000) 'The food system: a stranger to the planning field' *Journal of the American Planning Association* 66(2): 113–124.

Pretty, J., Brett, C., Gee, D., Hine, R., Mason, C., Morison, J., Rayment, M., Van Der Bijl, G., and Dobbs, T. (2001) 'Policy challenges and priorities for internalizing the externalities of modern agriculture' *Journal of Environmental Planning and Management* 44(2): 263–283.

Rossi, A. and Brunori, G. (2010) 'Drivers of transformation in the agro-food system: GAS as co-production of alternative food networks' *Proceedings of 9th European IFSA Symposium (July 2010), Vienna, Austria* IFSA.

Schuitmaker, T. J. (2012) 'Identifying and unravelling persistent problems' *Technological Forecasting and Social Change* 79(6): 1021–1031.

Seyfang, G. (2008) *The New Economics of Sustainable Consumption* Palgrave Macmillan.

Smith, A. (2007) 'Translating sustainabilities between green niches and socio-technical regimes' *Technology Analysis and Strategic Management* 19(4): 427–450.

Spaargaren, G., Oosterveer, P., and Loeber, A. (eds) (2012a) *Food Practices in Transition: Changing Food Consumption, Retail and Prouction in the Age of Reflexive Modernity* Routledge.

Spaargaren, G., Oosterveer, P., and Loeber, A. (2012b) 'Sustainability transitions in food consumption, retail and production' in Spaargaren, G., Oosterveer, P., and Loeber, A. (eds) *Food Practices in Transition: Changing Food Consumption, Retail and Production in the Age of Reflexive Modernity* Routledge.

Teufel, D. J., Baron, Y., Droste, A., Fibich, K., Gattermann, M., Grießhammer, P. D. R., Rietdorf, C., Schoßig, M., and Wackerhagen, C. (2014) *Ist gutes Essen wirklich teuer?* Öko-Institut e.V.

Tregear, A. (2011) 'Progressing knowledge in alternative and local food networks: Critical reflections and a research agenda' *Journal of Rural Studies* 27(4): 419–430.

UN FAO (2006) *Livestock's Long Shadow: Environmental Issues and Options* FAO.

USDA Foreign Agricultural Service (2012) *The German Food Retail Market* USDA.

Van Bavel, R., Herrmann, B., Esposito, G., and Proestakis, A. (2013) *Applying Behavioural Sciences to EU Policy-Making* Publications Office of the European Union.

Van Gameren, V., Ruwet, C., and Bauler, T. (2014) 'Towards a governance of sustainable consumption transitions: how institutional factors influence emerging local food systems in Belgium' *Local Environment* 20(8): 1–18.

Wekerle, G. R. (2004) 'Food justice movements: policy, planning, and networks' *Journal of Planning Education and Research* 23(4): 378–386.

7 Community energy as a site for social innovation

Iain Soutar

1 Introduction

The energy system in the UK and beyond is undergoing processes of profound change, not only in terms of the available supply technologies but also in terms of the social structures that define aspects of ownership, operation and governance within the system. Hastened by the climate change mitigation imperative, the general trend is towards more sustainable forms of energy production; that is, ones less dependent on fossil fuel-based technologies and thus less impactful in terms of GHG emissions and other pollutants (Mitchell 2016).

This deepening penetration of renewable energy technologies (RETs) is both necessitating and being supported by shifts in societal perceptions around and activities in energy systems (ibid.). This is demonstrable in cultural trends around increasing acceptance of novel energy technologies (Parkhill *et al.* 2013), institutional shifts such as in the development of novel energy supply business models (Hall and Roelich 2016), and changes to the economics of energy, such as the opening up of electricity generation and supply activities to an increasingly broad range of actors (Dahlmann *et al.* 2016; Ofgem 2016).

Although ostensibly driven by the climate change imperative, the shifts create new prospects for addressing key policy objectives such as energy security and affordability (Mitchell *et al.* 2013; Foxon and Pearson 2013). While the processes and outcomes of such shifts do not automatically imply progress towards wider social objectives (such as health and wellbeing, equity, justice and legitimacy) (Miller *et al.* 2013, 2015b), they do create opportunities for critical engagement with these issues within multiple arenas (Miller *et al.* 2015a; Goldthau and Sovacool 2012; Stirling 2014b).

In seeking to understand energy systems and processes of change therein however, the emphasis within both academic and political arenas has traditionally been on the development, deployment and integration of supply-side technologies, while the role of individual and collective behaviours has been underplayed (Sovacool 2014; Parkhill *et al.* 2013). Refocusing attention on the latter, i.e. towards social innovation, rather than just technological innovation, thus represents a key challenge for both research and policy practitioners (Burns and Watson 2016).

To help address this gap, this chapter draws on insights from 16 semi-structured interviews with stakeholders engaged in community energy (CE) practice throughout South West England, including practitioners but also representatives from the renewable energy (RE) industry, CE support organisations, and local and central government, undertaken throughout 2014–15. In addition, a household postal survey conducted with residents (n=321) of the town of Wadebridge, Cornwall, was carried out in June 2013 provided insights from local civil society stakeholders. Methods for both approaches are discussed in detail by Soutar (2016). The following questions are addressed: In what ways are forms of social innovation (SI) manifested within CE? How have different aspects of SI emerged within the CE movement? And to what degree can SI contribute both to sustainable consumption and to processes of transformation? In tackling these questions the chapter both draws on and enriches existing conceptualisation of SI as new ways of organising, knowing, framing and doing that challenge, alter and/or replace established institutions (Haxeltine *et al.* 2016).

The chapter is made up of three sections. The first considers how the CE movement has evolved as a site for the co-evolution of social with technological innovation within a range of local experiments. The next section focuses on the development of specific aspects of SI within CE, highlighting the development of novel forms of organisation within and beyond CE groups, and the development of shared values, knowings and framings of energy challenges and solutions. The final section then reflects on how CE within a broader ecosystem of energy system innovation can be considered transformative, in terms of challenging unsustainable modes of production and consumption in the energy system.

Under the broadest definition CE can be understood as a range of projects and initiatives led by, and for the benefit of, communities (of place or interest), and focusing on reducing energy use, managing energy better, generating energy and/or purchasing energy (DECC 2014). The range of initiatives and projects identifying with the notion of CE is thus considerable, encompassing a variety of actors, interests, motivations and activities (Seyfang *et al.* 2013; Coles *et al.* 2016) and thus varying both in terms of process (the degree to which communities participate) and outcome (the degree to which benefits accrue to communities) (Walker and Devine-Wright 2008). While not disregarding the role of CE as led by organisations other than communities themselves (which is discussed in the final section of this chapter), the primary concern of this chapter is with community-led, place-based initiatives, which in 2013 comprised the largest proportion of CE initiatives in the UK.

2 Synergies of innovation within community energy initiatives

In the UK, where the planning, ownership, operation and trading of energy has predominantly occurred within large-scale, centralised governance structures, place-based, community-led energy projects represent a novel set of approaches whereby energy options are discussed, invested in, managed and/or purchased within the context of local communities, and the places within which they reside.

While all CE projects by definition have an energy focus, practitioners identify with a plurality of economic, environmental, social, political and infrastructural objectives (Seyfang *et al.* 2013). These relate directly and indirectly to energy in terms of both expected outcomes (e.g. saving money on energy bills, reducing CO_2 emissions and increasing energy independence) as well as the processes undertaken along the way (e.g. skills development, enhancement of social cohesion and community empowerment). In addition, CE often takes place within the context of community-based sustainability movements, so may occur alongside experimentation with sustainable food or travel initiatives (such as within the Transition Network). As such, while CE contributes directly to energy policy objectives, it also seeks to identify and realise a wide range of sustainable production and consumption co-benefits beyond traditional energy policy objectives: that is, those relating to decarbonisation, energy security and affordability.

The centrality of technologies to the consumption and production of energy means that CE initiatives more often than not have strong technological dimensions, that is, they seek to materially change local energy flows, for example, through the deployment of small- and medium-scale technologies for electricity generation and heat production, as well as technologies for energy storage, energy efficiency, demand optimisation and low-carbon transport. In addition to exerting agency in terms of creating demand for such novel technologies, CE practitioners play a wide variety of functional roles understood to be important across multiple Technological Innovation Systems (as conceptualised in Hekkert *et al.* 2007), for example, experimenting with emerging RETs, contributing to knowledge exchange within communities around technological options, mobilising resources such as finance and land and counteracting the resistance of incumbents to the introduction of novel and potentially disruptive technologies.

In the same way that CE comprises technological innovation processes, CE groups also interact with a wider ecosystem of social innovations. For example, the CE sector has developed in parallel with the growth of the RET sector more generally, with government support for RET deployment (primarily the small-scale feed-in tariff) providing opportunities for revenue generation. Nor is an understanding of CE complete without reflecting on the ongoing evolution of information and communication technology (ICT) and its role as an enabling technology for CE and future energy systems more generally (Hilty *et al.* 2011). These include, but are not limited to social media as platforms for CE groups to engage with each other and with immediate and wider communities to shape local discussions and raise awareness about projects; and crowdfunding platforms, which offer CE hitherto difficult to access capital, while also satisfying nascent demand for RE investment opportunities.

In summary, CE both depends on, and contributes to, a wide range of processes within a diversity of social and technological innovation processes. Moreover, the relationship between social and technological is often symbiotic:

accessing the many benefits RETs have to offer is cited as a key driver of nascent CE projects, and the growth in the UK's CE movement can be correlated with increasing penetration of RE technologies more generally (Soutar 2016). Conversely, reductions in policy support for RETs has had the effect of reducing interest and activity within CE (Nolden 2013).

While social innovation within CE can be part and parcel of energy innovation as a whole, this chapter goes further to contend that it is the development of social innovation within CE – albeit alongside technological innovation – that has created the conditions for profound change within the energy system. Specifically, the CE movement in the UK can be understood in terms of the development of new social networks, whose understandings, practices and agency within the energy system represent a marked departure from established norms. As such, CE is representative of multiple aspects of SI: that is, of novel modes of organising, framing, knowing and doing, as proposed by Haxeltine and colleagues (2016).

This, for example, is evident in the adoption of formal constitutions for example within cooperative societies and community benefit companies, which combine democratic principles of control alongside directionality in terms of benefit-sharing and which represent a move towards more citizen-oriented representation of the like seen within Denmark and Germany (Nolden 2013). These (and other) organisational forms provide structured, legitimised spaces for framing key issues and imagining solutions, developing knowledges and competencies through which solution-focused practices can be planned, undertaken and appraised. The following section explores those aspects in more detail.

3 The formation of community energy institutions

3.1 Social organisation within community energy initiatives

A defining feature of CE is the materialisation of organised networks of individuals around energy issues, through which relationships can be formed, problem framings and visions agreed upon, and resources and responsibilities shared, such that practices can be carried out within the boundaries of established institutional norms. Examining CE in terms of the development of networks of trust, cooperation and contestation lends insights into the role of SIs as linkages between individuals and the wider social systems within which they operate. In particular the literature on social capital, broadly conceptualised as the resources within social networks, including norms, trust and reciprocity that help individuals to organise to meet agreed objectives (Putnam, 2000; Kay, 2003), can be instructive in helping to make associations between individuals and the networks formed within, between and beyond social innovation initiatives.

The composition within the community-led CE groups observed were typical of groups in general (Seyfang *et al.* 2013), with a small number of enthusiastic and committed individuals at the core, supported by a small group of active members and a larger membership of less-engaged supporters from the wider community. While expanding membership is important in terms of building legitimacy, having a strong core of active members is central, not least in terms of shaping initial visions and associated agendas. The development and strengthening of close-knit ties between individuals – termed 'bonding capital' within the social capital literature (Gittell and Vidal 1998) – thus provides the foundation upon which SI in CE can grow.

Bonding capital is thought to be most consequential where SI practitioners are working in close proximity to one another, as is the case in most CE initiatives, which are place-based. Having frequent, shared experiences a common sense of place help foster norms in mutuality, solidarity and reciprocity in resource-sharing in ways that can be difficult when interacting from afar (Coenen *et al.* 2010). Moreover, these processes are self-reinforcing; that is, simply working together in close proximity towards a common goal serves to bind the core group further and helps participants experience the benefits of social capital first hand (Putnam 2000).

Bonding social capital is in large part developed through the sharing of cognitive and non-cognitive resources and of the trust and reciprocity implicit in doing so (Putnam 2000; Aldridge *et al.* 2002). For CE (and indeed many SIs), the voluntary nature of the sector means that reciprocal arrangements between members are central to the ability to access key resources such as time, expertise and capital and, in turn, reinforce social relations, not least by requiring members to 'pull their weight' to remain involved.

3.2 Coherence of values

Whether newly created or formed out of existing social networks, the establishment of shared norms around both values and objectives appears to be a central feature to the success of CE groups. Shared values in particular have been found to be an integral part of social capital and the organisational manifestations thereof; they not only form the foundation of trust, facilitating mutual working, but also provide the core around which institutional norms and identity can become established (Evans 2003). For the CE groups surveyed here, such shared values revolved around notions of democratic participation in the pursuit of energy objectives. Such principles, which are often underpinned by cooperative models of organisation, are frequently framed as a counterpoint to undemocratic institutional norms within a centralised energy system.

While CE has been shown to be constituted by a range of drivers and motivations (Seyfang *et al.* 2013), the uniting framing that defines the movement as a whole is dissatisfaction with the current energy system in delivering adequately on a range of objectives. While the perceived failings of incumbent structures to address decarbonisation or affordability objectives features strongly within the CE movement, such failings are inextricably framed in the context of the availability of novel social and technological innovations and with them, new ways of satisfying those needs by alternative means, such as by owning and managing one's own energy supply. In this way, social and technological innovation can be seen as both highlighting deficiencies in existing systems while offering a range of options and associated value propositions with which they can be addressed.

3.3 Expanding social relations beyond initiatives

For CE, and indeed for other modes of SI who seek to change social relations and carry out practices, especially those seeking to benefit wider communities, cooperation inevitably goes hand in hand with contestation. While 'community energy' evokes connotations of participation and inclusion, this very much depends on the extent to which promised benefits can be realised, and the degree to which CE groups actually do so varies greatly (Walker and Devine-Wright 2008). As such, the success of CE schemes hinges not only on the outcomes of practices, but also importantly on the process taken in the pursuit of such outcomes (ibid.). Traditional structures of energy governance (energy supply companies in particular) traditionally suffer from low levels of trust by the public (Ofgem, OFT and CMA 2014; Butler *et al.* 2013). On the one hand, this can be seen as a stimulant for civil society to be alert to, and indeed actively search for, alternatives, such as CE; on the other, a heightened public awareness towards notions of value and fairness in energy services means that it is especially important that CE groups are scrupulous both throughout the process adopted and within the delivery of outcomes. In other words, the legitimacy of CE groups as modes of local energy governance is a resource that must be earned rather than a given.

Within those initiatives seeking to affect broader societal change, questions around whether, how and why wider communities can be engaged are inevitably raised. For CE, and especially where RE projects are concerned, garnering local support for projects can often be an instrumental factor determining the success or failure of a project, and, as such, community engagement of some form is often seen as a central theme across CE groups. For some CE groups, the existence of well-organised groups who seek community engagement to oppose RE projects make this an especially important priority. Beyond the necessity of garnering support for specific projects however, are expectations around how representative CE initiatives should be. Within CE groups, enabling and being able to demonstrate meaningful engagement, not just in the form of either support or lack of opposition, but through participation is a key principle (Walker and Devine-Wright 2008).

From the perspective of the wider communities in which local CE projects operate, CE initiatives carry, either explicitly or implicitly, promises and thus raise expectations around renewed opportunities for democratic change and representativeness in the securing of energy services. Furthermore, the centrality of these energy services to a broader set of aspects of human lives including economy health, housing and lifestyles means that CE initiatives can act as conduits through which individuals can access information and assistance around fundamental human needs (Soutar 2016). Additionally, many CE initiatives have experimented with sharing some of the financial benefits associated with RE generation: for example, by establishing community benefit funds. Under one such model, revenues are redistributed locally to other organisations, and can often include those engaged in social innovation towards a wider set of social and environmental objectives than those relating to energy (Walker and Devine-Wright 2008; Walker et al. 2010). By appealing to a broader audience than might be possible if operating purely towards energy projects, CE can develop membership from and legitimacy across a range of social spheres. Furthermore, this demonstrates how an underlying commonality in values and approaches (i.e. the pursuit of objectives deemed to be socially beneficial) can encourage mutual support, even between different domains of social innovation.

3.4 Knowings and framings within groups

Several discussions with CE practitioners echoed the literature in highlighting the importance of specific forms of knowledge and other cognitive resources throughout their activities. Even small CE initiatives can require a vast range of competencies in technical issues, community engagement (including website development and social media), finance and accounting, business planning and project management, planning and legal issues and project evaluation. Forming new (or strengthening existing) relationships under shared values and common goals forms the basis for individuals to offer and share a variety of cognitive, organisational and financial resources. For budding initiatives, having one or more key competencies present at an early stage is often cited as important in being able to identify perceived problems as opportunities for change.[1] However, the ability to acquire competencies (either by upskilling or expanding) can be considered as important as having them in the first place, particularly as different phases of CE projects often require a range of skills to be deployed at different times (Soutar 2016).

'Vision' refers both to the ability to envisage positive outcomes for SI practices and operationalise agendas to move towards these outcomes. Visions within CE are particularly useful as they help create salient narrative frames around local issues, enlighten others to both problems and setting expectations around potential solutions. In doing so they help to establish tangible, salient and specific expectations around the benefits to be gained from being involved, all of which are considered important processes within the development of niche innovations (Hargreaves et al. 2013; Coenen et al. 2010; Kemp et al. 1998).

3.5 Knowings and framings among groups

Strategic niche management (SNM) theory posits that networking between local 'niche' experiments, through intermediaries, results in the institutionalisation of local lessons and expectations and thus the development of coherence among emerging innovation experiments (Kemp *et al.* 1998; Hoogma *et al.* 2001). SNM thus understands the CE movement as resulting from progressively coherent networks of learning, developing from experimentation in local contexts and coordinated by intermediaries through which resources, including knowledge and guidance are transferred (Kemp *et al.* 1998; Seyfang *et al.* 2014; Hargreaves *et al.* 2013).

Such knowledge and guidance are typically understood to centre on practical aspects of doing, in terms of how local problems have been overcome, for example. Such networking, both between CE groups and through intermediaries can thus be considered crucial in terms of the transfer of both knowings and framings. For example, in such a resource-scarce environment, the success of projects can hinge on whether specific competencies can be accessed at the right time. Belonging to a rich network of practitioners 'who are in the same boat' appears to be of particular value, both in terms of being able to discuss in detail practical solutions to hurdles as they arise but also in terms of being able to air frustrations and exchange moral support.

Since CE initiatives comprise a variety of forms, visions and approaches, the value of networking to individual groups varies depends largely on the particular configuration of resource needs of the group at any one time (Seyfang *et al.* 2014). However, while reciprocal norms can be found throughout CE practices, resource scarcities and competition between groups (to attract limited funding, for example) can mean that the propensity to share resources and information can vary between contexts (Soutar 2016).

Although SNM theory proposes that networking between niche experiments eventually results in standardisation among networking social innovations, this does not yet seem to have occurred within CE (Seyfang *et al.* 2014). However, rather than somehow implying immaturity, the natural diversity of objectives and practices that characterise CE almost necessitates incoherence in some ways. In other words, incoherence in many ways represents the experimentation by an increasingly diverse set of actors and localities, interacting with an increasingly complex set of technological innovations and towards a multitude of transformative ambitions. Indeed for some, such diversity is at the heart of what it is to be transformative (Stirling 2014a).

4 Citizen-oriented energy and societal transformation

This chapter has so far explored social innovation largely in the context of networks of place-based, community-led energy initiatives, the impact of which locally towards social and environmental objectives has been well documented (Soutar 2016; Clore Social Leadership Programme *et al.* 2013; DECC 2014, 2015). Following the Conservative government's reduction of support for both RET deployment and CE projects more specifically, the growth of the CE sector slowed dramatically in 2016 (Cooperatives UK 2016). While this may have meant that community-led CE is in decline, it is not true that the prospects for all forms of citizen-focused energy initiatives are bleak. Rather, there is a burgeoning interest in the potential for local energy supply models, driven by local government and corporate actors, but also building on networks and learning from within the CE sector.

It is within these nascent activities that the new modes of organising, doing, knowing and framing encapsulated within CE continue to challenge incumbent institutions and have the potential to affect processes of societal change more profoundly. It is to these issues that this chapter now turns.

4.1 Institutionalisation of community energy

As noted above, CE comprises and has co-evolved alongside a range of synergistic social and technological innovations, including ICT as an enabler of both, and from the maturation of many innovations have come new challenges and thus opportunities for additional innovation to emerge. For example, the growth in demand for community-scale RE projects in south west England has in part been frustrated by the local electricity distribution network nearing technical capacity (Simonds and Hall 2013). However, rather than impeding RE growth altogether, the excessive cost associated with network reinforcement has provided the impetus for various forms of innovation around local demand optimisation grid management (Clark 2016). Importantly, this has been catalysed by the existence of established local visions, competencies and practices developed through CE networks as well as technological advances in terms of smart grid technologies. When taken together, the symbiotic relationship between SI, RE and ICT can thus be seen to challenge established ways of doing in terms of how conventional energy system challenges are being tackled.

A combination of deepening RE penetration, advances in ICT and social innovation within CE has also had a more profound effect on shifting dominant framing of the movement away from being just about local energy generation (which is then sold to a small number of electricity suppliers) towards being able to use generation assets to directly supply local customers. This is considered something of a natural progression from experiments in energy production carried out by conventional CE practitioners (Hall and Roelich 2015). Local supply models potentially give citizens far more control over the value associated with locally owned energy assets and invigorate discourses around notions of subsidiarity, energy citizenship and the democratisation of energy (e.g. Corbyn 2016). Such a shift can be understood as a significant change to dominant framings within the energy system: for example, by reframing the need for RET integration as an opportunity rather than a challenge (National Infrastructure Commission 2016). It also arguably challenges established objectives within energy policy-making and analysis to consider a broader set of societal preferences and objectives than has previously been the case.

Experimentation with new business models within these new market landscapes are increasingly attracting interest from a broader swath of actors, such as local authorities and social enterprises, but also new and incumbent energy supply companies (Hall and Roelich 2016; Ofgem 2015). In comparison to more 'traditional' community-led forms of CE, such initiatives are considerably less resource constrained and can operate on a larger geographical scale than their predecessors. Nonetheless, local supply market actors build on and reinforce the learning and competencies developed within community-led CE, such as that around community engagement, financing and effective principles of organisation. Rather than supplanting the traditional CE sector then, this suggests an ongoing role for community-led knowledge and competencies to feed in to these new experiments, and, indeed, the importance of involving local communities in visioning, supporting and enabling such models is being increasingly acknowledged.

In terms of sustainable consumption and production outcomes, there is no reason to suggest that these new models of citizen-oriented energy will necessarily result in a narrowing of the breadth of sustainability ideas CE identifies with. Rather, many of the key motivations of CE initiatives, such as local economic development, socioeconomic equity, environmental protection and self-governance, appear central to business models within local energy practitioners more generally (Hall and Roelich 2015). Furthermore, by involving actors such as local authorities who are already interested and engaged in addressing multiple objectives, such initiatives can be instrumental in coordinating a wide programme of activities. This may involve more strategic coordination of local energy systems, through better integrating heat, transport and electricity infrastructures to help balance local energy supply/demand patterns and/or deeper integration with other local objectives such as health and wellbeing by identifying and addressing inadequately insulated homes.

In terms of the final element of SI, knowing, the move to local supply arrangements and, indeed, related citizen-focused innovations, such as those in the smart grid ecosystem, will depend on the ability of energy system actors to develop new competencies that better serve the needs of a future energy system. This would include building expertise and competence in both energy policy and scholarship around a range of issues, such as the potential for behavioural change for demand reduction and demand management, how best to meaningfully engage with publics, how best to design and regulate local energy markets, and how to make the transition to more efficient local optimisation of energy systems (Hoggett 2016; Sovacool 2014; Roberts 2014; Ofgem 2015; Burns and Watson 2016).

In summary, it would not be premature to suggest that established institutions around organising, doing, knowing and framing within the UK energy system are being seriously challenged and, in some cases, altered and replaced by the pressure exerted by the combination of social and technological innovation. Such changes will not take place overnight and, indeed, will be subject to continued resistance, but, given the momentum behind both social and technological innovation and the emerging prospects for positive societal change, it seems clear that the pressure for institutional change can, and will be sustained.

5 Conclusions

In considering CE as a site of social innovation, this chapter has sought to explore SI in terms of novel forms of organising, doing, knowing and framing in the context of more sustainable production and consumption in the energy system. CE has a role within a number of functions within processes of system innovation, such as experimenting with, creating demand for and investing in RETs.

However, by engaging in a symbiotic relationship with such technologies, including ICT, the social innovations adopted and supported by CE can be considered vital components within ongoing processes of societal transformation in the energy system. Compared to incumbent-led, technologically focused and unidirectional system innovation, transformation refers to more fundamental, persistent and irreversible changes across society, which are frequently socially driven, diverse and unruly in structure and direction (Avelino *et al.* 2014; Stirling 2014a). CE has played a key role in both fostering discourse around and experimenting with novel energy systems, and it is within these initiatives, albeit reimagined, that ideas of sustainability in the energy system continue to be challenged. These ideas reach far beyond policy objectives of decarbonisation, security and affordability to encompass a far wider set of societal objectives, such as health and wellbeing, economy, equity, legitimacy and democracy. By seeking to realise such objectives through a range of social and technological innovations, which simultaneously and symbiotically address both processes and outcomes relating to energy system change, CE has played an instrumental role in helping to challenge established institutions within the energy system.

Note

1 The caricature of CE practitioners as 'retired engineers' (ECC Committee 2013) alludes both to the importance of problem-solving, technically minded 'tinkerers' in establishing CE projects, as well as the importance of having time and energy to spend on projects.

References

Aldridge, S., Halpern, D., and Fitzpatrick, S. (2002) Social capital (Performance and Innovation Unit discussion paper).

Avelino, F., Wittmayer, J. M., Haxeltine, A., Kemp, R., O'Riordan, T., Weaver, P., Loorbach, D., and Rotmans, J. (2014) Game-changers and transformative social innovation: the case of the economic crisis and the new economy (TRANSIT working paper 1) TRANSIT: EU SSH.2013.3.2–1 Grant agreement no. 613169.

Burns, W., and Watson, J. (2016) Energy systems research in a world in transition: challenges for policy and research (conference report, UK Energy Research Centre).

Butler, C., Parkhill, K., and Pidgeon, N. (2013) *Deliberating energy system transitions in the UK: transforming the UK energy system: public values, attitudes and acceptability* London: UKERC.

Clark, P. (2016) Centrica to trial unique green energy system in Cornwall *Financial Times* 2 Dec.

Clore Social Leadership Programme, National Trust and Shared Assets (2013) Social and economic benefits of community energy schemes, www.respublica.org.uk/disraeli-room-post/2013/09/05/economic-social-benefits-community-energy.

Coenen, L., Raven, R., and Verbong, G. (2010) Local niche experimentation in energy transitions: a theoretical and empirical exploration of proximity advantages and disadvantages *Technology in Society* 32: 295–302.

Coles, A.-M., Piterou, A., and Genus, A. (2016) Sustainable energy projects and the community: mapping single-building use of microgeneration technologies in London *Urban Studies* 53: 1869–1884.

Cooperatives UK (2016) *New data reveals 80 per cent drop in community-owned energy following government U-turns*, www.uk.coop/newsroom/new-data-reveals-80-cent-drop-community-owned-energy-following-government-u-turns.

Corbyn, J. 2016. Why Labour is putting energy reform at the heart of its green agenda *Guardian Environment Blog*, www.theguardian.com/environment/blog/2016/sep/07/why-labour-is-putting-energy-reform-at-heart-of-its-green-agenda-jeremy-corbyn.

Dahlmann, F., Kolk, A., and Lindeque, J. Emerging energy geographies: scaling and spatial divergence in European electricity generation capacity *European Urban and Regional Studies*, http://journals.sagepub.com/doi/pdf/10.1177/0969776416663808.

DECC (2014) *Community energy strategy: full report* London: Department for Energy and Climate Change.

DECC (2015) *Community energy strategy: update* London: Department of Energy and Climate Change.

ECC Committee (2013) *6th Report on Local Energy* London: Stationery Office Limited.

Evans, M. D. (2003) *The contribution of social capital in the social economy to local economic development in Western Europe (CONCISE)* Brussels: European Commission.

Foxon, T. J., and Pearson, P. (2013) *The UK low carbon energy transition: prospects and challenges* (working paper) Bath: University of Bath.

Gittell, R., and Vidal, A. (1998) *Community organizing: building social capital as a development strategy* Thousand Oaks, CA: Sage.

Goldthau, A., and Sovacool, B. K. (2012) The uniqueness of the energy security, justice, and governance problem *Energy Policy* 41: 232–240.

Hall, S., and Roelich, K. (2015) Local electricity supply: opportunities, archetypes and outcomes (IBuild report), http://opus.bath.ac.uk/46460/1/local_electricity_supply_report_WEB.pdf.

Hall, S., and Roelich, K. (2016) Business model innovation in electricity supply markets: the role of complex value in the United Kingdom *Energy Policy* 92: 286–298.

Hargreaves, T., Hielscher, S., Seyfang, G., and Smith, A. (2013) Grassroots innovations in community energy: the role of intermediaries in niche development *Global Environmental Change* 23: 868–880.

Haxeltine, A., Avelino, F., Pel, B., Dumitru, A., Kemp, R., Longhurst, N., Chilvers, J., and Wittmayer, J. M. (2016) A framework for transformative social innovation. (TRANSIT working paper 5) TRANSIT: EU SSH.2013.3.2–1 Grant agreement no. 61316.

Hekkert, M. P., Suurs, R. A., Negro, S. O., Kuhlmann, S., and Smits, R. E. (2007) Functions of innovation systems: a new approach for analysing technological change *Technological Forecasting and Social Change* 74: 413–432.

Hilty, L., Lohmann, W., and Huang, E. (2011) Sustainability and ICT: an overview of the field *Politeia* 27: 13–28.

Hoggett, R. (2016) Optimising the energy system from the bottom up *IGov New Thinking Blog*, http://projects.exeter.ac.uk/igov/new-thinking-optimising-the-energy-system-from-the-bottom-up.

Hoogma, R., Weber, M., and Elzen, B. (2001) Integrated long-term strategies to induce regime shifts to sustainability: the approach of strategic niche management (paper presented at the Towards Environmental Innovation Systems Conference, Eibsee, 27–29 Sept.).

Kay, A. (2003) Social capital in building the social economy in Pearce, R. (ed.) *Social enterprise in Anytown* London: Calouste Gulbenkian Foundation.

Kemp, R., Schot, J., and Hoogma, R. (1998) Regime shifts to sustainability through processes of niche formation: the approach of strategic niche management *Technology Analysis and Strategic Management* 10: 175–198.

Miller, C. A., Iles, A., and Jones, C. F. (2013) The social dimensions of energy transitions *Science as Culture* 22: 135–148.

Miller, C. A., O'Leary, J., Graffy, E., Stechel, E. B., and Dirks, G. (2015a) Narrative futures and the governance of energy transitions *Futures* 70: 65–74.

Miller, C. A., Richter, J., and O'Leary, J. (2015b) Socio-energy systems design: a policy framework for energy transitions *Energy Research and Social Science* 6: 29–40.

Mitchell, C. (2016) Momentum is increasing towards a flexible electricity system based on renewables *Nature Energy* 1, www.nature.com/articles/nenergy201530?WT.mc_id=TWT_NEnergy.

Mitchell, C., Watson, J., and Whiting, J. (2013) *New challenges in energy security: the UK in a multipolar world* Basingstoke: Palgrave Macmillan.

National Infrastructure Commission (2016) Smart power, www.gov.uk/government/uploads/system/uploads/attachment_data/file/505218/IC_Energy_Report_web.pdf.

Nolden, C. (2013) Governing community energy: feed-in tariffs and the development of community wind energy schemes in the United Kingdom and Germany *Energy Policy* 63: 543–552.

Ofgem (2015) Non-traditional business models: supporting transformative change in the energy market (discussion paper).

Ofgem (2016) *Retail energy markets in 2016*, www.ofgem.gov.uk/system/files/docs/2016/08/retail_energy_markets_in_2016.pdf.

Ofgem, OFT and CMA (2014) *State of the market assessment*, www.ofgem.gov.uk/ofgem-publications/86804/assessmentdocumentpublished.pdf.

Parkhill, K., Demski, C., Butler, C., Spence, A., and Pidgeon, N. (2013) *Transforming the UK energy system: public values, attitudes and acceptability: synthesis report* London: UKERC.

Putnam, R. D. (2000) *Bowling alone: the collapse and revival of American community* New York: Simon and Schuster.

Roberts, S. (2014) The missing ingredient in UK energy policy governance? *CSE Blog*, www.cse.org.uk/news/view/1839.

Seyfang, G., Park, J. J., and Smith, A. (2013) A thousand flowers blooming? An examination of community energy in the UK *Energy Policy* 61: 977–989.

Seyfang, G., Hielscher, S., Hargreaves, T., Martiskainen, M., and Smith, A. (2014) A grassroots sustainable energy niche? Reflections on community energy in the UK *Environmental Innovation and Societal Transitions*, 13: 21–44.

Simonds, V., and Hall, B. (2013) *Overcoming grid connection issues for community energy projects* (for Cooperatives UK and the Co-operative Group), www.localenergyscotland.org/media/33075/Cornwall-Energy-report_Overcoming-grid-connection-issues-for-community-energy.pdf.

Soutar, I. 2016. From local to global value: the transformational nature of community energy (PhD thesis, University of Exeter).

Sovacool, B. K. (2014) What are we doing here? Analyzing fifteen years of energy scholarship and proposing a social science research agenda *Energy Research and Social Science* 1: 1–29.

Stirling, A. (2014a) *Emancipating transformations: from controlling 'the transition' to culturing plural radical progress* Brighton, Suss.: Steps Centre.

Stirling, A. (2014b) Transforming power: social science and the politics of energy choices *Energy Research and Social Science* 1: 83–95.

Walker, G., and Devine-Wright, P. (2008) Community renewable energy: what should it mean? *Energy Policy* 36: 497–500.

Walker, G., Devine-Wright, P., Hunter, S., High, H., and Evans, B. (2010) Trust and community: exploring the meanings, contexts and dynamics of community renewable energy *Energy Policy* 38: 2655–2663.

8 Community agriculture and the narrative construction of change

Emese Gulyás and Bálint Balázs

1 Community supported agriculture and direct food-purchasing groups in Hungary

Farmers' markets, food cooperatives, pick-your-own harvesting and other forms of short food-supply chains have a long history in Hungary and, despite their declining share in household food sourcing, they are still regarded as the good old, traditional source of food. Growing demand for local food is fuelled by environmental concerns, explicit patriotic (political) attitudes and state support. Product features like "local", "regional" or "Hungarian" became values of their own in certain consumer segments. In Hungary, buying local and seasonal food is one of the most popular consumer behavioural forms to combat climate change (Eurobarometer 2014). Responding to open consumer attitudes, some forms of local food systems, like local food markets with strong sustainability missions, artisan food products and regionally labelled food, have been reinvented as well in the past decade. Their revival largely resulted from supportive governmental policies and the availability of public funds for infrastructural development, marketing promotions, and consumer campaigns.

Other forms of alternative food systems, like community supported agriculture (CSA) or direct purchasing groups, started to flourish around 2006. The first direct food-purchasing group in Budapest with a clear sustainability mission began to operate that year, and later it became a role model for several other initiatives. The first champion CSA in Hungary started in 1998 (Vadovics and Hayes 2010; Ángyán *et al.* 2003), but then it took more than a decade for others to emerge. A series of events and trainings organized by the Association of Conscious Consumers (ACC) and research organizations contributed to boosting a second generation of CSAs (Dezsény 2013; Dezsény *et al.* 2014). Dozens of farmers and several hundred consumers were inspired and equipped with proper knowledge to start and support CSAs. According to the directory of the ACC, there were 16 to 18 operating CSAs, and about 16 direct food-purchasing groups in Hungary in 2016. The actual number might be higher, but there is a clear tendency for the number of CSAs and food-purchasing groups to increase every year (Association of Conscious Consumers 2016). Both forms reflect the growing need and consumer demand for healthy, sustainable and just food, which previously was not met by other actors.

2 Social innovation in sustainable foodscapes

Academic and action research in Hungary documents well the flourishing of local food initiatives, and, in line with international literature (e.g. Chiffoleau and Prevost 2012; Blättel-Mink 2014; Möllers and Bîrhală 2014; Jaeger-Erben *et al.* 2015), much of the research conceptualizes direct purchasing groups and CSAs as social innovations spawning innovative practices.

Vadovics and Hayes (2010) studied the development of the first CSA in Hungary from a social-innovation perspective, implying that the CSA itself used to be an innovative farming and marketing method. Their case study described the life stages of the CSA. The authors concluded that the continuous adaptation to consumer needs and business constraints resulted in moving towards less innovative ways of operation. The CSA moved from the share model, in which all costs and harvest benefits were divided and shared among consumer members, towards a healthy-food delivery service that partly distributed its own organic produce.

Besides the share model described by Vadovics and Hayes (2010), there are other examples of innovations in CSAs. In a comparative case study of three CSAs, Dezsény (2013) identified several innovative practices. The first innovation was adopting the CSA model, which was relatively new in Hungary at the time of the research. He also found farmer-to-farmer knowledge sharing and cooperation among farmers, certain farming methods, new forms of contracting and marketing, discursive patterns and communication channels that he described as innovations. The research concluded that "these alternative enterprises are 'change agencies', promoting innovations" (ibid., 97).

CSA farmers themselves regard the CSA as an innovative practice (Balázs 2013). On the one hand, they regard CSAs as innovative marketing methods, which are capable of reducing production and commercialization costs and of simplifying the planning of human costs and sales; on the other hand, farmers gain more from the economic value created along the supply chain when compared to other forms of sales. The author (ibid.) concludes that CSAs in Hungary might be catalysing laboratories of social change, influencing the future of agrarian production.

The alternative food markets and ethical foodscape in Hungary emerged from intentional political activities and successfully created more sustainable alternatives to the dominant market provisions. One of the innovative features of CSA and other local food initiatives is addressing food-market failures: modern agriculture failed to provide a fair living to many farmers, just working conditions for workers, healthy food for consumers and sustainability. CSAs as social innovations respond to these failures (Möllers and Bîrhală 2014). Starting from the insight that individual-level sustainable consumption does not lead to transformation, community agriculture builds on the close socio-economic cooperation of farmers and consumers to generate more social connection and collaborative experience (Balázs 2012, 2013). Different forms of community agriculture reconnect consumers through market mechanisms to farmers in such a manner that strangers start to combine resources in ways that used to be confined to the realm of kinship and friendship (Schor and Fitzmaurice 2015). The typical forms of community agriculture are farmer-led CSA and consumers' buying groups. Through commercial activity and monetary exchange, these specific forms foster genuine community connections. Community agriculture as social innovation exhibits new ways of doing, organizing, knowing and framing (cf. Avelino *et al.* 2014).

In research on CSAs and direct food-purchasing groups, one apparent research gap is how consumers can contribute to the creation and spread of social innovations represented by community agriculture. Therefore, we turn in this chapter to an amended version of the narratives of change (NoC) analytical framework as developed by Wittmayer and colleagues (2015). We understand NoC as a discursive form which positions actors in a particular context and orders events or activities in (temporal) sequence towards a goal or future. Our analysis of the change narratives created by consumers in CSAs and buying groups in Hungary will show how consumers talk about the change needed in the food system and in society at large. Additionally, we zoom in on certain characteristics of the consumers engaging in CSAs and food-purchasing groups.

Following the NoC framework, we focus our research questions on the role of context, actors and plot. In terms of context, we analyse (1) why consumers consider change as necessary. As for the actors, we are interested in (2) who is or who could be driving change. And with regards plot, we analyse (3) how change is occurring. The first question focuses on describing the narratives by consumers themselves. For the second question, in addition to the NoC framework, we examine the social embeddedness of actors, thus their potential to drive change as well as the topic of trust and distrust. This focus is based on the assumption that social capital, the social embeddedness of actors and trust among them are necessary conditions of change. Loose or strong connections to other social networks may indicate a potential to diffuse the innovative practices between the various communities consumers belong to (cf. Granovetter 1973). High level of interpersonal and institutional trust may amplify societal change.

In the context of political consumerism, Neilson and Paxton (2010) argue that individuals are encouraged to follow certain consumption patterns for change in trusted environments they live in due to their rich social capital. The authors claim that social interaction between integrated, trusted individuals and institutions motivates and influences social change. People expect their environment to support and repeat their actions, which could increase the efficacy of their action. Therefore, we inquired into whom consumers of CSAs and direct food-purchasing groups trust and we analysed their narratives about trusting these actors. Regarding the third question, we describe consumer narratives about how change is occurring, how members can see their food communities and generally their consumer choices as steps towards the desired change.

As outlined in Figure 8.1 our research fields, CSA and direct food-purchasing groups, are regarded as social innovations, but narratives of change as shared

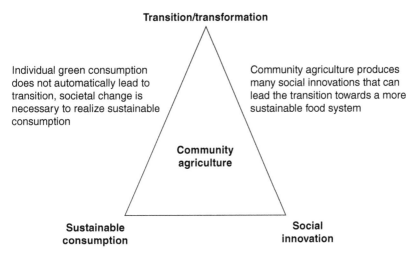

Transition/transformation

Individual green consumption does not automatically lead to transition, societal change is necessary to realize sustainable consumption

Community agriculture produces many social innovations that can lead the transition towards a more sustainable food system

Community agriculture

Sustainable consumption

Social innovation

Many forms of social innovations support sustainable consumption

Figure 8.1 Empirical observations on the relations of social innovation and sustainable consumption, based on the book concept.

Source: authors (adapted from Backhaus *et al.* in this volume).

construction and discourses about change may reinforce social innovation practices, which may lead to systemic changes (Wittmayer *et al.* 2015).

3 Methodological approach and empirical material

Our disposition towards CSA and buying-group members was self-reflective, sympathetic but critical. Interviewees were approached as sufficiently knowledgeable partners to contribute to the common understanding of social innovation potentials and to the clarification of benefits for the initiatives. Both authors are related to the Hungarian CSA movement. Emese Gulyás is affiliated with the Association of Conscious Consumers in Hungary. The research presented here had been designed to support the ACC's practice underpinned by social theory. Bálint Balázs at the Environmental Social Science Research Group has been promoting small-scale agricultural and agro-ecological models through various projects.

The research data was collected in two phases. In 2009 and 2010 we conducted 27 structured individual interviews with members of six Hungarian direct purchasing consumer groups: two were located in the capital and the other four in various cities or small towns. The members of these groups got access to natural (bio, biodynamic or organic) vegetables directly from farmers in their small region. The structured interviews covered four themes related to the buying group: (1) products and services, (2) motives for participating in the group, (3) members' lifestyle components associated with ethical consumption and (4) public participation attitudes.

While the 2009–2010 research applied qualitative methods, in 2016, the ACC made a quantitative follow-up. We were interested to see if, after the successful proliferation of innovative short food-supply chain practices, we could detect the same driving forces and motivations behind these initiatives than those established after the first phase. We asked respondents about (1) the motivations for participating in CSAs, (2) other sustainable consumption behavioural patterns, (3) embeddedness in other communities and relations to others and (4) other forms of political participation. Questions about motives and participation were derived from the results of the first phase and were used to validate these results. The survey was answered by 60 consumer members from 19 direct purchasing groups and CSAs in Hungary: CSAs are alternative food networks and in this sense similar to the purchasing groups, though they were not present at the time of the first study (see Table 8.1).

4 Consumers' narratives of change in local food initiatives

Consumers' narratives about the necessity of change (context) and the proposed solutions (plot) are many times interwoven, as they see food communities as solutions to specific problems: here we try to unwrap them according to the focal questions of our research.

4.1 Why is change considered necessary?

When talking about the goals purchasing groups may pursue and motivations for joining, the most prominent topics were health, critique of political regimes and their alternatives, environmental protection, community experience, fairness and solidarity, trust and patriotism. The interviewees spontaneously raised these topics. The interviewed consumers usually had a critical stance towards the mainstream food systems and towards capitalism and globalization in general because of their failure to contribute to the public good,

Table 8.1 Overview of research phases

Phases of data gathering	Source	Methods	Number of groups covered	Number of consumer respondents
2009–2010	Food-purchasing group members	Structured interviews; content analysis	6	27
2016	CSA and food-purchasing group members	Online questionnaire	19	60

including environmental sustainability and social justice. Several of the members mentioned the adverse effects of economic globalization on the environment, the unfairness of trade regimes for both producers and consumers, and a decline in health related qualities of products.

> [My opinion] is similar to the case of politics. They [big companies] only work for profit, many times they don't pay attention to humans and to the environment, this is not long term thinking.
>
> (Interviewee I, male)[1]

One of the most prominent themes was health, but this is only partly explained by the fact that the direct objective of the consumer groups had been buying healthier (organic) food. Like nearly all of the essential themes that had been mentioned, also the issue of health was linked with a critique of the system.

> The measure of economic stability is not that it grows three or four or five percent each year, but that it does not wear itself out. One way of achieving it is the way Attila [an organic farmer who sells to the group] farms. I know that his lands will be as fit for production a hundred years from now as they are now. He is not the only one thinking this way. If we could stick to his way, we could live in a better environment.
>
> (Interviewee M, male)

Disappointment in the dominant structures of economy and society motivated the interviewed group members to take action. Their attitudes reflected the need for and intention to change. Besides the topics mentioned like environment, justice and fairness, and health, an underlying, parallel narrative was frequently expressed, which we call the instrumentality of alternative food (and other) consumption practices. Instrumentality as a cross-cutting narrative means that for example, when consumers talked about health as an important motivation, they were critical about the healthiness of "industrial" food and they wanted to see and contribute to change.

The following quotation illustrates how the interviewed consumers constructed their belonging to the group as an alternative to globalization and as the manifestation of positive changes for a cause or the benefit of the wider society. Many of the interviewees mentioned anti-globalization among their motivations for joining the group.

> There have been some, who perceived the whole thing from the environmentalist perspective, as anti-globalization action. As the individual contribution in the whole struggle against globalization.
>
> (Interviewee V, male)

Future-oriented thinking appeared many times in the discourses about the groups. When members talked about the goals and objectives the group pursues, they often mentioned "access to healthy food" or "linking consumers and farmers" – both are essential features of food-purchasing groups. Nevertheless, in addition, a vision about a more sustainable world emerged. They perceive themselves as contributing to a solution that is an alternative to the harmful effects of globalization.

> It is good that initiatives come into being which are alternatives to big retail chains, which strengthen the direct relationship between the producer and consumers, which make the whole purchasing process controllable, which support local producers and organic farming and so on. Simply, the aim for which it was created, is good.
>
> (Interviewee H, male)

> I see [the group] as an alternative. We organize a business-like thing communally and help each other in a way that there are no mechanisms like capital accumulation, or hierarchy, where someone uses the others for something. I think this is imperative. There is this eco problem that we sit in the shadow of the eco-catastrophe. You can complain and say what is wrong, but then what is the other viable thing you can do?
>
> (Interviewee F, female)

> You can go and protest against multinationals to not sell potatoes at a dumping price in September, or you can contact a farmer, organize a group and buy. Both are activities, but maybe [the group] is more progressive.
>
> (Interviewee V, male)

The theme of trust and distrust came up in the first research phase. Distrust was expressed mainly towards the mainstream trade regime and its institutions. Disenchantment and mistrust motivated the group members to seek alternatives, such as to organize the buying groups.

4.2 Who is or who could be driving change?

Here diffusion potential is discussed from the perspective of trust, social capital and social embeddedness. Members surveyed in both phases were active citizens and strongly or loosely connected to other social networks.

On the societal level, the group members trusted advocacy and protest organizations (such as labour unions and environmentalist organizations), their own communities and their own efforts as consumers. However, they expressed great distrust towards large corporations and established political institutions (parties, parliament and government). If they trusted an institution, it was because they agreed and identified with its goals. An alignment of goals provided such a strong foundation of trust that it was not shaken, even if the respondents were critical of the actual operation of an institution – such opinions were often raised in regard to both environmentalist organizations and labour unions.

Accordingly, distrust was connected to goals with which the respondents disagreed.

> [Civil society organizations] work for values that are important for me. They work much more responsibly and thoroughly than any public body, and they take into account the interest of all stakeholders.
>
> (Interviewee Y, female)

The answers and opinions about institutional trust brought to the fore the future-oriented and socially sensitive thinking of the interviewed consumers. While their reflection on their groups revealed that they thought such groups could indeed contribute to an environmentally and socially sustainable future, their criticism of political institutions resulted from the opposite diagnosis.

The later, quantitative, survey confirmed that group members trust civil society organizations. When we asked them to what extent they trust environmental organizations on a 1–10 scale, 62 per cent of the respondents fell into the 6–8 categories, with more than 20 per cent of the interviewees in each percentile. About the same percentage (71 per cent) fell into the same categories (6–8) for trust in civil society organizations in general, and an additional 12 per cent marked category 9. In this survey, we asked about certain consumer behaviours that are only partly related to participation in the buying groups, but still indicate the diffusion potential of the members. In the previous 12 months, 60 per cent of the respondents had recommended a company for its corporate social responsibility (CSR) or environmental records and 39 per cent had discussed CSR issues in their private lives, which means that the group members frequently discussed or commented on progressive practices. 20 per cent of them had contacted politicians or decision-makers attempting to influence change.

Both field studies found that local food-purchasing groups and CSAs are collaborative achievements of farmers and their consumers. Our results suggest that trust drives participation. The trusting attitude of consumers in the groups was evident as a part of their narratives of change. They considered trustworthiness to be one of the most important characteristics of their value driven alternatives.

> His personality guarantees that this is locally grown, not chemically treated food…. This is trustworthy for me: I know the producer, I know how and where he farms.
>
> (Interviewee M, male)

The earlier, qualitative research also revealed that the interviewed group members had been engaged with other civil society organizations (CSO). A third of the interviewees were themselves CSO employees. This may indicate that buying groups were relatively new phenomena at that time, mainly endorsed by civil society organizations from which their membership had been recruited. Nevertheless, the interviewees named four other civil society initiatives or causes on average, which they supported independently of their occupation. At the same time, with few exceptions, they were not very active in the food communities, rarely attended community events and their main motivation for joining was not belonging or company.

The majority of the members are weakly connected to the buying group or CSA, but at the same time, they had links to other social groups. Their embeddedness in civil society and the riches of their social capital may assign them positive diffusion potential. Thus, the change that brought about the local food initiatives has windows of opportunities beyond its borders.

Among the respondents of the 2016 survey, 28 per cent were a member, donor or volunteer of one or two other CSOs. 25 per cent of them volunteered weekly or monthly with CSOs and another 41 per cent volunteered on a few occasions annually. This means a total of 66 per cent volunteer at least a few times a year, which indicates a stronger commitment to CSOs than the Hungarian average. However, besides food buying, only a smaller circle is very active in the CSA community (8 per cent), 15 per cent regularly or occasionally volunteers for the community, and almost half of the respondents do not participate in the community events of the farms.

We can conclude that the studied group members in both samples were not intensively connected to each other and to the groups themselves: they did not participate in joint events, and only a few of them volunteered with the groups, which implies that the co-creation of the change narratives did not happen within the groups.

4.3 How is change occurring?

Community agriculture has a very specific problem framing: a starting point for any CSA and buying group is that real change can start in empowered individuals only as a member of a supporting community through change maker activities that avoid dominant market solutions. Successful initiatives are therefore very much solutions-oriented (rather than problem-oriented). Their main position is political and ideological and reinforces the literature that the dominant agro-food supply creates adversaries that require community level actions (e.g. Balázs 2013; Bilewicz and Śpiewak 2015; Möllers and Bîrhală 2014). Communities see policy and governmental actors as allies only if they create more and more opportunities for community agriculture. CSAs and buying groups both act as laboratories that help people experiment with and prepare for change.

The groups and similar initiatives against consumer society and globalization can actively contribute to the fulfilment of a vision of sustainability, once they have more followers.

Then these things [like the group] will be the seeds of a sustainable world.

(Interviewee Z, male)

This is crucial from the environmental point of view. I cannot tell when, years or decades, but I can see that this is not sustainable.... The transportation of goods will fall apart, because of the oil prices and the environmental contamination. Then these [groups] will be the points, the food sources, which survived and which are sustainable.

(Interviewee G, female)

As this is a participatory action, this has a pedagogical and awareness raising power. If there is not only one like this [group], but many, this is a good example for others.... There is hopelessness in many places, many things could start in these places. You can calculate the number of families, if all of them would buy food from similar sources, what it would mean if only 1% would buy from similar sources.

(Interviewee A, male)

I think that an initiative like this, similarly all alternative initiatives, is useful for discovering paths, for developing new behaviours. Thus on top of being good for those of us involved, because we do good, we feel good, we think good, this [group] sets a pattern and this is vital.

(Interviewee D, female)

Consumers regarded food accessed through the food communities as an instrument for change. Another example is that they expressed dissatisfaction with the environmental impact of food chains, but they regarded their participation in the group as a means for change. Consumers wanted to take part in what they consider an alternative to economic globalization, which they assumed to have some negative effects. Beside access to healthy food, this was a major motive of joining the purchasing groups. Group members felt that the activities of their groups contributed to a model, which offers at least a partial solution to "the troubles of the world", and, through this, they contributed to solving social problems.

Purchases made within the consumer groups were considered to be behaviour that alleviates these effects and as an alternative to and protest against economic globalization. The term "purchase vote" (or "forint vote" referring to the Hungarian currency) was used multiple times during the interviews: consumers in the group support change with their money.

In fact, everything counts as a political organization. Inevitably so, since politics is the struggle for life. It would be rather naive to say that I am not participating in politics. It is already politics when one walks down to the shop and buys something.

(Interviewee Z, male)

We followed up these narratives in the 2016 survey. We were interested to find out what else motivates participation besides access to healthy, organic food.

The most standard answers describe how consumers perceive the transformative role of the groups. The majority of the respondents agreed that they joined their group because "I can directly support the farmer with my money, I can contribute to the fair livelihood of the farmer" (65 per cent) and because "I contribute to the diffusion of sustainable, eco-friendly solutions" (65 per cent). The popularity of these response options, supporting sustainable alternatives, again highlights that local food communities are not only an important source of sustainable food but possible means for systemic innovations in the field of sustainable food production and consumption. Members joined initiatives that applied a number of innovative practices starting from the way they farm, the way they communicate with members, the way they organize the community, to the way they provide an alternative to industrial food and large-scale food retail. At the same time, they perceived their participation as an active contribution to social change.

Talking about sustainable or ethical consumer choices, some of the first phase interviewees expressed their stand against consumer society with boycotts, even though they regarded them as merely symbolic. Several members mentioned fair trade and selective waste collection among the activities they were involved in. They chose such actions for ideological reasons most of the time or as a means of cultural resistance. They were also motivated by the idea that, with their consumer choices, they worked towards change. Some described their involvement in the group as an act of demonstration. Their participation in other sustainable or ethical consumption practices indicated a certain lifestyle, and many of its elements were meant to bring about or at least contribute to change.

> Direct purchasing comprises quite a lot of things, including the wish to protect the environment. And yes, it is a motivation to counter this negative effect of globalization. I think if we want to get by, either locally or at the regional level, we need to support each other. I can support the farmers by buying their products.
>
> (Interviewee V, male)

5 Discussion of results and conclusion: narrative construction of change in community agriculture

This chapter presented results from two phases of research conducted among Hungarian CSA and direct food-purchasing groups. We chose the narrative of change as an analytical framework to describe the discourses about the necessity of change and about how community agriculture may contribute to this change. We analysed the social embeddedness of the actors, and examined trust as a condition for leveraging individual practices to societal level change.

Results presented here show that members of these groups share narratives of change about how their consumer choices in general, and their participation in the groups in particular, may be the seeds of change within the food system (systemic change) or for larger scale societal change. We found aspirations to challenge capitalism as one of the key organizing structures of our societies. Change is considered necessary by the interviewed members because dominant market structures fail to bring about sustainability and social justice, while the studied groups present an alternative solution for the problems created by these structures. This result is in line with literature studying other or similar forms of individual sustainable or ethical consumption (e.g. Bock 2012; Balázs 2013, 2016; Balázs *et al.* 2016; Bilewicz and Śpiewak 2015; Goig 2007). Balázs (2013) observed similar narratives among CSA members who were regarded as opponents of the dominant consumer culture. According to his study, CSA consumers wish to change the power relations of the dominant food systems; they are not passive, adaptive captives of the hierarchical food chains, but rather conscious consumer–citizens who hope to regain control. Recent research on 12 active purchasing groups in Hungary also pointed out that consumers have become fed up with green campaigns built on deterrence and prefer gradual lifestyle change and green practicalities (Andrási 2016; see also Csutora 2012).

However, these narratives have most likely been constructed outside of the groups as the interpersonal relations within the communities are rather weak. This finding is similar to what Bilewicz and Śpiewak (2015) observed among "activist" Polish alternative-food-network members: they imported ideas and structures from their Western European counterparts, which may be regarded as an example of the international dimensions of diffusion potential. In Hungary, we were not able to find reference to global influence as it was outside the focus of the research.

Although this result is not related to consumers' narratives about the actors of change, but about consumers of CSAs and food-purchasing groups themselves, we found that the members had rich social capital and links to other communities. While according to a Eurobarometer (2011) survey, only 22 per cent of Hungarians volunteer occasionally or regularly, the members of our sample were more active and the embeddedness of our respondents in civil society groups indicates a stronger commitment than the Hungarian average. The richness of their network and their high level of activity may contribute to the diffusion of innovative practices between the various groups and may foster greater changes. Whether these sustainable food initiatives can leverage the diffusion potential of their members still needs to be investigated. However, currently there are spatial and policy barriers to their growth (Blättel-Mink 2014; Seyfang 2007). We also observed that members have a high level of trust towards potential change agents (e.g. environmental groups, protest groups) and show distrust in the established corporate and political institutions of the current system. The latter mirrors the opinion of the general public in Hungary (Boda and Medve-Bálint 2010, 2014).

Shared visions or problem framings, trust and social embeddedness are interdependent attributes. Trust or distrust in potential change agents is influenced by whether or not they share the same vision (at least partially) that group members do and to what extent they can contribute to the fulfilment of this vision. The shared vision also explains why group members join certain social groups: because they agree with the goals pursued. We interpret these results to mean that the mutually shared narratives about the necessity of change, the shared vision of empowered individuals about sustainability and social justice, trust and rich social links as diffusion potential are fundamental drivers for systemic changes in the field of food systems, production and consumption (cf. Avelino *et al.* 2014). Although these are necessary conditions, they only partially contribute to societal transformation. Several questions remain unanswered and are subject to further research: (1) what the transformative powers are that scale up individual action, like sustainable consumption practices, or small scale community actions, like CSAs or buying groups, to achieve societal level changes; (2) what the real change potential of the studied local food communities is; and (3) what leverages change mechanisms from the individual to the systemic and societal level.

Note

1 Interviewees and respondents have been granted anonymity and are therefore referred to using letters.

References

Andrási, K. (2016) Bevásárló Közösségek Magyarországon (Consumer buying groups in Hungary) (unpublished thesis, Szent István University, Gödöllő).

Ángyán, J., Milánkovics, K., and Hayes, M. (2003) A mezőgazdálkodás és a természetvédelem "újraegyesítése": a több-funkciós európai agrármodell. Gyakorlati esettanulmány: a helyi közösség által támogatott mezőgazdaság (CSA) működő modellje (Reunification of nature protection and agriculture: multifunctional European agrarian model: case study: local community supported agriculture (CSA) operating model) in Ángyán, J., ed. *Védett és érzékeny természeti területek mezőgazdálkodásának alapjai* (Foundations of agricultural practice on protected and vulnerable territories) Mezőgazda Kiadó: Budapest, 84–90.

Association of Conscious Consumers (2016) Működő közösségi gazdaságok, dobozrendszerek és bevásárlóközösségek (Operating CSAs and box schemes), http://tudatosvasarlo. hu/cikk/mukodo-kozossegi-mezogazdasagi-csoportok-bevasarlokozossegek (accessed 29 January 2017).

Avelino, F., Wittmayer, J.M., Haxeltine, A., Kemp, R., O'Riordan, T., Weaver, P., Loorbach, D., and Rotmans, J. (2014) Game-changers and transformative social innovation: the case of the economic crisis and the new economy (TRANSIT working paper 1) TRANSIT: EU SSH.2013.3.2–1 Grant agreement no. 613169.

Balázs, B. (2012) Local food system development in Hungary *International Journal of Sociology of Agriculture and Food* 19: 403–421.

Balázs, B. (2013) Civil élelmiszer hálózatok: A közösségi mezőgazdaság hazai tapasztalatai az érintettek szemével (Civil food networks: experience of community supported agriculture from the stakeholders' perspective) *Civil Szemle* 10(4): 107–126.

Balázs, B. (2016) Food self-provisioning: the role of non-market exchanges in sustainable food supply in Meybeck, A., and Redfern, S. (eds) *Sustainable value chains for sustainable food systems: a workshop of the FAO/UNEP Programme on Sustainable Food Systems* FAO: Rome, 73–78.

Balázs, B., Pataki, Gy., and Lazányi, O. (2016) Prospects for the future: community supported agriculture in Hungary *Futures* 83: 100–111.

Bilewicz, A., and Śpiewak, R. (2015) Enclaves of activism and taste: consumer cooperatives in Poland as alternative food networks *SOCIO.HU* 3: 145–166.

Blättel-Mink, B. (2014) Active consumership as a driver towards sustainability? *GAIA – Ecological Perspectives for Science and Society* 23: 158–165.

Bock, B.B. (2012) Social innovation and sustainability: how to disentangle the buzzword and its application in the field of agriculture and rural development *Studies in Agricultural Economics* 114: 57–63.

Boda, Zs., and Medve-Bálint, G. (2010) Institutional trust in Hungary in a comparative perspective: an empirical analysis in Füstös, L., and Szalma, I. (eds) *European social register 2010: values, norms and attitudes in Europe* MTA PTI and MTA SZKI: Budapest, 184–202.

Boda, Zs., and Medve-Bálint, G. (2014) Does institutional trust in East Central Europe differ from Western Europe? *European Quarterly of Political Attitudes and Mentalities* 3: 1–17.

Chiffoleau, Y., and Prevost, B. (2012) Les circuits courts, des innovations sociales pour une alimentation durable dans les territoires *Norois*, http://norois.revues.org/4245, (accessed 28 January 2017).

Csutora, M. (2012) One more awareness gap? The behaviour–impact gap problem *Journal of Consumer Policy* 35: 145–163.

Dezsény, Z. (2013) Emergence of community supported agriculture in Hungary: a case study of sustainable rural enterprises (unpublished thesis, University of California).

Dezsény, Z., Réthy, K., and Balázs, B. (2014) Alternative development on the organic sector horizon community supported agriculture in Hungary in Rahmann, G., and Aksoy, U. (eds) *Proceedings of the 4th ISOFAR Scientific Conference: "Building Organic Bridges"* (Organic World Congress, 13–15 Oct., Istanbul, Turkey), 587–590.

Eurobarometer (2011) *Volunteering and intergenerational solidarity* (Special Eurobarometer, Wave 75.2) TNS Opinion and Social: Brussels.

Eurobarometer (2014) *Climate change* (Special Eurobarometer 409) TNS Opinion and Social: Brussels.

Goig, R.L. (2007) Fair trade and global cognitive orientation: a focus on Spanish fair trade consumers *International Journal of Consumer Studies* 31: 468–477

Granovetter, M.S. (1973) The strength of weak ties *American Journal of Sociology* 78: 1360–1380.

Jaeger-Erben, M., Ruckert-John, J., and Schafer, M. (2015) Sustainable consumption through social innovation: a typology of innovations for sustainable consumption practices *Journal of Cleaner Production* 108: 784–798.

Möllers, J., and Bîrhală, B. (2014) Community supported agriculture: a promising pathway for small family farms in Eastern Europe? A case study from Romania *Landbauforsch* 264: 139–150.

Neilson, L.A., and Paxton, P. (2010) Social capital and political consumerism: a multilevel analysis *Social Problems* 57: 5–24.

Schor, J., and Fitzmaurice, C. (2015). Collaborating and connecting: the emergence of the sharing economy in Reisch, L.A., and Thøgersen, J. (eds) *Handbook of Research on Sustainable Consumption* Edward Elgar: Cheltenham, 410–425.

Seyfang, G. (2007) Cultivating carrots and community: local organic food and sustainable consumption *Environmental Values* 16: 105–123.

Vadovics, E., and Hayes, M. (2010) Open garden: a local organic producer-consumer network in Hungary: system innovation on a number of levels in Tischner, U., Stø, E., Kjærnes, U., and Tukker, A. (eds) *System innovation for sustainability III: case studies in sustainable consumption and production: food and agriculture* Greenleaf Publishing: Sheffield, 119–140.

Wittmayer, J.M., Backhaus, J., Avelino, F., Pel, B., Strasser, T., and Kunze, I. (2015) Narratives of change: how social innovation initiatives engage with their transformative ambitions (TRANSIT working paper 4) TRANSIT: EU SSH.2013.3.2-1 Grant agreement no. 613169.

9 Towards sustainable practices

A practice-theoretical case study of a cohousing project

Michaela Leitner and Beate Littig

1 Introduction: cohousing as a transformative niche?

Niches of socio-ecological transformation have gained attention in both scientific and public debates (Schellnhuber *et al.* 2011; Hargreaves *et al.* 2013). Innovative social experiments are perceived as lighthouses or pioneers of change, which could foster learning processes and might disseminate into the wider society (Moulaert *et al.* 2005; Haxeltine *et al.* 2013). Based on a case study we scrutinise the innovative and transformative potential and limits of such a pioneering social experiment, namely a new cohousing project in Vienna. We discuss in how far this kind of a niche experiment can be a space of learning and a laboratory of experimenting with more sustainable modes of living.

A cohousing project usually consists of private, single-household residences in an apartment building or single family houses in a housing estate and a variety of communal facilities like shared kitchens, play areas, open spaces and leisure facilities. The intentional community plans, manages and owns the building or estate and performs practices like cooking, eating, childcare, gardening and so on at least partly on a communal basis. The principles of cohousing are innovative and experimental in several aspects (McCamant and Durrett 1994, 38–58). The residents are involved in extensive participatory processes regarding the planning and running of the project. Furthermore, the overall architecture and infrastructure of the building promotes community life.

In a broader perspective, cohousing projects seek to address uncertainties, risks and constraints of (post-)modern societies. They aim to establish emancipatory ways of life by blurring the boundaries between the private and the public in favour of commonly shared and thus more sustainable facilities and practices (Grundmann 2011). Cohousing projects are experiments which endeavour to bring about lasting changes in behaviour by intentionally shaping the way people live, in this case by creating a new material infrastructure and promoting community-based forms of everyday practices. Consciously designed settings like cohousing projects can facilitate or promote new forms of work (e.g. home office or living and working under one roof), new forms of organising everyday life (e.g. collective organisation of housework tasks previously handled individually) and civic involvement. Such a reorganisation of work and the conduct of everyday life can also have gender-specific implications, since it means that informal or unpaid work frequently done by women can potentially be organised and distributed differently (Jurczyk *et al.* 2016). Furthermore, in comparison to individual forms of living, the social setting facilitates the adoption of environmentally friendlier practices (e.g. through the availability of readily accessible community facilities).

The case study[1] of a Viennese cohousing project (Wohnprojekt Wien) presented in this chapter is guided by the theory of social practices regarding data collection and analysis (Jonas and Littig 2015; Shove *et al.* 2012). It examines practices of sustainable living and working before and after the move-in of project members by analysing which elements of practices have changed, how and why they changed and whether practices became more sustainable. It thereby seeks to provide answers to the question whether and how practices can be lastingly transformed in a consciously designed and well-considered setting.

From a practice-theory oriented perspective, everyday practices cannot be classified as consumption practices. Instead, the usage of things (and bodies) is seen as a constitutive and necessary element of practices (Warde 2005). Thus, practices are (via their boundedness to materiality) relevant with regard to (ecological) sustainability. Consumption encompasses a broad range of practices, such as perceiving, acquiring, using and disposing of marketed and non-marketed entities (Jonas and Littig 2015).[2] Arguably, a cohousing project offers more sustainable (ways of utilising) material elements by creating new social and material (infra-) structures like shared laundry facilities; a food cooperative with organic and regional food; communal cooking of vegetarian food; car sharing; the sharing, giving away, lending and collective acquisition of things and the discussion, reflection and dissemination of knowledge regarding sustainable living. Research has shown that sustainable lifestyles are not consistent, but a summary of sustainable and non-sustainable behaviour and are usually based on alliances of motives: thus ecological motives exist beside others (Littig 1995; Barr *et al.* 2011).

Social innovation as a part of transformative social change can be considered as a new combination of practices or elements of these practices (Howaldt and Kopp 2012; Jonas in this volume). They involve new ways of doing, organising, knowing and framing and are socially transformative when challenging, altering or replacing dominant institutions (Pel and Bauler 2014). As we will demonstrate, all these characteristics apply to ecologically oriented cohousing projects like our case study, where certain elements of sustainability-related practices in areas such as nutrition, mobility, cooking, doing the laundry and energy consumption and routines connected with the performances of these practices are redesigned. By describing the stability and alteration of these elements, the development of practices and therefore of social transformation can be identified (Shove *et al.* 2012; Butzin *et al.* 2014).

In the following sections we will present and discuss several key findings of our case study. The new organisation of everyday practices follows two interlinked goals: the collectivisation of formerly "individualised" practices and the sustainability-oriented modification of practices. Our empirical research shows that this innovative reorganisation of everyday life leads to changes of (certain elements of) practices and at the same time to the persistence of previous practices. In our discussion of selected empirical results, we explain how and why practices have changed, why they persist and under which conditions changes are more likely. In the conclusions, we will relate these results to the debate about the transformative potential of innovative socio-ecological experiments on the niche level. With regard to the investigated cohousing project we detect the main potential for transformation in the collective learning process that is stimulated by the initiative.

2 Description and design of the case study

The Wohnprojekt Wien represents a trend of alternative housing, which can be observed in many countries. Various cohousing projects have been established over the last decades, following different concepts of participation of (future) residents in the planning and use of the new dwellings.

The residents of Wohnprojekt Wien explicitly strive to achieve environmental sustainability in everyday practices and to adopt a new collective organisation of care and household tasks. Partly in reaction to the general difficulty of organising practices more sustainably within isolated households, they created social and material conditions which promote the performance of alternative practices. These new conditions can (potentially) result in saving costs as well as time spent on organisation and know-how, which conventional households would have to invest in isolation. Therefore, this cohousing project seeks to realise the "promotion and implementation of sustainable living, housing and working in an intercultural and intergenerational community".[3]

In 2015, the cohousing project consisted of 38 households (66 adults and 30 children). The building offers 700 m² of shared space: a community kitchen, event rooms, guest apartments, a sauna, a library, a children's playroom and a meditation room. Environmental considerations feature both in the construction of the building and in its use: the building was constructed according to low-energy specifications and features a photovoltaic system. Furthermore, there are complex waste separation facilities, a mobility sharing system, a large storage room for bicycles, a bicycle workshop, a food-cooperative, a community laundry and shared freezers.

Many practices that have been performed within conventional households before the move-in are now at least sometimes carried out collectively, such as cooking, shopping and childcare. Furthermore, mutual neighbourly help, community outings and many organised get-togethers take place. In order to interact more with the surrounding area and the wider society, project members started several initiatives to address various social issues (e.g. projects with asylum seekers, a café on the ground level, etc.).

To realise all these plans, ideas and projects, residents agreed that each adult member contributes a total of 11 hours of unpaid work per month to the community during the planning phase and beyond. This work is performed in working groups, each of which focuses on a particular field, such as public relations, sustainability, community, solidarity, legal affairs and finance. Important decisions are always taken using the sociocracy[4] method, rendering them more socially robust (Buck and Endenburg 1984).

The data of the case study were generated at two points in time: the first approximately one year before the move-in to the cohousing project that took place in December 2013 and the second approximately one year after the move-in. The study examined environmental and social sustainability aspects of everyday practices, with a special focus on unpaid care and community work. It did so by using a comprehensive multi-method design, investigating the CO_2eq emissions generated by such work and by analysing its duration, significance and gender-specific distribution as well as the reconcilability of unpaid with paid work (Littig and Leitner 2017). Sustainability-related practices of the (future) residents of Wohnprojekt Wien were studied in central fields of everyday life: food consumption (cooking, eating behaviour, consumption and procurement), childcare, waste separation, doing the laundry, community-related work for the cohousing project, mobility, energy saving/energy use as well as activities with and support for neighbours.

To determine if these practices were performed in a more environmentally sustainable manner in the cohousing project, data regarding CO_2eq emissions generated by the residents before and after the move-in through their energy consumption, mobility and eating practices were collected and compared. The calculation of the emissions was carried out based on a life-cycle assessment (LCA) in line with IPCC guidelines (IPCC 2006; Solomon et al. 2007).[5] Changes in the area of social sustainability were analysed regarding gender-specific work distribution, support for and revaluation of unpaid work, its coordination with other practices (e.g. of paid work) and community solidarity based on a time-use study and on qualitative data (cf. Littig 2001, 2016; HBS 2001). The quantitative data regarding time use and CO_2eq emissions were collected by a self-observation list in which adult residents documented everyday practices performed during seven days and a subsequent online questionnaire. Additionally, a database of the cohousing project that keeps record of the time spent on community work by all residents was analysed. Of all households, 61 per cent which were present at the time of the second survey (38) took the quantitative pre- and post-survey. Eighteen adults living in twelve households were interviewed extensively before and after the move-in and were asked to make photos and a spoken digital diary documenting everyday practices for two days. Furthermore, participatory observation at meetings of the cohousing project, the analysis of selected minutes of such meetings and two group discussions regarding the perception of work took place.

3 Selected results: transformed practices in the Wohnprojekt

The collectivisation and sustainability-oriented design of practices, modifying some of their constituent elements and their social setting, create new relationships between actors and elements of practices. Especially the modified socio-material conditions, including shared spaces, facilitate more sustainable behaviour. In conventional, individual households particularly, the socio-material infrastructure can usually only be changed with considerable effort, which often encourages and reproduces non-sustainable performances of practices (Whitford 2002).

Despite these profound modifications, the quantitative data showed significant differences only in some aspects. Regarding the duration of examined practices, the pre–post comparison shows that the average duration of neighbourly contact increased significantly by seven times. Regular participants of communal meals cooked and bought food less frequently and spent less time on cooking than before the move-in. The gender-specific division of care and community work had not changed significantly.

Respondents reduced their CO_2eq emissions by 1.24 kg on average per person, per day, or 17 per cent – which does not present a statistically significant decline. Emissions emerging from energy consumption (electricity and heating of flats) were reduced by 28 per cent due to a higher consumption of green energy and the energy efficiency of the building. Emissions of mobility sank, not statistically significant, by 17 per cent, mostly due to a reduction in distances travelled by car. However, a threefold increase in air travel counteracted this effect, while the total amount remained below the Austrian average. CO_2eq emissions of food consumption increased by statistically insignificant 22 per cent. However, these emissions were already before as well as after the move-in more than half as low as the Austrian average.

Overall, the quantitative results indicate that the collectivisation of practices did not lead to time savings regarding their performance and a more equal distribution of care work between men and women. Furthermore, while reductions of emissions from energy consumption and mobility took place, overall CO_2eq emissions could not be significantly reduced by collectivisation.

At the same time, the quantitative results, only measuring time, frequencies and emissions of practices, fail to capture the many changes interviewees described with respect to their everyday lives. The performances of practices and some of their elements changed substantially regarding (a) aspects of the social setting within which everyday practices are performed, (b) the interaction with material objects and infrastructures, (c) the type of materials used as well as (d) know-how and meaning-related elements of different practices. For example, interviewees stated that their experience of neighbourhood has radically changed, now offering emotional and practical support and feelings of belonging and trust. This new social setting also influences the performances of practices of childcare and communal work. But not only meaning-related elements of practices, also several know-how-related and material elements changed within the new social setting. Regarding the areas of food provision, mobility, laundry washing and energy use, several factors were mentioned that facilitate a more sustainable way of living: material and social structures (waste room, food-cooperative, laundry room, low-energy house), the exchange of knowledge and items among residents and a reduction of necessary mobility and (administrative) effort.

4 Reasons for the persistence of practices

The few statistically significant results regarding ecological sustainability can be explained by various factors, for example a high variance between households, the fact that the behaviour of respondents was already more sustainable compared to the average Austrian population before the move-in (e.g. with respect to car ownership or meat consumption) and the fact that CO_2eq emissions cover just one specific aspect of ecological sustainability (e.g. savings concerning resource consumption were not investigated, but might have occurred due to the collective usage of facilities and objects).

Other explanations are equally relevant and concern the difficulty to coordinate new, partially collectivised performances of practices with "old" practices performed within the households. By analysing this difficulty, we aim to shed light on the question why many everyday practices of the residents seem to be rather resistent to change.

The aspired sustainability-oriented practices are mostly collectively organised and include taking part in common lunches or dinners, in the food-cooperative, in the mobility sharing scheme, using the laundry and communal work. To integrate these new practices into everyday life, new routines have to be established, which requires time, motivation, additional effort and learning processes. Therefore, the data represent only a snapshot of an ongoing process. The performance of these collectivised practices depends on commonly shared schedules and places. While many practices in the old living arrangements (like driving a car, shopping for food or cooking) were spatially and temporally flexible, flexibility decreases in the case of collectivised practices that rely on shared mobility, food provisioning or cooking schemes.

By the same token, emotionally and temporally dominant practices of paid work or childcare also require specific and individualised schedules and whereabouts and sometimes also a lot of temporal flexibility. Therefore, they are often not easily compatible with the requirements of the new, collective practices, which can prevent the recruitment of new practitioners. For example, schedules of paid work, school, kindergarten and children's leisure activities can collide with the schedules of communal meals or communal work (especially meetings in the evening).

The alignment of individuals with collective rhythms is – due to individualisation, the differentiation of lifestyles, flexibilisation of employment and the resulting absence of collective life rhythms of large population groups – a challenge that needs to be faced individually (Southerton 2003). The participation in a cohousing project takes place voluntarily, which implies an absence of social coercion to coordinate the different rhythms – yet many inhabitants try to structure their everyday lives according to the collective rhythms of the Wohnprojekt. Although many residents frequent various places in their everyday lives, the need for mobility in general is reduced, since the cohousing project offers different activities and facilities (library, sauna, seminar rooms) for which residents of conventional housing would have to leave the house. The extent to which residents achieve an integration of new practice performances into their everyday lives varies with different personal and employment-related circumstances, priorities and a willingness to change routines.

It is worth noting that collective usage requires "usage rules", which also have to be integrated into individual routines (e.g. rules for using the kitchen, laundry, car-sharing and the garbage room). When performing practices individually, rules can be more widely interpreted or can remain implicit, whereas when performing them collectively, rules are binding for all users, and therefore must be explicitly defined and formulated. One example is the replacement of kitchen utensils in their intended places in the communal kitchen to enable other users to find them, which is not equally necessary in the case of private cooking. Even if the integration of the rules into the individual routines succeeds, they must be interpreted in similar ways, which does not happen automatically and sometimes leads to conflicts or discussions. A challenge in this context is that there is no official authority (such as a property management) to sanction a violation of the rules. Problems with collective usage are discussed in the responsible working group and (a lack of) compliance is indicated to all inhabitants. Explicit and internalised social control, which is also present in conventional neighbourhoods, but due to the much closer relationships among residents more comprehensive in cohousing projects, seems essential for the compliance with usage rules.

Evidently, the collective usage of shared things like cars or washing machines relies on the temporal coordination of individual and collective practices and on binding rules. Individual availability is reduced and less flexible, as usage usually has to be planned in advance and organisation takes time and requires new practices, such as registering in advance to use the laundry, the car or the food cooperative. During interviews, residents frequently mentioned organisation and coordination efforts vis-à-vis the flexibility everyday life demands as obstacles to participation in these collective schemes. Interestingly, potential problems were in some cases more often mentioned by non-users than by actual users. A reason for this might be the anticipated necessary effort for changing routines and learning new habits, accompanied by worries about reduced flexibility. Another explanation might be the attempt to reduce cognitive dissonance triggered by an engagement in a less sustainable behaviour (Littig 1995).

5 Indications of enabling factors to change practices

Whereas the limiting factors described above help to explain the small amount of significant quantitative results regarding CO_2eq emissions, the significant ones give indications of factors or combinations of factors that presumably contribute to changes of practices.

One of these enabling factors is the new material infrastructure, for instance the common laundry room or the room of the food cooperative. Without them, a collective performance of laundering and food provision would be impossible.

The interplay of these material factors with personal motives led to an acceptance of these collective facilities by a significant amount of inhabitants. 55 per cent of the responding households used the laundry in the cohousing project, of which 70 per cent used it at least one to three times a month. Prior to the move-in, only 25 per cent of the households had access to or used shared laundry facilities. The food-cooperative was, despite its short running time at the time of our investigation, already used by half of the respondents (even though its usage did not lead to significant savings in time or CO_2eq emissions). In addition to creating the physical infrastructure, shorter distances for food supply and low membership requirements (compared to other food cooperatives) facilitated participation in this initiative.

The distinct rise in consumption of green electricity from 33 per cent to 90 per cent of the responding households also led to a significant reduction of the CO_2eq emissions resultant from electricity consumption. This major change can be explained by the easy knowledge exchange between the residents and the reduced effort to switch the supplier, including a quantity discount. In addition to this, the move to a new apartment created favourable conditions for contracting a new supplier.

Another significant result was delivered by the increased energy efficiency of combined refrigerator–freezers in the new homes of the households. (This holds also true for dish washers, ovens and stoves, but not significantly.) In this case a combination of several factors is likely: the move to a non-furnished apartment, which necessitated the new acquisition of many devices, the neighbourly dissemination of knowledge about energy-efficient appliances in the Wohnprojekt and the fact that today new devices require higher energy efficiency rates than older ones.

The most significant changes regarding the new living situation in comparison to the previous ones relate to the intense interaction in the neighbourhood. Neighbourly talks several times a week had become usual, while it was an exception before: before the move-in, 12 per cent of all respondents had contact with their neighbours several times a week or daily; after the move-in, all respondents reported this frequency. The average time spent with neighbours in the last seven days rose from 0.6 hours to 4.3 hours. The social setting of the neighbourhood has changed fundamentally in comparison to the old neighbourhoods and promotes common activities through similarities with and a high level of information about neighbours as well as material and social structures like common facilities and regular meetings.

Despite several changes that partly resulted in more sustainable performances of practices, the data also indicate rebound-effects or at least non-sustainable effects of the new living arrangements, for example in the areas of flying or heating. The pre- and post-analyses show a significant rise in private short distance flights (while the number of long distance flights stayed approximately the same): 27 per cent of the respondents used an aeroplane for short distance flights in 2012 compared to 64 per cent in 2014, the average number of flights has risen from 0.5 per year to 2. Accordingly, the CO_2eq emissions caused by flights have risen significantly. There may be various explanations for this development: the work-intensive time before the move-in and financial burdens due to the move-in might have led many to renounce trips by plane. However, a rebound-effect cannot be excluded: the many efforts of the Wohnprojekt members to enable a more sustainable life could have led to a reduction of ecological concerns and implicitly promoted individual flying. Another rebound-effect that is (also) produced by the new material infrastructure is the low air humidity common in low energy houses that is seen as negatively affecting well-being and health by many inhabitants. This has led to the purchase of air humidifiers that run in some flats for the whole day. Subjective well-being and health are, not surprisingly, prioritised over environmental protection.

The significant changes described indicate an interplay of material, social, financial or organisational elements, contexts and relations of practices or concern the changing social setting and living situation. Furthermore, alliances of different behavioural motives were an important factor for residents to change (elements) of their practices (Littig 1995). Motives regarding environmental protection exist alongside other, sometimes subjectively far more important, ones when it comes to the adoption of more sustainable or the rejection of less sustainable performances of practices by "carriers".

During interviews, many examples of convenient alliances of environmental with other motives were mentioned. For example concerning mobility, the choice for more sustainable or the rejection of less sustainable means of transport is not primarily based on environmental considerations: in addition, convenience, flexibility, healthiness, speed, savings in effort and money, and the experience, competence and affinity associated with different modes of travel are stated as relevant motives. The food-cooperative in the Wohnprojekt is also not always primarily used because of sustainability-related reasons. A general criticism of urban anonymity and the societal organisation of (over-)consumption (represented by anonymous supermarkets), the wish for an alternative shopping experience, healthy and tasty food, easy access to organic food and presumably the milieu- and value-specific similarities of the consumers have been found to be important reasons to choose this mode of food-supply. Communal cooking and dining are highly valued because of time savings and the feeling of belonging to a community associated with these practices. The laundry is used because of saving costs and space in the flat. Home heating temperature is primarily reduced because of health- and cost-related reasons. Alliances of motives also influenced the general decision to take part in the cohousing project. Sustainability issues mattered not for all participants in the same way and were not always decisive for the decision to join, but all respondents indicated the wish for a more communal life.

6 Ambivalences between the niche and socio-ecological transformation

Life in the Wohnprojekt can be interpreted as a voluntary attempt to transform individual lifestyles towards sustainability without being forced by external pressure or constraints. This niche form of living is, as outlined above, socially innovative and at the same time enables the actors to handle the material elements of practices in a more sustainable way. The problems that arise with the coordination of collectivised practices within the intentional community on the one hand and with practices performed within individual households on the other hand indicate a contradiction that underlies all cohousing projects: the collectivisation of personal lifestyles under conditions of modern individualisation and flexibility (Grundmann 2011).

In order for the Wohnprojekt to succeed as a community, participants with similar value orientations, high levels of reflexivity regarding their conduct of life, specific competencies (e.g. communicative skills, computer skills and capability of detailed planning) and willingness to dedicate much time to the communal work as well as to the change of individual routines are essential preconditions. In addition, the collective requires homogeneity of its members in respect to the compliance with rules and norms of collective practices. Therefore, the members of the Wohnprojekt form a community of attitudes (*Gesinnungsgemeinschaft*) based on similar value orientations mainly regarding living in the community, sustainability and a leftist-liberal political worldview. This homogeneity renders feelings of communality (*Gemeinschaft*), security, inclusion, acceptance and mutual trust possible, which are a prerequisite to reorganise formerly individual and private performances of practices collectively. Furthermore, the communal life influences the conduct of everyday lives of the inhabitants in various ways: regarding neighbourly activities and communal work, but also other everyday practices (depending on the degree the inhabitants accept their collectivised alternatives). Even if the heterogeneity of Wohnprojekt members in terms of life phases or professional backgrounds is valued, a high level of social homogeneity is necessary to make the community work. This homogeneity was achieved by the strict member selection process of the Wohnprojekt, which also leads to a social closure of the community.

The willingness to, at least partially, reorganise life in a collective context seems to be contradictory to a self-concept of many inhabitants that is shaped by individualistic norms: orthodoxies are rejected, diversity is highly valued and inhabitants are expected to act more sustainably based on insight instead of prescription. Many members of the project aim for self-actualisation, which becomes evident in the willingness to consequently reflect about their doings and sayings and to make new learning experiences. However, the fact that self-actualisation can never be fully achieved in a collective framework is noticed and considered at least by some participants of our study. According to one respondent, members of the Wohnprojekt have to "learn that not everyone will be able to self-actualise oneself. If everyone does this, then we are single, atomised individuals that are not joining forces." Another manifestation of the influence of modernist individualisation processes is the reflexive, highly rationalised and self-organised mode of the residents' communal work (Jurczyk *et al.* 2016). The tension between individualistic values and the necessities arising from (a desired) collectivity and the difficulty of realising these values in a partly de-individualised and collective context become visible in the narratives of the inhabitants.

By participating in the Wohnprojekt, inhabitants voluntarily accept the influence of a collective on the performance of practices that were formerly only conducted within individual households. Regarding the area of knowledge transfer, this influence is explicitly desired (e.g. sustainability-related knowledge that can become the basis of individual decisions), since it diminishes the burden of organising everyday life in a more sustainable way. The necessity of shaping (*Gestaltungszwang*) one's own life that came along with modernist individualisation processes (Beck *et al.* 1994) and the wish to be unburdened by the (partly) collective organisation of life makes the Wohnprojekt attractive for its members. The deliberate "de-individualisation" of their personal life is a means to reduce the impositions of reflexive modernisation (ibid.), like the need of its constant personal design, urban anonymity and the individualisation of life risks.

The question of whether cohousing projects contribute to societal transformation is not easy to answer based on the results of a case study. As outlined, these social experiments react to negatively perceived effects of reflexive modernisation and are, at the same time, a consequence of these developments. Cohousing residents actively oppose unsustainable, isolated, consumeristic and solely employment-oriented ways of life, which are dominant in modern society. The realisation of alternative lifestyles requires great efforts to survive within opposing dominant practices and socio-material infrastructures.

The ambivalences that we found regarding the establishment of alternative lifestyles in a niche can be traced back to the fact that it is impossible to fully encapsulate oneself from dominant societal structures and practices like paid work and the gender specific division of labour: they still shape the residents' lives. Niches are always exposed to societal dynamics "outside" of them – complete separation from them is impossible (Jonas 2017, in this volume). Hence, the members of the project have to deal with different dynamics they can barely influence and that impair their efforts regarding a more sustainable organisation of everyday life.

As Brand (2016) argues, incremental innovations like cohousing projects could spread further but would still only be accessible for a very small portion of the world population. As our research shows, various prerequisites, including motivation, skills, reflexive capabilities, knowledge and financial resources, are necessary to participate in a cohousing project. Additionally, its establishment requires particular legal, cultural and political conditions. Therefore, the necessary, more comprehensive social-ecological transformation is not possible without a radical change of economic and political institutions and structures and of the entire relationship between society and nature (Barth *et al.* 2016). The main role of niche experiments of socio-ecological transformation is to act as concrete utopias, as spaces of learning and experimenting with alternative and more sustainable modes of living. In this sense, they can be seen as "laboratories" of transformation, real life experiments, which contribute to the toolkit of societal innovation.

Notes

1 Supported by the Anniversary Fund of the Österreichische Nationalbank (project no. 15031).
2 (Consumptive) practices bring about effects of social distinction (Bourdieu 1987; Jonas et al. 2014).
3 Citations taken from the cohousing project homepage: www.wohnprojekt-wien.at (accessed 14 March 2017; translated by the authors).
4 "Sociocracy" is used to govern and take decisions in groups of equal individuals. Its core principles foresee that a decision can only be taken when none of the members of the group has any justified, strong objections and when all members have been involved in the decision-making process.
5 For this purpose project partner FiBL (Austrian Research Institute of Organic Agriculture) developed an environment assessment model, which is closely based on international environmental accounting guidelines.

References

Barr, S., Shaw, G., and Coles, T. (2011) "Sustainable lifestyles: sites, practices and policy" *Environment and Planning* 43: 3011–3029.

Barth, T., Jochum, G., and Littig, B. (2016) *Nachhaltige Arbeit: Soziologische Beiträge zur Neubestimmung der gesellschaftlichen Naturverhältnisse* Campus: Frankfurt a. M.

Beck, U., Giddens, A., and Lash, S. (1994) *Reflexive modernization: politics, tradition and aesthetics in the modern social order* Stanford University Press: Stanford, CA.

Bourdieu, P. (1987) *Die feinen Unterschiede: Kritik der gesellschaftlichen Urteilskraft* Suhrkamp: Frankfurt a. M.

Brand, U. (2016) "'Transformation' as a new critical orthodoxy: the strategic use of the term 'transformation' does not prevent multiple crises" *GAIA – Ecological Perspectives for Science and Society* 25: 23–27.

Buck, J., and Endenburg, G. (1984) *The creative forces of self-organization* Sociocratic Center: Rotterdam.

Butzin, A., Davis, A., Domanski, D., Dhondt, S., Howaldt, J., Kaletka, C., and Kesselring, A. (2014) *Theoretical approaches to social innovation: a critical literature review* SI-Drive: Dortmund.

Grundmann, M. (2011) "Lebensführungspraktiken in intentionalen Gemeinschaften" in Hahn, K., and Koppetsch, C. (eds) *Soziologie des Privaten* VS Verlag für Sozialwissenschaften: Wiesbaden, 275–302.

Haxeltine, A., Wittmayer, J.M., and Flor, A. (2013) "Transformative social innovations: a sustainability transition perspective on social innovation" (paper presented at NESTA Conference Social Frontiers: The Next Edge of Social Science Research, London), www.scribd.com/doc/191799102/Transformative-social-innovations-A-sustainability-transition-perspective-on-social-innovation.

Hargreaves, T., Longhurst, N., and Seyfang, G. (2013) "Up, down, round and round: connecting regimes and practices in innovation for sustainability" *Environment and Planning* 45: 402–420.

HBS (Hans Böckler Stiftung) (2001) *Pathways to a sustainable future: results from the work and employment interdisciplinary project* Setzkasten: Düsseldorf.

Howaldt, J. and Kopp, R. (2012) "Shaping social innovation by social research" in Franz, H.W., Hochgerner, J., and Howaldt, J. (eds) *Challenge social innovation: potentials for business, social entrepreneurship, welfare and civil society* Springer: Berlin and Heidelberg, 43–56.

IPCC (Intergovernmental Panel on Climate Change) (2006) *Guidelines for national greenhouse gas inventories* IGES: Hayama, Kanagawa.

Jonas, M. (2017) "Transition or transformation of societal practices and orders?" in Jonas, M., and Littig, B. (eds) *Praxeological political analysis* Routledge: London, 116–133.

Jonas, M., and Littig, B. (2015) "Sustainable practices" in Wright, J. (ed.) *The international encyclopedia of the social and behavioral science* Elsevier: Oxford, 834–838.

Jonas, M., Littig, B., and Penz, O. (2014) "Kaufen für eine bessere Welt? Das Beispiel Fairtrade" in *Österreichische Zeitschrift für Politikwissenschaft* 1/2014: 91–109.

Jurczyk, K., Voß, G., and Weihrich, M. (2016) "Conduct of everyday life in subject-oriented sociology: concept and empirical research" in Schraube, E., and Højholt, C. (eds) *Psychology and the conduct of everyday life* Routledge: New York, 34–64.

Littig, B, (1995) *Die Bedeutung von Umweltbewusstsein im Alltag. Oder: Was tun wir eigentlich, wenn wir umweltbewusst sind?* Peter-Lang-Verlag: Frankfurt a. M.

Littig, B. (2001) *Feminist perspectives on environment and society* Pearson Education, London.

Littig, B. (2016) "Nachhaltige Zukünfte von Arbeit? Geschlechterpolitische Betrachtungen" in Barth, T., Jochum, G., and Littig, B. (eds) *Nachhaltige Arbeit: Soziologische Beiträge zur Neubestimmung der gesellschaftlichen Naturverhältnisse* Campus: Frankfurt a. M., 75–97.

Littig, B., and Leitner, M. (2017) "Combining methods in practice oriented research: the case of sustainable cohousing" in Jonas, M., Littig, B., and Wroblewski, A. (eds) *Methodological reflections on practice oriented theories* Springer: New York, 161–176.

McCamant, K., and Durrett, C. (1994) *Cohousing: a contemporary approach to housing ourselves* Ten Speed Press: Berkeley, CA.

Moulaert, F., Martinelli, F., Syngedouw, E., and Gonzalez, S. (2005) "Towards alternative model(s) of local innovation" *Urban Studies* 42: 1969–1990.

Pel, B., and Bauler, T. (2014) "The institutionalization of social innovation: between transformation and capture" (TRANSIT working paper 2) TRANSIT: EU SSH.2013.3.2–1 Grant agreement no. 613169.

Schellnhuber, H.J., Messner, D., Leggewie, C., Leinfelder, R., Nakicenovic, N., Rahmstorf, S., and Schubert, R. (2011) *World in transition: a social contract for sustainability* German Advisory Council on Global Change WBGU: Berlin.

Shove, E., Pantzar, M., and Watson, M. (2012) *The dynamics of social practice: everyday life and how it changes* Sage: Los Angeles.

Solomon, S., Qin, D., Manning, M., Chen, Z., Marquis, M., Averyt, K., Tignor, M., and Miller, H. (2007) *IPCC climate change 2007: the physical science basis* Cambridge University Press: New York.

Southerton, D. (2003) "'Squeezing time': allocating practices, coordinating networks and scheduling society" *Time and Society* 12(1): 5–25.

Warde, A. (2005) "Consumption and theories of practice" *Journal of Consumer Culture* 5(2): 131–153.

Whitford, J. (2002) "Pragmatism and the untenable dualism of means and ends: why rational choice theory does not deserve pragmatic privilege" *Theory and Society* 31: 325–363.

10 The search for social innovations that are within ecological limits as well as more just

Edina Vadovics and Simon Milton

1 Introduction

Social innovation (SI) is not a new concept: it has a long history, and presently very important institutions, ideas and practices are the result of social innovation (e.g. fair trade and kindergartens). In recent years, SI has become an increasingly important topic of discussion about sustaining both the transition towards more sustainable lifestyles and, controversially, economic growth (e.g. Mulgan *et al.* 2007; Seyfang and Smith 2007; Seyfang and Haxeltine 2012; URBACT 2015). Due to this increasing popularity, SI is almost automatically considered to be a means of creating more sustainable practices, as a result of which the need for a more thorough analysis of SI-related initiatives has emerged (e.g. Demailly and Novel 2014; Gismondi *et al.* 2016; Sinclair 2014). In this chapter, we address this need and contribute to the dialogue about whether SI-related practices indeed lead to more sustainable lifestyles and forms of consumption: that is, lifestyles and consumption that respect ecological limits and are more just and equitable.

To accomplish this task, we directly address the social innovation–sustainable consumption–societal transformation nexus through an analysis of initiatives situated at this nexus. We identify the need for a framework which can be used in the assessment of the efficacy of organizations and initiatives located at this nexus, and propose one such analytical tool in an attempt to bridge this gap: the 'Convergence Mapping tool'. Conceptually, we also identify the need for more awareness-raising about the need for synthetic approaches that both tackle injustice and inequity and attempt to overcome environmental or resource-based challenges. The tool can also be seen as an educational and management device for this purpose.

We build on earlier work and research carried out in the CONVERGE project in which an international team of researchers and practitioners investigated initiatives that incorporated activities designed to promote equality and environmental sustainability. With regard to all other characteristics, the initiatives that were studied were very different: they include one-man projects, like No Impact Man, and community initiatives, like local exchange systems, transition towns, business ventures, faith groups, policy initiatives, and so on.

However, as the focus of this research team was to study how these very different initiatives were attempting to promote social equity and living within ecological limits, the need to develop a means of comparison emerged. 'Convergence Mapping' is the resulting tool, and this chapter describes how the tool was conceptualized and used, as well as how it can be used in the study of social innovation. While doing this, we also reflect on whether and how these examples and the efforts behind them could contribute to making transformative changes and increase social and environmental sustainability.

To illustrate how the mapping tool works, we have selected three of the sustainability initiatives that were studied in the CONVERGE project: a carbon reduction club from the UK, a transition-town initiative in Hungary, and a kitchen garden and fruit tree afforestation initiative in India. All of these initiatives we consider to be examples of social innovation in the sense that they meet social needs currently unmet or not sufficiently met by existing alternatives, and they create new social relationships or collaborations. We claim that 'they are innovations that are not only good for society but also enhance society's capacity to act' (BEPA 2011, 33; see also Jégou and Manzini 2008), or, in other words, they constitute a change in social relations involving new ways of doing, organizing, knowing, and framing (Haxeltine *et al.* 2016).

All three can also be considered sustainable consumption initiatives that subscribe to the notion of strong sustainable consumption which 'is based on the assumption that changes in consumption levels and patterns are necessary to achieve sustainable consumption. … and accepts the social embeddedness of consumption decisions' (Lorek and Fuchs 2013, 38). However, none of them focus solely on promoting one style of consumption, preferring, as we show below, to adopt a lifestyle and systems-based perspective.

In the following section, we first describe the conception of the Convergence Mapping system and include details about the methodology that was used. We then introduce specific examples of SI to show how the mapping tool can be used for analytical, visual representation, and communication purposes. Following this, we reflect on the innovation and transformational potential of the diverse initiatives. Finally, we conclude by providing suggestions about how the mapping tool can be used, and how it could be developed further.

2 Background to Convergence Mapping: the CONVERGE project and the concept of contraction and convergence

The aim of the CONVERGE project, funded by the European Union's 7th Framework Programme, was to 're-think globalization' by studying the implications of a 'convergence' approach to global development based on more equitable access to the life-support capacities of the planet and fair livelihoods within planetary boundaries through a transdisciplinary systems approach (Fortnam *et al.* 2010). Convergence advocates socio-ecological justice and calls for wealth, well-being, and consumption to converge across and within nations to a level that the biosphere can support (see arrow in Figure 10.1).

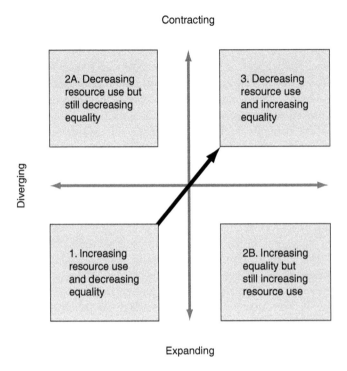

Figure 10.1 Schematic overview of the process of convergence.

Source: Roderick in Vadovics et al. 2012.

Although convergence has been a subject of study in economics literature since the mid-1980s, the concept of contraction and convergence (C&C™) from which the CONVERGE project originated comes from Aubrey Meyer and the Global Commons Institute (GCI). C&C™ is a global climate policy framework which was proposed to the UN in 1990 as one way to manage and reduce anthropogenic carbon dioxide through a burden-sharing approach (Meyer 2000), and has since been endorsed by various UN bodies and reports. It suggests combining a recognition of planetary limits with an equity approach, a principle that has been formally recognized in European Parliament resolutions (European Parliament 1998), is supported by numerous policy makers, academics, NGOs, and lay people, and was examined as an emissions allocation approach by the IPCC (IPCC 2007, 2013).

In the CONVERGE project we examined how the principles of the C&C™ framework for carbon emissions could be applied to other resources. Our objective was to link the scientifically validated need to reduce (i.e. to contract) resource use with a justice-based approach to apportioning the responsibility for doing so (to converge) and to identify examples from all fields of life that already seek to do this in practice (Vadovics *et al.* 2012). Here, we take this work a step further and connect it to social innovation. We look at some initiatives studied in the CONVERGE project as examples of social innovation. In this context innovation partly refers to the fact that the studied initiatives are seeking to follow the principles of justice and equity while simultaneously fostering the idea of living within ecological limits, albeit these goals are in many cases dealt with separately.

In this chapter and in our work related to Convergence Mapping, we use the terms 'limits/contraction' and 'equity/convergence' in the following way:

- 'Limits/contraction' is used to mean progress, development, or movement towards ensuring that resources, ecosystem, and planetary limits (or 'boundaries') are observed and respected.
- 'Equity/convergence' is used to mean progress, development, or movement towards the more equal sharing of both the benefits (e.g. food, fuel, clean air) and burdens (e.g. responsibilities to reduce carbon dioxide emissions, adverse impacts) of resource use. It therefore relates to normative concepts such as justice and rights.

'Convergence' – in the term 'Convergence Mapping' – is also used to refer to 'equity within planetary limits' or simultaneous 'contraction and convergence'.[1]

3 The methodology behind Convergence Mapping

The Convergence Mapping tool was constructed after identifying, through literature research and empirical methods, different initiatives (communities, municipalities, policies, companies, etc.) which appeared to be engaging in convergence-type activities (i.e. were making attempts to address resource limits, were addressing the issue of how Earth's biocapacity is shared, or were seeking to promote justice and equity).

During the four-step initiative selection and analytical process, the research team gathered an initial list of about 200 initiatives (through a process of brainstorming and a review of general sustainability and development literature) which were shortlisted to 51 initiatives following a shallow research process and progressed to the detailed study of 28 initiatives. The final selection process involved an evaluation employing three main criteria: (1) how the initiatives addressed the issue of limits/contraction, (2) how they addressed equity/convergence, and (3) their scale and potential impact. Detailed data about the 28 initiatives was collected between September 2010 and July 2012 using a semi-structured survey format and a diversity of investigative techniques including field work, unstructured and semi-structured interviews, and document reviews (see more detail in Vadovics *et al.* 2012).

The Convergence Mapping tool developed to illustrate the convergence features of these initiatives uses an ascending five-item scale (see Annex for details) which can be used to quantify activity in the areas of limits/contraction and equity/convergence. The five-item scale for equity/convergence built on work by Agyeman about 'just sustainability' (2005) as well as work by Roderick and Jones (2008). The limits/contraction scale was created based on the authors' earlier work (Vadovics 2009) and a literature review. The appraisals of initiatives are necessarily subjective but nonetheless illustrative of how different initiatives address ecological limits and equity-related issues.

The outcomes of Convergence Mapping – the 'convergence map' of the relevant initiatives, along with a text detailing the analytical process and findings – were shown to initiative representatives who were invited to comment on them. Based on these comments the convergence maps were amended in a few cases, but no substantial changes were required.

4 Results of Convergence Mapping

Even though the initiatives we researched are very diverse in terms of type and goal, they can be clearly located in the top right-hand quadrant of Figure 10.1 when plotted using the two scales, and thus are useful illustrations of the concept, as well as practice, of convergence or 'equity within limits'. Below we briefly introduce three of the initiatives.[2]

4.1 *Fownhope Carbon Reduction Action Group (CRAG)*

Fownhope CRAG is a voluntary, grassroots carbon rationing action group (CRAG)[3] set up in 2007 in the village of Fownhope, UK, with the primary goal of reducing the carbon footprint of its members (Figure 10.3 shows CRAG members at a group meeting). Fownhope CRAG was also part of the at-the-time very active wider CRAG network. Members support the goal of reducing their personal carbon footprints to a sustainable and equitable level (Fawcett *et al.* 2007; Howell 2012; Hielscher 2013).

In time, the original focus on carbon reduction of Fownhope CRAG widened in scope, and its members became involved in a number of related projects such as providing locally sourced alternative energy, decreasing food miles, and promoting other sustainability goals.

Convergence elements

The primary aim of the initiative is to contract the carbon footprint of its members in all areas of household consumption, not only those related directly to energy. However, members of the CRAG also 'support each other in reducing those footprints, sharing skills and knowledge in lower carbon living and promoting awareness and practical action in the wider community'.[4] Practical activities they have been involved in include planting trees around the village of Fownhope, participating in local sustainable energy events and actively promoting the use of renewable energy.

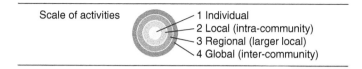

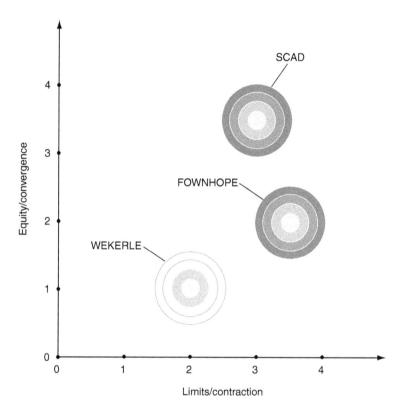

Figure 10.2 Placement of the three initiatives on the convergence map.
Source: GreenDependent.

CRAGs were started because people realized that carbon emissions need to be contracted in the richer parts of the world, as well as converged (or made more equitable) worldwide. CRAG members urge governments to adopt a universal and equitable framework for achieving this goal, while, in CRAGs, individuals implement this approach at a community level. In local groups, members support one another to reduce carbon footprints towards a sustainable and equitable level, as well as measure progress against carbon allowances.

The desire to adhere to the principles of contraction and convergence are evident in the way Fownhope CRAG operates, as well as in the activities its

Figure 10.3 Members of Fownhope CRAG at a meeting.
Source: Fownhope CRAG.

members are engaged in. Group decision-making is participatory, and group members also participate in local community events and activities for the purpose of sharing knowledge and information. Finally, members of the CRAG have voluntarily supported a tree-planting project in the Gambia to combat climate change-induced desertification that also produces a renewable form of heating oil. Engagement in this planting project, although later reconsidered by members, illustrates how responsible citizens in a rich country can support contraction efforts through voluntarily supporting communities in poorer countries. It also shows how equity may be promoted through offering voluntary support for environmentally appropriate projects which have additional socio-economic benefits.

4.2 Climate-Friendly Wekerle (Transition Wekerle)

The Climate-Friendly Wekerle initiative, located in a Budapest residential area called the Wekerle estate, is the first transition initiative in Hungary. The initiative was started by a group from the largest local NGO (Wekerle Társaskör Egyesület). Their aim is to inspire local residents to shift towards a more sustainable way of living. They seek to build on local resources, needs, and ideas while adapting the transition model to their ambitions.

The long-term objective of this initiative is to reduce the food and energy dependency of the Wekerle estate in various ways: for example, by setting up infrastructure for community composting, an organic food-box scheme, 'edible gardens', and a local food market. Members also seek to localize services, reduce waste, support direct trade with nearby producers (within a 50 km radius), and promote cycling and modes of community transport. The whole process is designed to be realized with the cooperation of the local community, based on active citizen participation in decision-making (Figure 10.4 shows residents at a participatory consultation meeting about waste collection on the estate).

Convergence elements

The long-term aim of Climate-Friendly Wekerle is to reduce consumption and environmental impact. At the time of the research, members were mostly

Figure 10.4 Climate-Friendly Wekerle participatory consultation about selective waste collection.

Source: Climate-Friendly Transition.

engaged in carbon-footprint reduction initiatives such as their own energy brigades programme which helps people insulate their homes. Although a lot of effort has been made towards reduction, concrete reduction targets have not been established.

The group experiments with the techniques of participatory democracy, operates with a low level of hierarchy, and all members have an equal say in discussions over strategic and operational issues. The core group also initiated community planning events in the estate to involve local residents in the renewal and design of public spaces.

The overall aim of the initiative is to improve local resilience and self-sufficiency, which includes strengthening the connection between producers and consumers. Thus, the initiative has an influence at the individual, local and regional level. At the time of the study, apart from the recognition of global challenges (climate change and peak oil), there was no active focus on global equity or environmental justice issues.

4.3 SCAD Kitchen Gardens and Fruit Tree Afforestation

SCAD (Social Change and Development) is a non-profit organization based in Tamil Nadu, India. Their mission is to support people and communities to lift them out of poverty. SCAD, with input from UNCCD and European partners, set out to find a sustainable way of addressing these challenges and decided upon the establishment of organic kitchen gardens and the planting of fruit trees (see Figure 10.5), both with the involvement of the local community. Both of these programmes started in 2008 and have been successful at fighting the effects of climate change, as well as improving the health and nutrition of rural communities. SCAD trains villagers – with the help of women's self-help groups – about organic vegetable growing and composting. Apart from gardening, people also learn how to conserve their resources through harvesting and using grey water.

Convergence elements

In this initiative, there is explicit recognition of ecosystem limits, and a very clear effort to actively protect and maintain resources. SCAD's organic kitchen gardens and tree-planting projects are an excellent example of a poor yet developing region choosing to take a sustainable path of development. SCAD works towards justice and equity at individual, local, and regional levels through ensuring that the basic needs of people and communities are met. Using a participatory approach, both kitchen gardens and the planting of local trees can help to lift people out of poverty over the long term and increase the resilience and self-sufficiency of communities.

SCAD uses indicators to measure the success of their activities. Examples include the income earned from kitchen gardens, the minimum amount of vegetables consumed by individuals, number of trees planted, amount of CO_2

Figure 10.5 SCAD Kitchen Gardens and Fruit Tree Afforestation initiative tree
        planting.
Source: SCAD.

sequestered, and the extent to which food miles are reduced through the establishment of kitchen gardens.

5 Discussion

5.1 Innovation and the transformative potential of the three initiatives

As already suggested in Section 2, we consider the initiatives introduced here to be
innovative because they explicitly focus on issues related to both living within ecological limits and promoting equity and because they connect these two goals in
various ways. Based on the Convergence Mapping tool analysis (see Figure 10.2),
the most innovative example in this regard at the time of research is the SCAD
kitchen gardens and fruit-tree afforestation initiative. Fownhope CRAG is less
innovative in terms of its attempts to address equity concerns, but slightly more
innovative as concerns supporting ways of living within planetary limits, mainly
because it employs concrete reduction targets. At the time of data collection, we
found Climate-Friendly Wekerle to be the least innovative initiative in this regard.

In addition to this, all three initiatives help meet social needs that are currently not satisfied and by doing so enhance society's capacity to act through creating new ways of doing, organizing, knowing, and/or framing. Below, we provide a summary of how the three initiatives accomplish these goals. However, a more thorough analysis could be carried out following the methodology used by McFarland and Wittmayer (in this volume).

Fownhope CRAG

Faced with a lack of ambitious government, shared societal objectives and concrete action to prevent runaway climate change and the lack of active involvement of citizens in creating and working towards such objectives, Fownhope CRAG shows how a group of concerned citizens can develop and adopt clear objectives and steps for action.

Members of Fownhope CRAG have voluntarily agreed to contract their carbon footprints to a level that is considered both environmentally sustainable and just, based on available scientific information. They have also developed a simple tool that allows them to monitor their footprints. Thus, they have clear reduction targets and by calculating where they stand in relation to these targets have contributed to creating new ways of doing and knowing: this includes new types of accounting and incentivising structures that help households try to live within ecological limits. Due to their recognition of potential limits to individual and household level effort and by relying on self-organized participative processes, they have also managed to move towards action at the community and regional level. Furthermore, they have even experimented with taking more global responsibility for their carbon footprints through supporting climate adaptation in a developing country.[5]

The innovation potential of CRAGs and the lessons that can be learnt from their small group-based attempts at voluntary carbon accounting and reduction have been studied by several authors, especially in terms of the implications for the introduction of policies for personal carbon trading (Fawcett 2010; Howell 2012). This provides an example of how grassroots, citizen-led social innovation can help test and formulate new policies, as well as more sustainable lifestyle choices and consumption patterns. It also hints at the yet unexploited role of such initiatives in policy-making, suggesting how important social innovation will be in the transformative change towards greater sustainability.

Transition Wekerle

At the moment, governmental and societal strategies that help prepare for life without fossil fuels on a planet with different climatic conditions, as well as the involvement of citizens and community groups in creating and implementing such solutions are lacking. Transition Wekerle, a member of the international Transition Network, is reacting to this need by creating new ways of doing and organizing and new ways of community building and engagement. Using innovative and highly participative methods, the members of the organization seek to envision and create a decarbonized future (i.e. to use a new process of framing) using experiential and social learning. During this process, a great many activities and initiatives have been created that are resulting in more sustainable consumption practices (such as local food-box schemes, community composting, energy brigades for promoting energy efficiency, and an improved cycling infrastructure).

Just like the CRAG network, the Transition Network has also been studied widely with respect to its innovation and transformation potential (see e.g. Alexander 2014; Alloun and Alexander 2014; Longhurst and Pataki 2015; Westley *et al.* 2011). Studies agree that the innovation potential of the initiative and its methodology is significant, and that 'it is one of the most promising and coherent social movements focused on building the alternative society' (Alexander 2014, 5). Transition Wekerle – and, indeed, the Transition Network as a whole – shows how social innovation can contribute to developing methods and participatory structures for dealing with global environmental and societal challenges, and ultimately for creating more sustainable lifestyles and communities.

SCAD Kitchen Gardens and Fruit Tree Afforestation

The SCAD initiative focuses on alleviating poverty and providing adequate nutrition in a way that observes ecological limits and the principles of strong environmental sustainability. This example is different from the other two in that it is situated in a region where the basic needs of people are not met. In this context, staying within ecological limits has to be framed and communicated in a completely different way than it does to members and stakeholders of the other two initiatives. Here the focus needs to be on increasing the ecological footprint in a way that does not contribute to overshooting ecological limits. By doing exactly this, SCAD not only seeks to promote equity within limits but is also creating a new way of framing positive local change around the issues of poverty, development, and climate change.

In terms of how the initiative is organized, SCAD, a non-governmental organization, actively manages the diffusion of the innovation in the communities it works with (about 500 villages in Tamil Nadu). Through new, innovative ways of organizing, which include working with women's self-help groups, SCAD manages to lift families and households out of poverty and to involve them in creating more sustainable lifestyles: organic gardens provide nutrition and additional locally generated income in a way that respects resource boundaries.

In summary, we conclude that all three initiatives rely on participative, voluntary action, engage in local community building, and encourage community action and responsibility-taking for humanity's shared resources, such as fossil fuels, a well-regulated climate, productive soil, water, and so on. In all three examples, social innovation or, in other words, new ways of doing, organizing, knowing, or framing contribute to creating more sustainable consumption patterns and lifestyles. The initiatives are thus situated at the nexus of sustainable consumption, social innovation and societal transformation. The Convergence Mapping tool helps with understanding how such initiatives are located in terms of sustainability and how they address justice and equity issues. Moreover, the tool provides an indication of elements of the initiatives – if any – that could be further developed. It can therefore be considered a tool for guiding transformative science and action.

5.2 The use and further development of the Convergence Mapping tool

In the introduction to this chapter, we identified the need for a tool that can help assess whether some social innovation initiatives represent more sustainable practices and options compared to others. Through the example of three initiatives, we have demonstrated that the Convergence Mapping tool can indeed be used for such purposes, and that it is able to illustrate the outcomes of analysis in an easily understandable graphical format. For this reason, apart from its use in scientific research, the instrument could also be used as:

- a (self-)assessment tool for initiatives and organizations to see where they stand in relation to addressing the issues of limits/contraction and equity/convergence (see the potential steps of such an assessment outlined with the use of concrete examples in Vadovics and Milton 2013); and
- a tool for identifying different developmental paths that may assist initiatives/organizations as they decide how to move forward.

Furthermore, along similar lines, Convergence Mapping

- could form part of the periodic sustainability evaluation and reporting of all types of initiatives and organizations, with the results of mapping shown in (annual) reports in which development over time could be depicted; or
- could be used to assess (research) project proposals prior to the distribution of funding to ensure that funded projects incorporate concerns about both equity and ecological limits in their work. Minimum achievable scores for funding could be established, requiring at least an explicit recognition of both principles and an analysis of their relevance to the proposed project.

Although the tool could be used for these purposes in its current form, there are different ways in which it could be developed further. One obvious way would be to incorporate the activities of initiatives even better in the analysis process. At the moment, the tool is not designed to facilitate the analysis of activities in detail. Although a mix of organizational principles, mission, objectives, and activities are considered during the analysis process, activities are not the focus. It may be interesting and revealing to compare the convergence (or contraction and convergence) map of the principles and mission of some initiatives and organizations with a map of their activities. Such a process could inspire new ways of developing and would entail defining universally applicable indicators for both scales to help in the analytical process. Literature is available that could help in this regard (e.g. Gismondi *et al.* 2016; Holden *et al.* 2014; Leppänen *et al.* 2012; Raworth 2012, 2017; Rockström *et al.* 2009; Steffen *et al.* 2015). Later, universal indicators could be supplemented with regionally and locally specific ones (e.g. for some of the resources). A third way of improving the tool would be adding a third dimension to the system: well-being or prosperity. Again, work is available which could be used for this purpose (e.g. Holden *et al.* 2014; Fritz and Koch 2014), but further research is needed to develop and test methodological approaches that would potentially fit and could be used with the tool.

6 Conclusions

Given the grave environmental and social challenges human society is now facing (Oxfam 2017; IPCC 2013), sustainability initiatives, social innovation, and transformative change should be studied together and must be considered in the framework of strong sustainability. To facilitate this change, it is important to be able to identify, analyse, and support (social innovation) initiatives that help us foster social justice and equity within ecological limits. It is of utmost importance that social innovation is connected to strong environmental sustainability (Melamed *et al.* 2012; Westley *et al.* 2011), and the consideration of ecological limits is a first step in this process.

The Convergence Mapping tool may be a useful instrument in this effort: it can play a role in awareness raising and conducting a primary analysis of initiatives, and can also be used to suggest a developmental path for initiatives. However, to ensure that initiatives, including social innovation initiatives, continue to foster strong and just sustainability (Agyeman 2005) and improve their performance in this regard, it is important that they regularly use these and other such tools to understand their position in relation to contraction and convergence. This process would also help ensure that such initiatives are dynamic enough to contribute to the transformative change that engenders more societal sustainability. While innovative, grassroots, community initiatives are essential for this purpose, there is also a need for tools and methods that help set a course in the direction of strong and just sustainability. We believe that Convergence Mapping is the first version of one such tool.

Annex: scales used in the Convergence Mapping tool

A.1 *Limits/contraction*

−1 Mention of resource, ecosystem, or planetary limits or boundaries in core mission statement or in prominent, contemporary textual, or programmatic material but no obvious mechanism for, or attempts to, reduce consumption of resources or reduce pollution. Initiative activities may even contribute to increases in resource consumption/pollution.

0   No mention of resource, ecosystem, or planetary limits or boundaries in core mission statement or in prominent, contemporary textual, or programmatic material. The initiative's main goals are not related to reducing consumption of resources or of reducing pollution in any obvious way.

1   Implicit. No explicit mention of resource, ecosystem, or planetary limits or boundaries in mission statement. May have limited mentions of limits and resource issues in associated prominent, contemporary textual, policy, or programmatic material. However, despite the lack of formal references to limits, the initiative is involved in activities to reduce resource consumption and/or decrease pollution.

2   Explicit. Resource, ecosystem, or planetary limits or boundaries are mentioned in core mission statement or/and in prominent, contemporary textual, or programmatic material, and the initiative is clearly engaged in attempts to reduce consumption and/or reduce pollution. Specific quantitative reduction targets or goals may or may not be defined.

3   Explicit + targets/indicators. Core mission statement/prominent, contemporary textual or programmatic material relates to resource, ecosystem, or planetary limits or boundaries and reducing consumption. Specific limits are identified and/or specific contraction targets are detailed. There are transparent and accountable methods for contracting resource use and tracking results (e.g. use of indicators).

4   Explicit + targets that are defined based on available (scientific) information about resource, ecosystem, or planetary limits or boundaries. Clear efforts are being made to connect limits-related science with practice. Transparent and accountable methods for contracting resource use and tracking the results (e.g. use of indicators) are in place.

A.2 Equity/convergence

-1 Mention of equity or justice in core mission statement or in prominent, contemporary textual, or programmatic material but no indication of activities relating to promoting equity or justice. Initiative activities may even contribute to increasing inequality/hindering justice.

0   No mention of equity or justice in core mission statement or in prominent, contemporary textual, or programmatic material. No evidence of an equity/justice/re-distributional focus to the initiative's activities.

1   Implicit or limited mention. No explicit mention of equity or justice in core mission statement. Limited mention (once or twice) in prominent, con-temporary textual, or programmatic material. The initiative's activities involve attempts to address the issue of justice/equity.

2   Explicit mention. Equity or justice mentioned and reference given to either intra- or inter-generational equity in core mission statement. Limited mention (once or twice) in prominent, contemporary textual, or

programmatic material. The initiative's activities involve attempts to address the issue of justice/equity.

3   Explicit mention of and reference to both intra- and inter-generational equity or justice in core mission statement. Limited mention (once or twice) in prominent, contemporary textual, or programmatic material. The initiative's activities have a focus on addressing the issue of justice/equity. Specific quantitative targets or goals relating to Equity may or may not be defined.

4   Explicit mention + targets/indicators. Core mission statement relates to both intra- and inter-generational equity and justice and/or justice and equity occur in same sentence in prominent, contemporary textual, or programmatic material. The initiative's activities have a focus on the issue of justice/equity. There are transparent and accountable methods for fostering equity and tracking the results (e.g. use of indicators) are in place.

Acknowledgements

Part of the research presented here was funded by the European Commission's 7th Framework Programme through the CONVERGE project (Rethinking Globalisation in the Light of Contraction and CONVERGEnce), grant agreement number 227030. The sole responsibility for the content of this chapter lies with the authors.

Notes

1 For more details about the background to the CONVERGE project and Convergence Mapping, see Vadovics *et al.* 2012, 2013.
2 As the data about the initiatives was collected between 2010 and 2012, re-mapping using current data may produce different results.
3 Even though the network calls itself Carbon Rationing Action Groups (CRAGs), Fownhope CRAG prefers to call itself Carbon Reduction Action Group but uses the same acronym.
4 www.fownhopecrag.org.uk (accessed 8 August 2016).
5 It should be noted that even though the CRAG network has mostly disappeared (Hielscher 2013), Fownhope CRAG is still active.

References

Agyeman, J. (2005) *Sustainable communities and the challenge of environmental justice* New York University Press.
Alexander, S. (2014) 'Disruptive social innovation for a low-carbon world' (working paper for the Visions and Pathways project).
Alloun, E., and Alexander, S. (2014) 'The Transition Movement: questions of diversity, affluence and power' (Simplicity Institute Report 14g).
BEPA (Bureau of European Policy Advisors) (2011) *Empowering People, Driving Change: Social Innovation in the European Union* European Commission.

Demailly, D., and Novel, A-S. (2014) *The sharing economy: make it sustainable* (Study no. 03) IDDRI.

European Parliament (1998) 'Resolution on climate change in the run-up to Buenos Aires' (B4–0802/98).

Fawcett, T. (2010) 'Personal carbon trading: a policy ahead of its time?' *Energy Policy* 38: 6868–6876.

Fawcett, T., Bottrill, C., Boardman, B., and Lye, G. (2007) *Trialling personal carbon allowances* UKERC.

Fortnam, M., Cornell, S., Parker, J., and CONVERGE Project Team (2010) *Convergence: how can it be part of the pathway to sustainability?* (CONVERGE Discussion Paper 1, CONVERGE deliverable 11) Department of Earth Science, University of Bristol.

Fritz, M., and Koch, M. (2014) 'Potentials for prosperity without growth: ecological sustainability, social inclusion and the quality of life in 38 countries' *Ecological Economics* 108: 191–199.

Gismondi, M., Connelly, S., Beckie, M., Markey, S., and Roseland, M. (2016) *Scaling up: the convergence of social exonomy and sustainability* Athabasca University Press.

Haxeltine, A., Avelino, F., Pel, B., Dumitru, A., Kemp, R., Longhurst, N., Chilvers, J., and Wittmayer, J. M. (2016) 'A framework for transformative social innovation' (TRANSIT working paper 5) TRANSIT: EU SSH.2013.3.2–1 Grant agreement no. 61316.

Hielscher, S. (2013) *Carbon Rationing Action Groups: an innovation history* University of Sussex.

Holden, E., Linnerud, K., and Banister, D. (2014) 'Sustainable development: *Our Common Future* revisited' *Global Environmental Change* 26: 130–139.

Howell, R. (2012) 'Living with a carbon allowance: the experiences of Carbon Rationing Action Groups and implications for policy' *Energy Policy* 41: 250–258.

IPCC (2007) *Climate change (2007): the physical science basis: contribution of Working Group I to the Fourth Assessment Report of the Intergovernmental Panel on Climate Change* Cambridge University Press.

IPCC (2013) *Climate Change (2013): the physical science basis: contribution of Working Group I to the Fifth Assessment Report of the Intergovernmental Panel on Climate Change* Cambridge University Press.

Jégou, F., and Manzini, E. (eds) (2008) *Social innovation and design for sustainability* Edizioni POLI.design.

Leppänen, J., Neuvonen, A., Ritola, M., Ahola, I., Hirvonen, S., Hyötyläinen, M., Kaskinen, T., Kauppinen, T., Kuittinen, O., Kärki, K., Lettenmeier, M., Mokka, R., and SPREAD Project Team (2012) 'Scenarios for sustainable lifestyles 2050: from global champions to local loops' (SPREAD Sustainable Lifestyles 2050 project deliverable 4.1).

Longhurst, N., and Pataki, G. (2015) 'The transition movement' (WP4 case study report) TRANSIT: EU SSH.2013.3.2–1 Grant agreement no. 613169.

Lorek, S., and Fuchs, D. (2013) 'Strong sustainable consumption governance: precondition for a degrowth path?' *Journal of Cleaner Production* 38: 36–43.

Melamed, C., Scott, A., and Mitchell, T. (2012) *Separated at birth, reunited in Rio? A roadmap to bring environment and development back together* (background note) Overseas Development Institute.

Meyer, A. (2000) *Contraction and convergence: the global solution to climate change* (Schumacher Briefings 5) Green Books.

Mulgan, G., Tucker, S., Ali, R., and Sanders, B. (2007) *Social innovation: what it is, why it matters and how it can be accelerated* Young Foundation.

Oxfam (2017) 'Just 8 men own same wealth as half the world', www.oxfam.org/en/press-room/pressreleases/2017-01-16/just-8-men-own-same-wealth-half-world (accessed 16 Jan. 2017).

Raworth, K. (2012) *A safe and just space for humanity: can we live within the doughnut?* (Oxfam discussion paper) Oxfam.

Raworth, K. (2017) *Doughnut economics: seven ways to think like a 21st-century economist* Random House Business Books.

Rockström, J., Steffen, W., Noone, K., Persson, Å., Chapin, F. S., III, Lambin, E. F., Lenton, T. M., Scheffer, M., Folke, C., Schellnhuber, H. J., Nykvist, B., De Wit, C. A., Hughes, T., Van der Leeuw, S., Rodhe, H., Sörlin, S., Snyder, P. K., Costanza, R., Svedin, U., Falkenmark, M.., Karlberg, L., Corell, R. W., Fabry, V. J., Hansen, J., Walker, B., Liverman, D., Richardson, K., Crutzen, P., and Foley, J. A. (2009) 'A safe operating space for humanity' *Nature* 461: 472–475.

Roderick, I., and Jones, N. (2008) 'The converging world' in Blewitt, J. (ed.) *Community, empowerment and sustainable development* (Converging World Series) Green Books, 17–33.

Seyfang, G., and Haxeltine, A. (2012) 'Growing grassroots innovations: exploring the role of community-based initiatives in governing sustainable energy transitions' *Environment and Planning C: Government and Policy* 30: 381–400.

Seyfang, G., and Smith, A. (2007) 'Grassroots innovations for sustainable development: towards a new research and policy agenda' *Environmental Politics* 16(4): 584–603.

Sinclair, H. (2014) 'Does microfinance really help poor people?' *Guardian*, 8 Oct.

Steffen, W., Richardson, K., Rockström, J., Cornell, S. E., Fetzer, I., Bennett, E. M., Biggs, R., Carpenter, S. R., De Vries, W., De Wit, C. A., Folke, C., Gerten, D., Heinke, J., Mace, G. M., Persson, L. M., Ramanathan, V., Reyers, B., Sörlin, S. (2015) 'Planetary boundaries: guiding human development on a changing planet' *Science* 347: 6223, DOI: 10.1126/science.1259855.

URBACT (2015) *Social innovation in cities: URBACT II capitalisation* URBACT.

Vadovics, E. (2009) 'Understanding and enhancing the contribution of low-carbon communities to more sustainable lifestyles' (thesis prospectus, Central European University).

Vadovics, E., and Milton, S. (2013) *Equity within planetary limits: where do you stand? Introducing the convergence mapping system: a sustainability assessment tool* GreenDependent Institute.

Vadovics, E., Milton, S., and CONVERGE Project Team (2012) *Case studies ('initiatives') illustrating contraction and convergence: equity and limits in theory and practice* (CONVERGE deliverable 33) GreenDependent Institute.

Vadovics, E., Milton, S., and CONVERGE Project Team (2013) *Case studies ('initiatives') illustrating contraction and convergence: equity and limits in theory and practice* (background paper to complement CONVERGE deliverable 33) GreenDependent Institute.

Westley F., Olsson P., Folke, C., Homer-Dixon, T., Vredenburg, H., Loorbach, D., Thompson, J., Nilsson, M., Lambin, E., Sendzimir, J., Banerjee, B., Galaz, V., and Van der Leeuw, S. (2011) 'Tipping toward sustainability: emerging pathways of transformation' *AMBIO* 40(7): 62–780, DOI: 10.1007/s13280-011-0186-9.

11 North American perspectives of societal transformation

Philip J. Vergragt

1 Introduction

Reflecting on the themes of the book from a US perspective, it is worthwhile to realize differences in the cultural and political landscapes of the United States and Europe. No one would expect a swift and radical transformative change toward a sustainable society in the current Trumpian political climate in the US. Rather, the political switch toward a right-wing populist government signals trouble for the sustainability agenda. However, the US is not a monolith but a historically and culturally diverse country with many contrasting regional cultures (Woodard 2011). In addition, the constitution which created the US in 1798 was in essence a compromise balancing regional with federal interests (Larson 2014). The ensuing nineteenth-century wave of industrialization, infrastructure development and rapid economic growth paved the way for what is now known as consumer society. Consumer society has been intentionally constructed after WWII in order to redirect war production capacity toward peaceful products, to create jobs for military veterans, and to create a cultural counterweight to Soviet communism (Brown and Vergragt 2016).

Present day capitalist-consumerist society in the US can be culturally characterized as a mixture of belief in the "American Dream" and a deep disappointment and scepticism about it. This dream still lures immigrants from across the globe, promising financial security, a large house in the suburbs with multiple bathrooms, a spacious green yard and a multiple-car garage, a job, and a better life for the next generation. However, for many this dream has become a nightmare, with widespread, often race-based poverty, inequality of incomes and wealth, erosion of jobs and the middle class, less security of employment, health care and retirement benefits, soaring college tuitions and debts, a crumbling infrastructure, and political corruption and stalemate. In addition, consumer society has created massive ecological devastation, including climate change.

Historically, ecological degradation was more a concern of the highly educated elite, starting with Theodore Roosevelt who created the National Parks to protect wilderness and wildlife against mining, industrialization and large-scale agriculture. In the industrial inner-city slums, ecological degradation is largely experienced as health problems due to air, water, and soil pollution, which affect mostly poor citizens and immigrants. These problems gave rise to environmental justice movements which still play a prominent role in the environmental movement in the US.

In the following, I sketch how the themes of this book – societal transformation, sustainable consumption, and social innovation – play out in this US American context of diversity and ambiguity in relation to the American dream.

2 Conceptual/intellectual approaches to societal transformation

The Tellus Institute in Boston was an early frontrunner in thinking about societal transformation and systemic change.[1] In 1995, Tellus was one of the conveners of the Global Scenario Group that developed long-range scenarios for the twenty-first century. Their work – updated in 2010 (Raskin *et al.* 2010) – was popularized in 2002 in an essay *Great Transition: The Promise and Lure of the Times Ahead* (Raskin *et al.* 2002) in which the historic roots, current dynamics, future perils, and alternative pathways for world development are described. It advances a "great transition" as the preferred route, identifying strategies, change agents, and necessary value shifts for a new global agenda. Based on this essay, the Tellus Institute initiated the Great Transition Initiative[2] to promote the great transition and to help catalyze a "global citizens movement" toward a transition to a sustainable society (Raskin 2016).

A related initiative is the Next System Project, initiated by the Democracy Collaborative.[3] The latter works to create a "vision of a new economic system where shared ownership and control creates more equitable and inclusive outcomes, fosters ecological sustainability, and promotes flourishing democratic and community life." The Next System Project seeks to "launch a national debate on the nature of 'the next system' using the best research, understanding and strategic thinking, on the one hand, and on-the-ground organizing and development experience, on the other," through publication of a bundle of essays on their website.[4]

The analysis of what could catalyze a societal transformation has in the US most clearly been addressed by Eric Olin Wright (Wright 2010; see also Cohen *et al.* 2017). Echoing Polanyi (2001) and the multilevel perspective as discussed in Chapters 3–4 of this book, Wright sees most promise in "interstitial" strategies, making use of the cracks and fault lines of the existing system, rather than in "symbiotic" or even "ruptural" changes. He argues that most historic transitions can be explained this way, for instance the capitalist system growing in the apertures of feudal society.[5]

3 Sustainable consumption: action and research

The New Dream initiative, which emerged from the Center for a New American Dream, has raised awareness of the negative impacts of a consumerist culture, helped define conscious consuming and green living, focused on down-shifting and life–work balance, and helped large institutional buyers shift their procurement to greener alternatives.[6] It seeks to change social norms around consumption and consumerism and to support the local movements of individuals and communities pursuing lifestyle and community action.

The Sustainable Consumption Research and Action Initiative (SCORAI) is more research oriented. It was founded in 2008 and is a

> knowledge network of professionals working at the interface of material consumption, human well-being, and technological and cultural change. It aims to foster a transition beyond the currently dominant consumer society. It provides a forum for scholars and practitioners striving to understand the drivers of the consumerist economy in affluent technological societies; to formulate and analyze options for post-consumerist lifestyles, social institutions, and economic systems; and to provide the knowledge for emergent grassroots innovations, social movements, and public policies.[7]

It is a network organization of nearly 1,000 researchers and practitioners focused on North America but spread across the globe, with sister organizations in Europe, Israel, and China. Since its inception, SCORAI has organized numerous presentations, workshops, two international conferences, several special journal issues and several books (the most recent is Cohen *et al.* 2017).

In the last few years, SCORAI has closely collaborated with USDN, the Urban Sustainability Directors Network, to help create an understanding of sustainable consumption for city managers and policy makers – an effort that culminated in the Eugene Memorandum.[8] SCORAI also supported USDN in creating a toolkit for city sustainability managers[9] which is presently piloted in several cities (see Bonneau and Jégou in this volume). More recently, SCORAI has been involved in an emerging Future Earth Knowledge Action Network on "Systems of Sustainable Consumption and Production."[10]

4 Social grassroots innovations

The concept of social innovation in the US goes back to Benjamin Franklin, who discussed small modifications within the social organization of communities that could help in solving everyday problems. In the US, there are many grassroots and social innovations comparable to those described in Chapters 6–9, like cohousing, local currencies, community supported agriculture, and community energy. What stands out in the US is very active grassroots activism for social and environmental justice, especially in Southern and Midwestern cities in states which are generally associated with a more conservative electorate. One of the most visible network organizations is the New Economy Coalition,[11] which has its roots in the E.F. Schumacher Society[12] and in the New Economics Foundation in the UK.

The New Economy Coalition (NEC) is a network of [currently 201] organizations imagining and building a future where people, communities, and ecosystems thrive. Together, we are creating deep change in our economy and politics—placing power in the hands of people and uprooting legacies of harm—so that a fundamentally new system can take root.

This network focuses on grassroots organizing and fostering different types of cooperatives.

A few examples from recent participatory observation in Chicago's Little Village neighborhood highlight the diversity of activities. The New Era Windows Coop[13] is a workers' cooperative founded in 2012. When the factory was first closed in 2008, it was occupied by the workers, which brought about nation-wide attention and endorsement by the bishop and even by President Obama;[14] next it remained partially open under new ownership. When the factory was closed again in 2012, it was occupied again; and this time the workers were able to buy the company with support from the Working World,[15] a not-for-profit organization that started in Latin America that supports worker's cooperatives with management and funding.

A second example is the Self-Help Federal Credit Union.[16] Originally, this was a local credit union providing loans for small businesses, start-up firms, and cooperatives and providing protection against predatory lenders. The depositors are the coop members: they have 120,000 members and $7 billion in assets. In 2008, during the financial crisis, the big banks were bailed out but the small banks and local credit unions were not: which many people still consider a blatant injustice.

A third example is the Little Village Environmental Justice Organization.[17] Since 1994 it has been fighting against neighborhood health problems, most notably caused by local coal power plants and a Superfund waste dump. With the organization's support the plants were closed in 2012. The waste dump was also closed, capped and turned into a huge new park, La Villita, which was established in 2015.

Another active organization is the US Solidarity Economy Network.[18] This network is part of a global network promoting the solidarity economy and is rather similar to the New Economy Coalition. The two organizations have different histories, however, with the solidarity economy originating from social justice organizations mainly in the global South, especially Latin America.

Other social innovation networks are more oriented toward environmental sustainability, comparable to those in Europe (cf. Haxeltine *et al.* in this volume). Examples include the Earth Day network,[19] Transition US,[20] the US Climate Action network,[21] influential websites like Yes! Magazine[22] and Shareable,[23] and organizations of scientists such as the Union of Concerned Scientists.[24]

5 Reflections

On the level of conceptual thinking, connections between societal transformation, social innovation, and sustainable consumption are well developed in the

US, but less so in practice and policy. Grassroots networks and networks of academics are loosely connected and much more could be accomplished. Those networks and alliances should be prepared to take advantage of windows of opportunity, like the financial crisis in 2007.

Social innovations and sustainable consumption practices and experiments could play important roles even before such windows of opportunity open. First, they create spaces for learning and experimenting with different economic models and with enacting different social norms by bringing together different stakeholders and creating communities of practice. Second, by reflecting on their learning processes, they could improve their effectiveness and efficiency without giving up the value of sufficiency. Third, they could experiment with different governance models, for instance participatory democracy. Societal transformation could further be guided and enabled by a possible cultural transformation beyond consumerism, materialism, competition, efficiency, extremely hard work, and careerism that may be led by millennials (Brown and Vergragt 2016).

Notes

1 www.tellus.org.
2 www.greattransition.org.
3 http://democracycollaborative.org.
4 www.thenextsystem.org.
5 www.youtube.com/watch?v=X-KcHtYCtTs.
6 www.newdream.org.
7 http://scorai.org.
8 http://scorai.org/eugene-memorandum.
9 www.usdn.org/public/page/94/Sustainable-Consumption-Toolkit.
10 http://futureearth.org/future-earth-sscp.
11 http://neweconomy.net.
12 www.centerforneweconomics.org.
13 http://newerawindows.com.
14 See the documentary by Michael Moore at https://vimeo.com/33260810.
15 www.theworkingworld.org/us.
16 www.self-helpfcu.org.
17 http://lvejo.org.
18 https://ussolidarityeconomy.wordpress.com.
19 www.earthday.org.
20 www.transitionus.org/home.
21 www.usclimatenetwork.org.
22 www.yesmagazine.org.
23 www.shareable.net.
24 www.ucsusa.org.

References

Brown, H.S., and Vergragt, P.J. (2016) "From Consumerism to Wellbeing: Toward a Cultural Transition?" *Journal of Cleaner Production* 132: 308–317, http://dx.doi.org/10.1016/j.jclepro.2015.04.107 (accessed May 25, 2017).

Cohen, M., Brown, H.S., and Vergragt, P.J. (2017) *Social Change and the Coming of Post-Consumer Society* Routledge: New York.

Larson, E.J. (2014) *The Return of George Washington: Uniting the States 1783–1789* Harper Collins: New York.

Polanyi, K. (2001 [1944]) *The Great Transformation: The Political and Economic Origins of Our Time* Beacon Press: Boston, MA.

Raskin, P.D. (2016) *Journey to Earthland: The Great Transition to Planetary Civilization* Tellus Institute, Boston, www.tellus.org/pub/Journey-to-Earthland.pdf (accessed May 25, 2017).

Raskin, P., Banuri, T., Gallopin, G., Gutman, P., Hammond, A., Kates, B., and Swart, R. (2002) *Great Transition: The Promise and Lure of the Times Ahead* Stockholm Environmental Institute: Boston, http://greattransition.org/documents/Great_Transition.pdf (accessed May 25, 2017).

Raskin, P.D., Electris, C., and Rosen, R.A. (2010) "The Century Ahead: Searching for Sustainability" *Sustainability* 2: 2626–2651.

Woodard, C. (2011) *American Nations: A History of the Eleven Rival Regional Cultures of North America* Penguin: New York.

Wright, E.O. (2010) *Envisioning New Utopias* Verso: New York.

12 Commentary from a Japanese perspective

Tapping into traditions for transitions and societal transformations

Satoru Mizuguchi

1 The rise of European theories and practices for transformations

Promising theories and practices for social innovation, sustainable consumption, and societal transformations are already emerging in Europe (IPCC 2014). Examples include Sweden's SymbioCity approach, as well as the Netherlands' transition management approach, which has become the backbone of the European Environment Agency's quest to realise the circular economy (EEA 2016). I have become familiar with both approaches, which have been tried in Japan within the past decade. Sweden's SymbioCity urban innovation initiative made Stockholm the first green capital of the European Union in 2007. The flagship project for the circular economy was Hammarby Sjostad, where a former brownfield area was transformed into an attractive district of 11,000 apartments and 10,000 workplaces. The Hammarby model has set a new world standard for future sustainable housing development, with its integrated planning approach. The innovation consisted of a system-based approach to architecture and planning of energy efficient housing; automatic underground waste collection systems; solar-powered hot water and electricity; biogas from household sewage water and waste; collection and filtration of runoff water; and super-efficient buildings, triple glazed windows, green roofs and so on (Government Offices of Sweden n.d.).

The Hammarby model also made Malmö a best-practice example of sustainable urban development. Rusty industrial districts were transformed into sophisticated residential ones. Malmö even went further than Stockholm did. Working with Skane County, Malmö converted public hospitals into "sustainable hospitals", where the "nexus of hospital resources" was created (Mizuguchi 2013). Slum apartment complexes at Augustenborg were transformed into a popular eco-district, where elders run a cafe and put on plays at the local theatre and are able to enjoy living among younger generations. Residents can stroll on the green roof gardens and practise urban gardening on the roofs as well as inside or outside their houses (Malmö stad 2010). The former mayor had strongly applied a boundary-spanning approach to governance since the 1990s. The model has been widely adopted beyond the Swedish context, for example in Paris, Moscow and Tangshan in China (Mizuguchi 2016).

Examples of the transition management approach, such as MUSIC (mitigation, urban setting, innovation of cities), an EU urban innovation and climate mitigation project and InContext, an EU local revitalisation project, have followed. Transition management approaches have been implemented in Japan, Taiwan, Pacific islands, Australia and Africa.

2 Synthesizing SymbioCity and transition management

Although the two approaches developed from different backgrounds, they both employ backcasting, boundary spanning/crossing and system-based methods for eliciting change. There are minor differences between SymbioCity and transition management. However, SymbioCity has a major focus on the "physical space" of the nexus of urban resources and is thin on the "process of social dynamics", while transition management is the reverse. In SymbioCity, project managers, often civil engineers, sit at the centre of the planning teams. They facilitate, record and organise whole discussions. They invite sector specialists serially. Sector specialists take turns to take part in planning sessions, but the project managers are always at the centre. They put ideas visually on semi-transparent paper on the physical map of the city. As the series of sector sessions continues, the semi-transparent papers make layers, integrating sector ideas and laying the ground for boundary crossing. In the process of transition management, the transition management team plays a similar role to that of the project manager; however, their focus is on handling the interaction/social dynamics between niche-regime and niches. They manage transition process rather than physical space. In other words, transition management handles "time" while SymbioCity handles "space". The combination of the two approaches would benefit each other.

3 European approaches to managing transitions: implications of variable success

Through the eyes of non-Westerners other European methods for enabling transitions have similarities with SymbioCity and transition management in terms of relying on backcasting, boundary crossing, and system-based approaches. Examples include Natural Step and Arup's integrated urbanism methodology. These methods have also had some success in Europe and less success outside Europe (Mizuguchi 2017a). Since territories outside Europe and other developed countries will constitute a major share of global production and consumption in the near future, the unpopularity in the non-Western world of promising European approaches to effecting transition and transformation may cast a shadow on global sustainable development unless non-Western people are able to develop methods appropriate to local contexts and cultures.

I have followed and reflected on the introduction and implementation of SymbioCity, transition management, Natural Step, and Arup's integrated urbanism methodology in Japan and participated as an acting member of the

Japanese governmental panel on the FutureCity Initiative where various European methods for urban transition have been studied and applied. I have also researched SymbioCity in Sweden and China and transition management in the Netherlands, while making study visits in each country and undertaking or attending interviews, workshops, and lectures on it. In Japan, system-based approaches have attracted little interest among bureaucrats and business people even when they have been discussing sustainable urban development. The transition dynamics of transition management perplexed managers of municipalities and central government even when they have been discussing social innovation. Participants found it difficult to categorise their ideas into "vision, guiding principle, strategy, and the first step" at a backcasting session in the University of Tokyo: their sheet of matrix factors was a mess. The eco-city project in a district of Tangshan, China, where the Swedish applied SymbioCity, was introduced as a promising practice of sustainable development by the Swedish government during a side event of COP15 of the United Nations' Framework Convention for Climate Change in 2009. Five years later, a UK broadsheet newspaper described the district as a "ghost town" (*Guardian* 2014). Through Swedish involvement in urban projects in Asia, SymbioCity manuals have since been revised, to focus more on governance aspects than in the original approach.

My hypothesis is that Europe's common tools – backcasting, boundary crossing, and system-based approaches – are deeply rooted in the Western intellectual tradition and cause Japanese (and other Asian countries) problems in adopting and applying such methods. People tend to tap into their tradition or narratives of transition when they need fundamental change. Tradition or narratives provide people with a sense of who they are, where they come from, and how they have previously accomplished transitions/societal change (Yoichiro 2000).

In the West, the biblical story of the Exodus offers a foundation narrative for transitioning to a new society. An example of this is the making of America, which is a story about leaving the oppressions of the Old World, and venturing into a wilderness and creating a new promised land (Brooks 2017). In the Exodus story, Moses presented the Israelites a vision of "freedom from slavery", the Ten Commandments as guiding principles for change and displayed a "sign" as a first step to convince them to follow him. Although God encouraged Moses, he had perhaps "invented" backcasting, another gift for transition-minded Europeans. Asia has no comparable pan-Asian narratives like Exodus.

In Exodus, Moses encouraged people to step forward, however, the new course created another boundary. Even during the Exodus, divisions of labour, the rise of the priesthood and tribalism developed. The New Testament seems to present a remedy, a state of mind for boundary crossing. Practising boundary crossing requires a specific state of mind. The first is a willingness to cooperate and compromise with stubborn people, even with the enemy. Second, cooperation and compromise processes require tolerance and respect for everyone. And tolerance and respect for everyone may originate in the concept of equality among people before God or without God. I imagine that Jesus' command that one should "love your neighbour, love your enemy" provides a foundation for the state of mind required for boundary crossing.

4 Social innovation without European methods

There seems to be no comparable pan-Asian concept of "love" for boundary crossing. Buddhism is excellent for attaining mindfulness, but less social. Confucianism provides a foundation for social harmony at the expense of human equality and freedom. Upanishad Hindu treatises mention little about love and respect. Asia has no Moses or Jesus on a pan-Asian scale; however, Asia has local versions of "Moses" and "Jesus".

More than 300 km away from Tokyo lie Toyama and Higashiomi, both of which practise boundary-crossing governance. Toyama is famous for being a compact city amid high ownership rates of car and suburban housing. Higashiomi is known for its community business projects called Welfare Mall, clustered local production of food, energy, and elderly care in one shopping mall-like venue. In both regions, Japan's radical Buddhism reformation movement spread from the sixteenth century to the seventeenth century: the Buddhist farmers ruled their land by themselves for nearly a century. The founder of the movement organised people by preaching "justification by faith alone" like Paul the Apostle, a founder of the early Christian church, which had characteristics one might now associate with the "sharing economy", in which members consume and produce cooperatively. In Toyama and Higashiomi, people could see vibrant interactions among niche innovations as well as between niches and local regimes across sectors, creating room for social transformations (Mizuguchi 2016, 2017b), which might be the legacy of the local "Paul". Additionally, both regions are the birthplace of a prototype of the modern Japanese merchant, whose pragmatic philosophy is known as "do well for seller, well for buyer, and well for society", which might substitute for system-based approaches.

5 Tradition for societal transition and personal transformation

Moses and Jesus apparently provide Europeans with the psyche and self-confidence for change. The non-Western world should have had similar figures and narratives locally; however, it was lost during the colonial period (Voth 2007). The system-based approach, seemingly a synthesis of mathematics, science and philosophy, is attributable to Hellenism, the Greek civilisation, where they invented mathematics, science, and philosophy (Russell 1980). Three days' attendance at SCORAI Europe/TRANSIT and Horizon 2020 workshop and meetings at Vienna in 2015 induced me to imagine the atmosphere of the agora in ancient Athens, where policy makers, sophists (social scientists), and promising youth discussed current issues and theories for sustainable urban (city-state) development.

Both China, the first inventor of the printing machine and the compass in the world, with its failure at early industrialisation, and Japan, with its lack of military strategy in the age of three major "navy states" (Huntington 1957), exemplify their weak traditions of synthesizing mathematics, science, and philosophy and in relation to system-based approaches. Japan proved that leap-frogging economic growth is possible, such development being partly due to military and industrial pressures and philosophical influences from the West on societal transformation over the century from the mid-1850s, though without Moses, Jesus, and Hellenism. Asian "tigers", China, and other developing countries followed Japan's lead. However, sooner or later they might face long periods of stagnation like Japan has done over the past two decades. Then, they may need to find their Moses, Jesus, and Hellenism to transform from the inside. Europe also could unlock its full potentiality for fundamental change if it tapped into its root traditions for personal, and ultimately societal, transformation (c.f. Rotman 2015).

References

Brooks, D. (2017) "The Four American Narratives" *New York Times* (Japanese edn) 27 May.

EEA (European Environment Agency) (2016) *Sustainability transitions: now for the long term* (Eionet report 1/ 2016) EEA: Copenhagen.

Government Offices of Sweden (n.d.) "Take a deeper look, holistic approach to sustainable urban development" *SymbioCity* 17.

Guardian, The (2014) "Caofeidian, the Chinese eco-city became a ghost town" 23 July.

Huntington, S. (1957) *The soldier and the state* Harvard University Press: Cambridge, MA.

IPCC (2014) *Climate Change 2014* (WGII AR5) Cambridge University Press: Cambridge.

Malmö stad (2010) *Ekostaden Augustenborg: On the Way Towards a Sustainable Neighbourhood*, http://climate-adapt.eea.europa.eu/metadata/case-studies/urban-storm-water-management-in-augustenborg-malmo/augustenborg-brochure.pdf.

Mizuguchi, S. (2013) "Creating comfortable hospitals" *Housing Tribune Magazine* 10 50–51 (in Japanese).

Mizuguchi, S. (2016) "Interactions Among Multiple Niche-Innovations and Multi-regimes" in Loorbach, D., Wittmayer, J. M., Shiroyama, H., Fujino, J., and Mizuguchi, S. (eds) *Governance of Urban Sustainability Transitions. European and Asian Experiences* (Theory and Practice of Urban Sustainability Transitions Series) Springer Japan: Tokyo, 69–90.

Mizuguchi, S. (2017a) "Shock and transition: exploring difference among Japan, China and the West" (slideshow, Policy Platform Seminar 55, University of Tokyo).

Mizuguchi, S. (2017b) "Toyama as a model of compact city" *Housing Tribune Magazine* 10: 40–41 (in Japanese).

Rotman, J. (2015) "How game changers deal with radical innovation" (lecture at Transition Academy, DRIFT and Impact Hub, Amsterdam, 11 December).

Russell, B. (1980) *History of Western Philosophy* Unwin Paperbacks: London.

Voth, G. (2007) *The History of World Literature* Pt 4, Teaching Company: Chantilly, VA.

Yoichiro, K. (2000) "Role of local museum" (lecture paper) (in Japanese).

13 Conclusions

How social innovations become transformative and help increase sustainability

Sylvia Lorek and Edina Vadovics[1]

As stated in the Introduction, this book is the outcome of collaboration between a European research project, TRANSIT,[2] which investigates transformative social innovation, and the SCORAI Europe community,[3] which is primarily involved in studying sustainable consumption, largely to inspire and instigate transformative change. Part of the motivation for the cooperation between these two groups of researchers and practitioners was the desire to investigate the nexus of and define the links between social innovation, sustainable consumption and societal transformation.

'Social innovation', 'sustainable consumption' (as a contribution to sustainability) and 'societal transformation' – all three terms have received a great deal of attention in terms of practical experimentation as well as academic debate. However, what has been lacking is a discussion about how these different strains of thought and practice relate to one another, especially as regards how social innovation initiatives can contribute effectively to sustainability and the relationship between social innovation(s) and societal transformation. Based on the insights provided by the nine chapters and two commentaries of this book, in this concluding section we return to the questions posed in the Introduction and identify the opportunities and challenges for social innovation in terms of how it can play a significant role in transforming societies by increasing their sustainability.

We first elaborate what is needed for (and from) social innovation for it to become transformative. Furthermore, we identify a variety of preconditions for the integration of sustainability into social innovation processes. Finally, we specify criteria for linking social innovation, sustainable consumption and societal transformation with the transformation to sustainability. An overview of the challenges that remain completes this chapter.

1 What makes social innovation transformative?

Social innovation (SI) is an ongoing social process and contributes to the "evolution" of society in terms of how it deals both with change and challenge (Mulgan *et al.* 2007). However, not all social innovations are immediately recognised as such. Such innovative potential is quite often masked behind the perception that the innovation is largely technical in nature. Take information technology (e.g. the development of internet, computers and smart phones) as an example. These technical developments have resulted in social innovation that has significantly reordered human relationships in the shape of new forums and styles of communication (Facebook, Twitter, etc.) and also new ways of working (the home office, co-working spaces and other internet-based work spaces). Moreover, the same technical innovation has also facilitated the dissemination, multiplication and upscaling of numerous social innovations (consider, for example, the current popularity of car-sharing initiatives or the increase in number of participants and activity of local food networks such as those analysed by McFarland and Wittmayer in Chapter 6, as well as Gulyás and Balázs in Chapter 8). Lacking the widespread use of internet and smart phones, such innovation would be almost unimaginable.

Indeed, as Soutar (Chapter 7) notes, "social and technical innovations happen simultaneously and symbiotically". But whether occurring independently or in tandem with technological innovation, the authors of this book have strived, using different frameworks, to highlight where and how social innovation has created – or has the potential to create – conditions for profound change:

- Drawing on four different conceptual approaches (social practice theory, socio-technical transitions, neo-institutionalism and Karl Polanyi's *The Great Transformation*), Backhaus and her colleagues investigate the sharing economy (Chapter 3);
- Combining two schools of thought – reflexive governance and public administration – Bonneau and Jégou focus on SI in governance for use by city governments (Chapter 5);
- Taking a transformative social innovation perspective, McFarland and Wittmayer explore the transformative potential of a specific type of food network: a community pick-up point scheme in Berlin (Chapter 6);
- Focusing on relevant fields of consumption, Soutar explains how social and technological innovation, linked with energy communities, is able to influence and challenge the incumbent energy system in the UK (Chapter 7);
- Applying a "narrative of change" framework, Gulyás and Balázs analyse community-supported agricultural initiatives in Hungary and consider why their participants believe that change is necessary (Chapter 8);
- Inspired by practice theories, Leitner and Littig take a close look at a case of cohousing in Vienna, investigating how the innovative reorganisation of everyday life around shared spaces and practices can lead to change (Chapter 9); and
- Using the analytical Convergence Mapping tool, which links an assessment of environmental and social sustainability with the transformative social innovation perspective, Vadovics and Milton investigate various types of SI initiatives in terms of their transformative sustainability potential (Chapter 10).

Based on the work of these authors, we conclude that social innovation, albeit often defined by the authors in slightly different ways, has the potential to contribute to societal transformation in various formats. First, for those involved, social innovation initiatives create the opportunity and means for them to meet otherwise unmet needs or to meet their needs in alternative, more socially and environmentally sustainable ways, which may be quite experimental and as yet unexplored.

In terms of governance, there are two additional benefits. On the one hand, social innovation gives active citizens and diverse stakeholders an opportunity to get involved in a variety of forms of decision-making, including in local government and local planning initiatives. On the other hand, social innovation can permit various levels of public administration to engage new actors in planning and decision-making.

Nevertheless, several authors (e.g. Backhaus et al. (Chapter 3), Haxeltine et al. (Chapter 2), Leitner and Littig (Chapter 9), McFarland and Wittmayer (Chapter 6), and Vadovics and Milton (Chapter 10)) stress that social innovation and societal transformation are far from being synonymous. Furthermore, social innovation initiatives may not have the goal of increasing sustainability. In fact, for 'sustainability transformation' to occur, social innovation, societal transformation, and a higher level of sustainability must be combined under specific conditions.[4] Nevertheless, various factors can be identified, based on the analyses carried out in the chapters in this book that appear to lead from social innovation to sustainability transformation. We first summarise which factors appear to be indispensable for social innovation to become transformative. We then consider the sustainability potential of social innovation initiatives. Following this, we comment on the synthesis of these.

To take the definition provided by Haxeltine and his colleagues, "a truly transformative social innovation challenges, alters, replaces or supplements the dominant institutions that are reproducing the 'unsustainability' dynamic in the societal context" (Chapter 2). The challenge for SI is first to address a persistent problem. Then, in order to motivate transformative change, SI initiatives need to progress from being marginal phenomenon to initiatives capable of instigating deeper, systemic change. If they fail in this, they will not create any meaningful and significant transformation. To be transformative, social relations – that involve new ways of doing, organising, framing and knowing – need to both understand and challenge dominant ways of doing, organising, framing and knowing (i.e. "dominant institutions") (Haxeltine et al. 2016). In addition, the sustainability impacts of specific SI initiatives are proportional to the change they bring about in social relations and institutions, and cannot be assessed only in terms of material outcomes such as decreases in ecological footprints or carbon emissions (McFarland and Wittmayer (Chapter 6); Haxeltine et al. (Chapter 2)).

1.1 Factors that support social innovation: unlocking the potential of social innovation

Various factors which enable transformative social innovation can be identified. Bonneau and Jégou (Chapter 5), for example, describe a range of conditions under which change becomes more probable. First, leaders and motivators of change processes who can both maintain vision and coordinate practical activity are needed. In addition, people from a variety of backgrounds are required to discuss, share and carry out work. In the context of municipal development – the case described by Bonneau and Jégou – enthusiastic members of the Amersfoort and Gdańsk administration and outsiders enriched a process of innovation with their abilities and energy. Backhaus and colleagues (Chapter 3) note that recent trends in political devolution may play into the hands of local governments that seek to take matters into their own hands and to take citizens along. Moreover, the collective ownership and governance of local resources and infrastructures represent social innovations in and of themselves compared to current arrangements.

In this respect, Bonneau and Jégou (Chapter 5) show that to enable broader outreach and recognition, as well as to obtain acceptance by the community, the trust of stakeholders and citizens in the process of change had to be won, but such stakeholders also had to be awarded trust in the form of empowering them to play a role in city governance. Open and honest conversations created a good basis for this (Genus 2016). The role of trust is also highlighted and validated by Gulyás and Balázs (Chapter 8) in their analysis of community-supported agriculture initiatives. In these examples, the authors show how trust in the initiatives was based on the agreement and identification of members with their goals.

Furthermore, as experience shows, the first quick results (sometimes called "low-hanging fruit") can be used to clarify the benefits of a change process and maintain momentum. In the social innovation processes in the cities of Gdańsk und Amersfoort, for example (Bonneau and Jégou (Chapter 5)), early wins were first obtained through a process of informal collaboration between the administration and citizens, and only later were formal processes developed.

Finally, research has identified the greater transformation potential of SI initiatives anchored in real communities, rather than virtual ones (Bonneau and Jégou (Chapter 5), Soutar (Chapter 7), Leitner and Littig (Chapter 9), Gulyás and Balázs (Chapter 8)). The bonding capital of personal exchange may be an important factor in this regard (Soutar (Chapter 7)). Whether this finding can be generalised, however, is uncertain – other readings suggest that virtual communities facilitate "stranger sharing" and are more prone to allow strangers to become acquaintances, a situation with its own specific potential (Schor 2014).

1.2 Challenges related to the implementation and consolidation of social innovation

To contribute to sustainability transformation, SI initiatives must overcome two different challenges. First, they need to respond to internal (group) challenges.

Then, they must deal with issues that arise as a result of the spread, multiplication or growth of the initiative.

Leitner and Littig (Chapter 9) investigated the internal challenges that participants in a cohousing initiative faced. Through blurring the boundaries between the private and the public by creating more sustainable shared facilities and practices, participants in this initiative hoped to reduce CO_2eq emissions and better manage care work. However, in the specific initiative Leitner and Littig studied, neither of these outcomes materialised. Instead, what the authors observed is that the collective use of shared items such as cars or washing machines relied on the temporal coordination of individual and collective practices and on binding rules of use. Availability was not ensured at all times, use usually had to be planned in advance, and the related organisational activity demanded time and the development of new routines. Thus, the collectivisation of practices did not lead to time-saving, nor to a more equal distribution of care work between men and women. As a result the envisioned sustainable lifestyles did not materialise in a consistent way. Instead, a mix of sustainable and non-sustainable practices emerged, based on alliances of motives.

Collectivised practices developed alongside the "older" practices within the households. Regarding ecological gains, despite several changes that partly resulted in more sustainable practices, non-sustainable impacts of the new living arrangements (for example, an increase in electricity consumption) also occurred. Moreover, in "compensation" for the presumed benefits of living in a cohousing project and making greater effort to create a sustainable lifestyle, members of the initiatives may tend to increase ecological impact in other areas: for example, using aeroplanes more often (Siman and Herring 2003; Leitner and Littig (Chapter 9)).

Besides the personal and internal challenges associated with SI initiatives, they are also exposed to significant external challenges as they spread and grow. For example, McFarland and Wittmayer (Chapter 6) suggest that, alongside modifying purchasing behaviour (in the context of community pick-up point schemes, a type of alternative food network), the owners and members of initiatives also actively need to engage in lobbying decision-makers in (food) systems in order to make a real transformative impact.

Furthermore, SI initiatives must continuously update and adapt their portfolio of strategies, narratives and theories of change in order to maintain their radical core, while also adapting to changing circumstances. This works best if the knowledge they produce and its framing is credible and trustworthy (Gulyás and Balázs (Chapter 8)).

Perhaps counterintuitively, another challenge related to the spread and growth of SI initiatives is the fact that policy-makers and/or other important decision-makers that are associated with currently dominant and unsustainable institutions may lend them support. In this way the dominant institutions (i.e. the norms, rules, conventions and values thereof) will inevitably also influence the processes by which SI initiative strategy is formulated and created. As a result, the very processes that lead to success in the form of wider uptake of an innovation can also lead to the loss or dilution of core vision and values. Haxeltine and his colleagues

(Chapter 2) recommend that proponents remain aware of the fact that social innovation initiatives may be required to walk a tightrope between morphing into something which ultimately strengthens an unsustainable dominant regime or remaining isolated local experiments.

2 Support mechanisms for social innovation: increasing the capacity for sustainability transformation

The impact of SI initiatives, even if it is transformative, is not necessarily synonymous with sustainable development, sustainable lifestyles or sustainable ways of consuming and producing. A specific set of conditions is required for sustainability transformation to occur.

As a basic condition, initiatives must address specific environmental and social problems. Moreover, they must do so in ways that navigate and transform systemic patterns of unsustainability that society is locked into by dominant, incumbent institutions. Building on work by Haxeltine and his colleagues (Chapter 2), the following questions may be posed about an SI initiative to better understand and encourage its potential:

- What are the specific (transformative) sustainability ambitions of the SI initiative?
- What social innovations does the initiative employ to achieve its sustainability ambitions?
- What are the specific strategies and tactics that the SI initiative employs in attempting to increase its (transformative) sustainability impacts?
- How and to what extent does the SI initiative challenge, alter, replace or supplement (which) dominant institutions?

Sustainability transformation is a process of institutional transformation that involves broad structural changes in the institutional arrangements (Genus 2016) and the social relations (Haxeltine *et al.* (Chapter 2)) of a society towards more sustainable arrangements and patterns. Therefore, SI initiatives are required to employ explicitly political tactics and strategies to ensure that they are not influenced or captured by currently dominant institutions. As an example, we may think of the success of Airbnb that, surfing on the wave of "digital capitalism" (Theurl *et al.* 2015), commercialised and captured the market for sharing unused private rooms and, in doing so, negatively influenced the traditional tourist industry (Zervas *et al.* 2017), resulted in a reduction in the number of "normal" apartments on offer for rent in often frequented cities (Van der Zee 2016) and, in addition, increased the travel footprint by reducing overall travel costs (Ting 2016). Such developments call for local initiatives to be tailored to local conditions and needs, to ensure that benefits are shared and outweigh costs. This, in turn, requires the active involvement of local government and, as discussed above, the strategic partnering with stakeholders (Backhaus *et al.* (Chapter 3); Van der Zee 2016).

The need for an explicit political strategy and active involvement with policy change is highlighted by McFarland and Wittmayer (Chapter 6), who point out that in the cases when policy plays a major role in shaping production and consumption systems (e.g. with food systems), transformative change cannot occur without the transformation of policy. The authors argue that, in the case of the food system, consumption is only one contributor to sustainability problems, so it is unrealistic to expect social innovation that enables "sustainable consumption" to deliver a transformation to a sustainable food system by itself. Initiatives which do not seek to effect change through channels other than through consumption behaviour and which fail to address political, social or other solutions to food system problems will not replace dominant institutions but instead act within them. McFarland and Wittmayer conclude that "if policy can be redesigned to better support environmentally, socially, and economically sustainable food chains … innovative initiatives will be able to translate transformative potential into transformative impact and help solve persistent systemic problems".

In order to support transformative social innovation for greater sustainability or, in other words, to guide transformative change, two methodologies are proposed in this book: Vadovics and Milton (Chapter 10) introduce "Convergence Mapping", a tool which may be used to analyse how and to what extent different initiatives address the dual challenge of sustainability, described as increasing equity within ecological limits. McFarland and Wittmayer (Chapter 6), meanwhile, show how the transformative potential of SI initiatives can be assessed.

2.1 Unfolding the sustainability potential of social innovation

Vadovics and Milton (Chapter 10) have created an assessment tool that they name "Convergence Mapping" which can be used to examine the efficacy of organisations and initiatives located at the social innovation–sustainable consumption–societal transformation nexus. The Convergence Mapping tool can help to determine how "sustainable" initiatives are from an internal and external perspective in terms of addressing both justice and equity issues and ecological limits. The tool also suggests directions for development and can help assess whether SI initiatives are engaged in more sustainable practices than preexisting ones. The Convergence Mapping tool generates findings in an easy-to-understand figure which may invite members of initiatives to further develop their concepts and extend their ambitions.

2.2 Identifying the transformative potential of social innovation

For research to better support and help develop social innovations with true transformative potential, it should empirically identify and appraise the activities SI initiatives are engaged in. Such an investigation should involve an analysis of whether and to what extent an SI initiative displays characteristics that challenge, modify, or replace dominant institutions. "Challenge" in this context refers to questioning the legitimacy or existence of dominant institutions (i.e. currently dominant ways of doing, organising, knowing and framing). "Altering" refers to actually changing some or all of a dominant institution, while "replacing" means that a social innovation takes the place of (a) dominant institution(s) (Haxeltine *et al.* (Chapter 2), McFarland and Wittmayer (Chapter 6)).

Taking an example from the food sector, McFarland and Wittmayer (Chapter 6) inquire whether a specific case of more sustainable food provision challenges, alters or replaces currently dominant institutions in (1) retail sector market dominance, (2) the externalisation of environmental impact, (3) internationalisation and standardisation and (4) a lack of clarity about which actors are responsible for food-system-related sustainability issues.

2.3 Connecting sustainability and transformative potential

Going further, these two methods of analysis (convergence mapping and the analysis of transformative potential), could and should be combined to arrive at an analysis of transformative sustainability potential. Vadovics and Milton (Chapter 10) make an initial attempt at this through the three initiatives that they discuss (a transition-town initiative in Hungary, a grassroots carbon reduction action group in the UK and a fruit-tree planting and organic gardening initiative in India). Backhaus and her colleagues (Chapter 3) also connect these two methods, albeit at a more theoretical level. The potential for combining these two methods could be investigated and taken further as a part of future research, action or even policy initiatives.

3 Social innovation: a necessary but not sufficient condition for transformative change towards more sustainability

As Jonas (Chapter 4) argues,

> sustainable consumption practices that often entail social innovations as important ingredients can ... be grasped as necessary, but not sufficient, parts or aspects of the cosmopolitan practice/arrangement configurations of societal transformation that are needed to create a more equal and sustainable world society, the realisation of which remains open and contested.

Several authors agree with this conclusion that SI initiatives are part of the "solution", but are not a panacea (McFarland and Wittmayer (Chapter 6), Soutar (Chapter 7), Vadovics and Milton (Chapter 10)). However, they, along with others, also highlight the fact that SI initiatives have great potential to contribute to and catalyse transformative change, and, among other things can:

- be "laboratories" of transformation, or real-life experiments, which contribute to the toolkit of societal innovation (Leitner and Littig (Chapter 9), Vergragt (Chapter 11));

- play an instrumental role in challenging established institutions (Soutar (Chapter 7)); and
- translate transformative potential into transformative impact, and thereby help solve persistent systemic problems (McFarland and Wittmayer (Chapter 6)).

It is also important to remember that there is no "one-size-fits-all" approach: those who attempt to spread or upscale a successful initiative should bear in mind the new circumstances and characteristics of different contexts, as highlighted by Mizuguchi in his commentary (Chapter 12). Mizuguchi draws attention to the challenges implicit in importing Western European ideas and methods to Asian countries, but we may note that similar challenges apply to transposing initiatives between more similar socio-political environments, like those of Eastern and Western Europe.

Furthermore, to promote transformative change for sustainability, social innovation must occur simultaneously at different levels: in households, between households at a community level, in business and between businesses, in municipalities, as well as at national and international levels. Bonneau and Jégou (Chapter 5) note that local authorities can facilitate the creation of public innovation spaces to change the way policies are made and how public services are provided. Even though SI is often associated with grassroots initiatives, it can benefit (and eventually grow and spread) as a result of support from institutions, as observed by Bonneau and Jégou (Chapter 5) and Backhaus and her colleagues (Chapter 3). The reverse is also true.

Finally, although there is general agreement that social innovation has the potential to increase the sustainability of society and may contribute to transformative change towards greater sustainability, there is a need to adopt a more critical approach towards it. First of all, social innovation initiatives should be evaluated not only from the perspective of strong environmental (Lorek and Fuchs 2013) and just sustainability (Agyeman 2005), but also from the perspective of their transformative potential, and the connection between them (Backhaus et al. (Chapter 3), Haxeltine et al. (Chapter 2), McFarland and Wittmayer (Chapter 6), Vadovics and Milton (Chapter 10)). Furthermore, in parallel with adopting a more critical approach, there is a need for more awareness-raising and training to ensure that SI happens in a way that society desires and benefits from, as observed by Bonneau and Jegou (Chapter 5) and Vadovics and Milton (Chapter 10).

To conclude, as shown in Figure 13.1 – a redrawing of the original figure in the Introduction – there is need for more research and action at the nexus of sustainable consumption, social innovation and societal change within the framework of strong and just sustainability. In other words, as Raworth has aptly put it, "humanity's challenge in the 21st century is to eradicate poverty and achieve prosperity for all within the means of the planet's limited natural resources" (2012, 1) As described in this book, social innovation has a very important role to play in this endeavour through its great potential to contribute and offer a diversity of

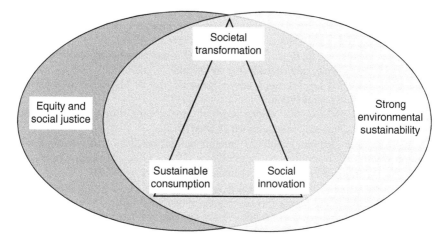

Figure 13.1 Sustainable consumption, social innovation and societal transformation within the framework of strong and just sustainability.

ways of developing. However, social innovations are presently somewhat like seeds and seedlings: for their potential to be realised, they need the help of farmers; the initiators and members who sowed or planted them, and who continue to take care of them. But they also require the nurturing and support of policy and research-based decision-making if they are to develop and grow to fruition.

Notes

1 Names of co-authors of this chapter are listed alphabetically.
2 More information about TRANSIT (Transformative Social Innovation Theory) may be found at www.transitsocialinnovation.eu.
3 More details about the SCORAI (Sustainable Consumption Research and Action Initiative) Europe community can be found at http://scorai.org/europe.
4 By "more sustainability" or "higher level of sustainability" we mean a move towards a state where the principles of strong environmental sustainability and just social sustainability are observed.

References

Agyeman, J. (2005) *Sustainable communities and the challenge of environmental justice* New York University Press.
Genus, A. (2016) "Sustainability transitions: a discourse-institutional perspective" in Brauch, H., Oswald Spring, Ú., Grin, J., and Scheffran, J. (eds) *Handbook on sustainability transition and sustainable peace* Springer, 527–541.
Haxeltine, A., Avelino, F., Pel, B., Dumitru, A., Kemp, R., Longhurst, N., Chilvers, J., and Wittmayer, J. M. (2016) "A framework for transformative social innovation"

(TRANSIT working paper 5) TRANSIT: EU SSH.2013.3.2–1 Grant agreement no. 61316.

Lorek, S., and Fuchs, D. (2013) "Strong sustainable consumption governance: precondition for a degrowth path?" *Journal of Cleaner Production* 38: 36–43.

Mulgan, G., Tucker, S., Ali, R., and Sanders, B. (2007) *Social innovation: what it is, why it matters and how it can be accelerated* Young Foundation.

Raworth, K. (2012) *A safe and just space for humanity: can we live within the doughnut?* (Oxfam discussion paper) Oxfam.

Schor, J. (2014) *Debating the sharing economy*, www.greattransition.org/publication/debating-the-sharing-economy (accessed 15 May 2017).

Simon, K.-H. and Herring, H. (2003) "Intentional communities and environmental sustainability" in Christensen, K., and Levinson, D. (eds) *Encyclopedia of Community: From the Village to the Virtual World* Sage Publications, vol. 2, 690–693.

Theurl, T., Haucap, J., Demary, V., Priddat, B. P., and Paech, N. (2015) "Ökonomie des Teilens: nachhaltig und innovativ?" *Wirtschaftsdienst* 95: 87–105.

Ting, D. (2016) *Airbnb's impact on online travel agencies and hotels is different than you thought*, https://skift.com/2016/06/06/airbnbs-impact-on-online-travel-agencies-and-hotels-is-different-than-you-thought (accessed 15 May 2017).

Van der Zee, R. (2016) "The 'Airbnb effect': is it real, and what is it doing to a city like Amsterdam?" *The Guardian* 6 Oct., www.theguardian.com/cities/2016/oct/06/the-airbnb-effect-amsterdam-fairbnb-property-prices-communities (accessed 15 May 2017).

Zervas, G., Proserpio, D., and Byers, J. W. (2017) "The rise of the sharing economy: estimating the impact of Airbnb on the hotel industry" *Journal of Marketing Research*, https://doi.org/10.1509/jmr.15.0204.

Index

Page numbers in **bold** denote figures and those in *italic* refer to tables.

Taylor & Francis eBooks

Helping you to choose the right eBooks for your Library

Add Routledge titles to your library's digital collection today. Taylor and Francis ebooks contains over 50,000 titles in the Humanities, Social Sciences, Behavioural Sciences, Built Environment and Law.

Choose from a range of subject packages or create your own!

Benefits for you
» Free MARC records
» COUNTER-compliant usage statistics
» Flexible purchase and pricing options
» All titles DRM-free.

Benefits for your user
» Off-site, anytime access via Athens or referring URL
» Print or copy pages or chapters
» Full content search
» Bookmark, highlight and annotate text
» Access to thousands of pages of quality research at the click of a button.

| REQUEST YOUR **FREE** INSTITUTIONAL TRIAL TODAY | **Free Trials Available** We offer free trials to qualifying academic, corporate and government customers. |

eCollections – Choose from over 30 subject eCollections, including:

Archaeology	Language Learning
Architecture	Law
Asian Studies	Literature
Business & Management	Media & Communication
Classical Studies	Middle East Studies
Construction	Music
Creative & Media Arts	Philosophy
Criminology & Criminal Justice	Planning
Economics	Politics
Education	Psychology & Mental Health
Energy	Religion
Engineering	Security
English Language & Linguistics	Social Work
Environment & Sustainability	Sociology
Geography	Sport
Health Studies	Theatre & Performance
History	Tourism, Hospitality & Events

For more information, pricing enquiries or to order a free trial, please contact your local sales team: **www.tandfebooks.com/page/sales**

 Routledge Taylor & Francis Group | The home of Routledge books

www.tandfebooks.com

For Product Safety Concerns and Information please contact our EU
representative GPSR@taylorandfrancis.com
Taylor & Francis Verlag GmbH, Kaufingerstraße 24, 80331 München, Germany